DATE

Welfare at Work

Modern Management Series

118013

HD 7696.97

Welfare at Work

A. O. MARTIN

B. T. Batsford Ltd London

First published 1967

© A. O. Martin 1967

Made and printed in Great Britain by
William Clowes and Sons Ltd, London and Beccles
for the publishers B. T. Batsford Ltd
4 Fitzhardinge Street, London W1

Contents

Acknowledgments

This book was stimulated by five rewarding years spent as Welfare Adviser to the General Post Office. I have a deep sense of gratitude to all those past and present members of the GPO, particularly its welfare officers, who contributed so much to my thinking about welfare at work. And there are many others, both inside and outside the field of welfare, who may not know how much they helped.

I am trying to thank them all by putting some of the shared experience on paper—but I do not commit any of them to the opinions thus expressed. I take full personal responsibility, as a private individual, for what is in this book. In particular, although I learned much from the GPO and have the highest admiration for its attitudes to people at work, what I have written must not be interpreted as official GPO policy on staff welfare or on the employment of welfare officers. Similarly, my views on the occupational welfare officer function and its relation to other 'personnel' functions and to outside social workers are not necessarily those of the GPO or any other government department.

Special thanks go to those personal friends who read the text with such constructive criticism and who encouraged me to take the argument to a wider readership. In particular, they pointed to the danger of trying to write with one eye on the practitioner and his colleagues, and the other on the social scientist. This book is therefore in the form of a sandwich. The Foreword and Postscript present the theoretical setting; the practical detail is in the numbered chapters, with references and footnotes on theory for those who wish to follow them up. I hope this arrangement will prove palatable.

ALEC MARTIN

London, 1967

Foreword

Some people in industry and commerce are a little uneasy about 'Welfare'. Others are downright sceptical. They seem to want to get away from a term which in their eyes conjures up a confused picture of mother-and-baby clinics, old people in institutions, social workers in inevitable hats, and fringe benefits which directors think they must lay on but do not really want. To them, welfare smacks of cosseting, ill-suiting a climate of opinion chilled by the need for sheer economic survival. This is not really surprising. The word has been pressed into the service of so many causes that specific meanings are being lost in a general vagueness which encourages its debasement. Should we connive at debasement, or are we prepared to do something about it before it is too late even to try?

It is my own belief that in the world of work 'welfare' is a term worth rehabilitating. This book is offered to managers, supervisors, trade unionists, 'personnel' people and welfare officers particularly, as a small contribution to the examination which must precede rehabilitation. I write it as an ex-practitioner who has helped in the selection and training of welfare officers and in the education of managers and others in the proper use of their services; and as a social scientist working for industry and commerce who is interested in the contribution social scientists can make to welfare at work.

I have tried to produce something in the nature of a handbook, a guide to welfare at work in the limited sense of the work of occupational welfare officers. For the most part, the treatment will be severely practical; day-to-day involvement with occupational welfare is often with practical points which may seem trivial from a distance but which are in reality the flesh and blood on the bones. But in welfare, practice cannot be sound unless it is firmly related to principles. Its essence dies if the right things are done for the wrong reasons. Indeed, confusion amongst the practitioners over principles is probably one of the main justifications for the sceptics' label 'woolly welfare'.

I shall be concerned only with the occupational welfare officer— the scope and limits of his activity, how his job may be analysed, how he can be selected, trained, kept informed and effectively employed, how his expert work dovetails with the welfare responsibilities of others. For brevity, I shall not always spell out *Occupational* Welfare Officer; this should be taken as read. However, it is important to stress that comparable studies of welfare officers working in other fields, who similarly merit their full titles, have yet to be made. We do not really know how much—or how little—they have in common with occupational welfare officers, but meanwhile a lot of confusion could be avoided if we insisted on the prefix Social, Educational, Mental, etc., where applicable, except in contexts such as the present one where repetition would be tiresome.

The use of prefixes is a useful step towards precision, since they relate one's thinking to an actual welfare context. However, it is necessary to glance at the generality of welfare before going into the occupational context in detail. Dictionaries are by no means infallible guides to actuality, because definitions represent no more than a consensus of received opinion—opinion which may be ill-informed or based on faulty interpretations of actuality. But they are starting points which give the roots of words; furthermore, successive editions indicate the history of change in meaning.

The *Concise Oxford Dictionary* (of *Current* English, to give it its full title) shows us the mediaeval roots of 'Fare' and 'Well' and offers the broad definition of 'Satisfactory state, health and prosperity, well-being'. The Third Edition (1934) also gives '*Welfare work*, efforts to make life worth living for workmen, etc.' The Fourth Edition (1951) substitutes *employees* for workmen (a change of received opinion) and adds '*Welfare State*, one having national health, insurance and other social services'. The Fifth Edition (1964) makes no change. This is instructive, for it shows that welfare work was originally conceived as welfare *at* work, or at least as welfare related *to* work. Welfare in the broader social and community sense—leading to the Welfare State— developed out of this. The *Penguin English Dictionary* (1965) does not relate welfare work specifically to employment. Its definition broadens to 'Any activity designed to improve the social conditions of an individual or group'. Definition of this breadth is hardly definition at all, for a great many human activities, such as those of technology, politics and the arts, could be held to improve social conditions but could scarcely be described as welfare work.

What constitutes an improvement of individual or group social conditions is entirely relative to existing conditions. Thus there are no absolutes; we are talking about social norms, social values and social aspirations, which derive initially from the leadership provided by the beliefs of individuals. Since there are no absolutes, the practice of welfare cannot rest on them. It is normally seen as the means by which those who do not enjoy a 'satisfactory state' are helped to do so. Welfare work is thus the antithesis of exploitation, and must be related to an underlying philosophy which itself rejects exploitation. In practical terms this means that 'welfare at work' should be provided for its own sake, accepting any economic return as incidental. To 'invest in welfare' *in order* to gain an economic return is fundamentally a very mild form of exploitation. However, we cannot live comfortably on such lofty moral pinnacles. I hope in the first chapter to show that a practical and commonsense approach can readily accommodate the moral issues which must underlie good welfare at work, and that there need be no conflict between the moral and the economic case.

Whatever axiom or set of values we start out from, it cannot reasonably be denied that we are interdependent; we meet our own needs by providing goods or services for others. But we cannot provide goods or services for others if our own needs are so urgent that they must be dealt with first. At the basic physiological level this is self-evident. We must have sleep, food, shelter, we must eliminate waste products, before we can be of any use to anyone else. We must be in a relatively 'satisfactory state' physiologically.

What is self-evident at this level applies to two other levels as well, although with less force or different emphases. While we can look at man as a physiological system, we can also look at him in social groups—the viewpoint of the sociologist. We can also look at him as an individual, thinking, feeling and behaving person—the viewpoint of the psychologist. These viewpoints provide a useful way of examining welfare at work. What I shall call social group needs and personal psychological needs are of course less tangible than physiological needs and thus more difficult to recognise, but they are there all the same.

I should make it clear that my approach is to the *individual as a member of a working group*. It therefore differs from those who study the group as such—as a corporate entity. It has been pointed out that apart from the technical reasons for its existence a working organisation has social and psychological requirements in its own right.[1] A considerable amount of research effort is now being devoted to the nature of these requirements. These are of course related to the individual's personal psychological and social group needs, but they are much more concerned with the processes of information, control and renewal of the group entities themselves. The application of such research findings in the growing field of industrial administration will certainly contribute to welfare at work in the larger sense, just as social administration will contribute to welfare in the community sense.

Thus we can begin to classify welfare. We can label as *Social Welfare* the provisions made for the whole community, with such subdivisions as may be necessary, without reference to occupation. These sub-divisions could well be the already distinctive fields of social-work activity—with children, old people, immigrants, offenders and prisoners, hospital patients or the mentally disturbed. We can distinguish this main group from *Occupational Welfare*, which relates exclusively to people at work, whatever their age, sex, source, conduct, sickness or health. Within Occupational Welfare I suggest that we can classify on a different basis—Physical, Group and Personal Welfare—catering broadly for physiological, social and psychological needs at work, respectively.

I shall give Physical Welfare very scant attention indeed, not because it is unimportant but because it is so important that its provision is largely governed by law. Organisations may provide over and above the requirements of such legislation as the Factories Acts and the Offices, Shops and Railway Premises Act, but inspection should ensure that they do not drop below the legal minima. In considering priorities above the minima, managers could well give thought to the priority of physiological needs of men and women. Adequate lavatories, adequate in quality as well as in quantity, should be the prime consideration. We should know by now that poor hygiene leads to sickness, yet commonsense is often forgotten. Murals on canteen walls are admirable, but are no substitute for cleanliness in the kitchen behind them. After lavatories and cleaning, human decencies and en-

---

[1] A. T. M. Wilson, 1955, and subsequent writing in industrial administration and industrial sociology. Lupton, 1966, provides some useful references.

lightened self-interest demand proper clothes-drying facilities, good lighting, heating and ventilation; and the law now helps to press home the demand.

The first battle has been won and we need not re-fight it here. Those who need the detail can go straight to the Acts, to H.M.S.O. popular guides to them, to more general publications (e.g. Mitchell, 1965) which summarise the law, or direct to central and local government inspectors. This is not to say that the only foreseeable development in Physical Welfare will be the gradual improvement of existing standards. On the contrary, the science of ergonomics (see Murrell, 1965, and the H.M.S.O. series of pamphlets on the subject) should in time make a significant contribution to aspects of the physical environment, the importance of which is as yet barely recognised.

A great deal has also been achieved in catering for social and psychological needs at work. Indeed, the last few years have seen in swift succession several Acts of Parliament which have narrowed the limits of 'voluntary' action by firms for the social and psychological welfare of employees—witness the Contracts of Employment, Redundancy Payments, and Industrial Training Acts. However, legislation in these two spheres is more difficult and inevitably lags behind control of the physical environment. One can lay down standards for the supply of drinking water, or the guarding of machines, which will be universally applicable. One can deal with social and personal problems only within the context of individual firms, with limits set by legislative safeguards of the kind quoted above.

Attention will thus be focused on the two areas of Personal and Group Welfare. The first will be given pride of place, because personal problems most need specialist help. Group Welfare is by its nature much more of a team effort, the main driving force coming from volunteers who will none the less need expert help from time to time. By analysing the Occupational Welfare Officer's function I hope to show that his role is limited—but essential. Too large and too indefinite a claim has been made in the past, so large that it has often been ignored and so indefinite that it has not always been understood. A smaller and more precise claim may be heard and understood—and also accepted. How occupational welfare officer work can best be limited, staffed, organised, encouraged and integrated with the work of others in industry and commerce is therefore the burden of this book.

Part one

SCOPE AND LIMITS

1 Why Welfare Officers?

Summary   Some guiding principles are established in making the case for the employment of occupational welfare officers. Most of them relate to his *personal welfare* job. Many personal problems are in the man-at-work context, and the firm should deal with as many of these problems as it can. Managers must accept the prime responsibility for the welfare of all staff under their control, but managers are not selected primarily to deal with difficult personal problems, for which special areas of knowledge and skill are required. Even if managers had the time, knowledge and skill, many employees would still be reluctant to expose personal worries to those in authority over them.

Personal welfare work cannot be done satisfactorily by other specialists, who should be fully loaded already, and who stand in a particular relationship with the man with a problem. Trade unions should be involved with physical welfare provision, to a lesser extent with group welfare and to a still more limited extent with the detail of personal welfare. Managers, supervisors and trade union officials will handle a certain amount of simpler personal welfare, but should refer the more difficult or time-consuming cases to the specialist. The individual in trouble must be given the right of direct access to the welfare officer, although he should also be able to make his approach via manager, supervisor or trade union official if he wishes.

The provision of an occupational welfare officer service is based on a humanitarian appreciation of individual needs and individual worth, but experience shows that such a service is also an aid to efficiency. The service itself must be managed efficiently; there is no conflict between the humanitarian basis and the businesslike and unsentimental attitudes which welfare officers and their supervisors must adopt.

The Growth of an Organisation

A one-man firm does not need a welfare officer. It does not need a
salesman, pay-clerk, shop-steward, buyer, typist or manager either;
all the functions are rolled into one and the man fends for himself. As
the firm grows, people are employed, roles are differentiated, but
still the owner takes full personal responsibility for all aspects of day-
to-day running. If he wants to keep his staff, he must comply with the
law on working and pay conditions, and beyond this he has to see that
they are content with their lot. If growth continues, problems of
human beings at work become more complex, functions are separated
out and specialist 'personnel' work is identified. It may be spread
around line managers and supervisors or one man may have the
whole gamut to look after. On behalf of line managers, he may recruit
and select, train, consult, negotiate, promote and retire; he may run a
benevolent fund or sports club, look after a staff canteen, control the
work of the First Aider and advise his directors on legal requirements
concerning working conditions—and he may be expected to deal with
such personal employee problems as come his way. Just as the owner's
varied tasks were once rolled into one, so in the firm just big enough
to employ a single specialist all the personnel functions may be the
responsibility of one individual. More growth, and eventually there
will be specialist recruiters, selectors, negotiators, retirers, discipline
and wages experts, trainers and others. At some point, someone will
be charged with the oversight of physical, group and personal welfare.
There may be one welfare officer—or there may be one hundred if the
organisation is big enough.

This is the traditional pattern in Britain, but we shall not be concerned with the organisational relationships between welfare officers
and other personnel specialists, nor with the history of what is now
broadly called 'personnel management', until much later. Our question is, why welfare officers ? To answer it we must go back to the
owner or manager who must comply with the law and see that his
staff are content with their lot. The 'one-man firm' can exploit *himself* almost as much as he chooses (almost, because family and friends
may impose some constraints), but the law forbids any gross exploitation of others. Full employment reduces the possibility still further,
and the need for positive attempts to attract and keep staff would
seem to rule it out completely. This is the stage when the manager or
owner thinks in terms of 'fringe benefits'—he *invests* in welfare provision in order to gain an economic return. One might also call it the

stage of enlightened self-interest, and it is a major step forward from reluctant compliance with the law. Yet, as argued in the Foreword, investment in welfare for an economic return is still a very mild form of exploitation; true welfare work is by definition the antithesis of exploitation and must be related to a philosophy which explicitly rejects it.

The Purpose of Work

Such a philosophy is by no means difficult to find.[1] It can be based on the simple axiom that without people there would be no work in the human sense of the word. Work therefore exists solely for the satisfaction of human needs, and the purpose of working organisations is to provide for the needs of the community of which these organisations are part. If we accept this, we are led quite inescapably to a rather unusual conclusion. If working organisations serve the community as a whole, thus contributing to its welfare (satisfactory state, health and prosperity, well-being), it must follow that at least in part they exist to promote the welfare of the people who operate them, for these people are part of the whole community. This is readily apparent in the one-man firm, yet it may sound absurd to say that one of the purposes of the National Coal Board (or any other organisation at the giant end of the scale) is to promote the welfare of its employees. But once exploitation is rejected as an alternative, it is none the less true. Perhaps we are beginning to realise the truth of it as we pay increasing attention to 'social cost and benefit' in our economic thinking and planning.

Doubtless, many people of an authoritarian cast of mind will not accept this 'satisfaction of human needs' view of work and will look around for a sterner ethic. To them it seems too permissive,[2] too slack, too mushy, and, dare one say, too simple possibly to be true? They seem to start from a different axiom: that work is a duty, that as good medicine it should taste nasty, that suffering is good for the soul. Perhaps it is—for those whose souls are already strong enough to cope, who are already in a 'satisfactory state'—but this logic seems to

---

[1] Michael Fogarty, 1964, has developed the theme of the nature and purpose of work in considerable detail. See also his article 'In Search of Business Ethics', *New Society*, 26 May 1966.

[2] C. H. and W. M. Whiteley, 1964, give a philosopher's view of the 'permissive morality' and its implications.

do nothing at all about human suffering and its milder forms of anxiety and fear. It seems rather to lead to exploitation.

The Manager's Responsibility

In modern society, with its accelerating trend towards larger industrial and commercial undertakings, the owner/manager is becoming rare. The manager acts as the owner's agent and discharges the owner's responsibilities, which are also growing in complexity. Complexity is such that the present century has seen an enormous expansion in the literature about management, from supervision at the lower end of the scale to industrial administration at the upper end. Principles are being established in place of rules of thumb, and manager training seeks to get them into practice. What principles have emerged in the personal problem area, which is our main concern ?

One is accustomed to hearing the transposition into industrial terms of the armed services' doctrine that the first responsibility of the officer is the well-being of the men under his command. This is usually given in precept form at manager training courses as 'the prime responsibility for staff welfare is with line management', accepted with wise nods and not examined further. There is nothing wrong with the doctrine; it is completely acceptable. But one may question the usefulness of telling managers that they are responsible for staff welfare without showing them, possibly through discussion of actual cases, just what this really means in practice. Does it mean the adoption of the 'ever-open door' policy, inviting staff to stroll in and air their grievances when they wish ? Does it mean taking occasional trips through works or office desperately trying to remember first names and asking kindly after the children ? Does it mean dragging reluctant staff from their work from time to time and asking busy-body fashion whether they have any problems ? Or does it mean dealing with welfare in terms of managing by exception—only coming in when things have gone wrong ?

These are loaded questions. The actual behaviour of the manager (or supervisor, in the same context) will depend on what kind of person he is, how well he recognises his limitations of knowledge or skill in handling personal problems and, most fundamental of all, what is his attitude to staff with those problems. Some managers will blame, despise the 'weakness' they intuit in the character of the individual needing help, and offer advice of the 'pull your socks up and take a grip of yourself' variety. Others may have an almost neurotic desire to please, or a wish (perhaps born of personal insecurity) to be regarded as a father-figure wise in the ways of men and able to make god-like decisions about the troubles of lesser mortals. Through bitter personal experience, or through the grape-vine, staff will quickly identify managers and supervisors who go into the personal problem business with motives which appear to them suspect.

However, lack of the right attitudes, knowledge or skill in some managers is only a small part of the case for employing specialist welfare officers. Even if all managers and supervisors were perfect personality-wise, had time to develop the necessary knowledge and skill, and further time to put it into practice, members of their own staffs might still be reluctant to take their personal problems to them. No manager need feel dismayed about this. It is one of the facts of life that we frequently prefer to discuss personal problems with a complete stranger than with somebody emotionally close to us. 'My wife/husband/supervisor does not understand me' is one of the commonest complaints that a welfare officer hears. Managers do not always appreciate that people under their command stand in peculiar relationship with them, in which emotional reactions to authority play a large part. An individual needing help is already in a vulnerable position; emotional needs have put him somewhat off balance. By seeking help from the boss, the individual puts himself in a 'one-down' position at the very time he needs support to face life—and much of life is spent at work. 'What will he think of me if I tell him about it? How will this affect my prospects?' are questions which are present in one form or another in the mind of the individual who considers opening his soul to the scrutiny of another who is in authority over him.

The dismayed manager might reply to the effect that a welfare officer is similarly not a stranger to staff—or shouldn't be—and if the 'stranger' argument is valid why does the employee not go to doctor, parson, solicitor or the Citizens' Advice Bureau? There are several answers to this. In the first place, people do seek expert external advice to a far greater extent than managers realise. But not all of these agencies are open in the evenings—and not all of them are free. It is a matter for conjecture how much casual absenteeism is due to people taking time off to cope with personal problems which could have been dealt with more economically during working hours. It is similarly for conjecture how much certificated sick absence can be laid at the door of busy medical practitioners who may suspect that a headache, sleeplessness or a 'run-down' feeling is caused by personal trouble which they have no time to deal with except by prescribing aspirin, barbiturates or rest. Second, in his own thinking the individual needing help has already ruled out the possibility of medical, religious or legal advice because he knows that his problem has nothing to do with any of these spheres of expertise. Third, he may be in a mental state which prevents him thinking rationally about which outside agency is in a position to help him; or he may be of an intelligence or educational level which does not even know of the existence of outside agencies.

The fourth answer is probably most important of all. It is that a great many personal problems have to do with the man or woman *in the context of work*. If wife or aged parent is ill enough to need care but not ill enough to go into hospital, the problem is thought of not in isolation but in terms of 'Can I get off early ?' 'Can I catch a later bus ?' 'Shall I go off sick?' 'Will I still get my money ?' and so forth. Furthermore, staff spend at least half their waking time at work or in getting to it or leaving it. They know they contribute *to* the organisation when they are reasonably free from worry, and they feel, perhaps inarticulately, that when they are in trouble they are due to get something back *from* the organisation. People are entitled to be treated as full human beings with personal needs, hopes and anxieties; they are employed as *people*, they bring themselves to work, not just their hands, and they cannot readily leave their troubles at home. This is part of the simple philosophy of work which has been suggested as the basis of true welfare. The phrase 'hands wanted' is taking an unconscionable time a-dying; we should now insist on its final funeral.

The unconvinced manager will still suggest other possibilities, rather than accept the need for an expert welfare officer. He is very likely to offer trade union branch secretaries, industrial nurses, training officers, safety officers, First Aiders or personnel selection officers as suitable candidates to take on the welfare officer function. But by doing so he ignores important points, some of which have already been dealt with. He ignores the fact that all of these people have been elected or selected for other work which may need different personal qualities and different areas of knowledge and skill. And just as the manager cannot devote all of his time to personal, group or physical welfare, so these other experts should be employed to cover full-time posts. Most important, all these people stand in a specific existing relationship with the employee needing personal help; he sees them

in a defined role which in his mind is quite different from the one he
seeks.

Role of the Unions

Historically, trade union office-holders may have accepted a welfare
officer role, but that is no reason for their continuing to exercise it.
As industry is at present organised, local trade union officers are
mainly concerned to get the best possible pay and conditions for
their members, even though the unions at national level play an increasingly important role in the *general management* of industry (e.g.
productivity councils, industrial training boards and the like). Staff
may be encouraged by enlightened firms to belong to a trade union,
but very few firms—and not many unions—will accept the principle
of the closed shop. Welfare must cater equally for the trade unionist
in the firm's majority union (which might have a good supply of
active officers), for unionists in minority unions, and for non-
members. This is a comparatively simple point; a far more fundamental one is that by leaving welfare officer work to trade unions the
manager effectively abdicates his own responsibility, offending the
accepted doctrine that the prime responsibility for the welfare of
staff must rest with the line manager.

Trade unions will of course have a part to play in welfare provision,
but their contribution will be most effective in the physical welfare
sphere. One would also expect them to be represented on many of the
group welfare bodies within the firm—benevolent funds, sports and
social councils, First Aid committees and all the other organisations
which are dealt with in subsequent chapters. They may also claim a
watching brief on welfare officer complements, duties and organisation, and it is right that they should be concerned with personal welfare provision at this level. Yet again, trade union officers will rightly
consider it part of their function to seek welfare officer help for their
members when they need it, either as a matter of routine or when a
personal problem comes to their attention which they have not the
resources of knowledge, skill or time to deal with themselves. In
other words, good trade union officers will act precisely as good
managers and supervisors will act. If a problem comes to them which
they cannot handle, they will call in the welfare officer. But trade
union officers, managers and supervisors alike need to be well informed about what a welfare officer does, where he fits into the
organisation, and what are the limits of his function as compared with

the welfare functions of government, local authority or voluntary social agencies. They must also recognise their own limits, not trying to deal with problems outside their competence because of a misguided sense of duty or because of the satisfaction derived from having power over the private life of an individual in trouble. It goes without saying that the welfare officer himself must avoid these pitfalls; later chapters may help in identifying them more clearly.

The Economic Case

So far, the case for employing specially selected and trained welfare officers has been built on a simple philosophy of work—that work exists solely for the satisfaction of human needs. From it we derived the proposition that if the organisation exists to serve the community generally, so it also exists for those it employs. It follows from this that good welfare provision requires no other justification. But this is a hard moral pill for some to swallow; economic justification is sought by those who cannot get it down. Some are quite blunt and straightforward—'I am in business only to make profits, and I am not interested in doing more for my employees than the law dictates, unless it is profitable.'

'Profitability' has been increasingly fashionable in the last few years, and this is a healthy trend. No one will deny that private commercial and industrial organisations cannot survive unless they are profitable. On the other hand, a business enterprise can be profitable without being efficient: efficiency is therefore a sounder criterion than profitability, and it is one which can be applied equally to public enterprise, where 'profitability' may be a meaningless term. Most managers are probably neither 'profitability' nor 'morality' extremists. They appreciate that profitability can never be the end, only the means, since one must ask: profitability for what? The answer can only be related to the well-being of the community as a whole. They are likely to settle for efficiency (or 'productivity') which carries with it a community imperative which 'profitability' lacks, but yet does not introduce the tinge of sanctimoniousness which some find in 'morality'. The question they would like answered is: Is good welfare equally good business? Many more firms would be prepared to take a hand in it if this could be proved to their satisfaction. The answer is almost certainly positive, if by 'good welfare' we also mean 'efficient welfare'.

The Need for Research

The economic case for employing welfare officers should become clearer when we consider what they actually do and how they should do it. No welfare officer service should fear investigation by the cost accountant or research worker. If investigation is feared, it can only be because welfare methods are not as businesslike as they should be. None the less, one must point out quite firmly that no proper research has been done, and one of the purposes of this book is to throw out a challenge to research interests on the one hand and to those who may find themselves 'researched upon' on the other. In making the challenge, one may also point to a trap for the unwary, the trap of 'morale'.

If there is an economic or productivity case for a welfare officer service, it should be shown to reduce accidents, sick absence, casual absenteeism. It should improve quality of production or service. It does this by supplying to individuals information which can lead direct to change of behaviour, or by reducing the anxiety which attends difficult personal problems, thus allowing individuals to operate at something nearer their maximum level of efficiency. One should not rest an economic case on assumptions about 'improving morale' and on further assumptions that such improvements lead to the right sort of behaviour. One can hardly define 'morale', let alone try to measure it. In fact, one of the best-known definitions of morale—'satisfaction with, desire to continue in and willingness to strive for the goal of each task, on the part of those actually performing that task' (Smith and Weston, 1951)—is really so obscure that it has been interpreted in the sense of liking the job, wanting to keep at it and to do more of it. This has led to the assumption that good morale should mean more output, etc., less absence, etc.,—'more' or 'less' of many aspects of behaviour which can be measured. This is of course little more than rubbish. I can be in a 'good state of morale' painting a door, mowing the grass, or just idling, quite satisfied with what I am doing, wanting to continue doing it—at least *for a while*—and willing to strive for whatever goal I have set for myself. But I might also enjoy myself more if I stopped even my idling for a cup of coffee; and speed is rarely of the essence in mowing the grass as it might be in the factory flow-line or at the office desk.

Thus, while we may all claim to have a pretty good idea of what we mean by 'morale', it cannot be measured directly. One should certainly not make the gross mistake of assuming its behavioural consequences, measuring them and then attributing the results to 'changes in morale'. Handyside and Speak, 1964, have pointed out that there is no scientific evidence to support the view that efficiency goes hand in hand with good morale, 'however the latter may be defined or measured'.[1] An odd finding for some people, but it is even more odd that a causal connection should have been assumed to exist.

We are on safer grounds with 'anxiety' than with 'morale', for there is some research evidence which we can take into account. *Mild* anxiety (in the sense of 'expectancy tension') acts as a drive to work well; and learning theory suggests that learning takes place, thus improving performance if it is correct learning, when anxiety is *reduced*. At the other extreme, acute anxiety can be a complete barrier to effective learning and performance. The welfare officer is not concerned with mild anxieties and minor problems of the kind which stimulate effort and give zest to life, but with the grosser types which may lead to day-dreaming, distraction, even paralysis of thinking, thus possibly to accident or absence, which have a definitely negative effect on efficiency. None the less, one would not try to measure anxiety as such. The assessment of the effectiveness of welfare provision should concentrate on aspects of *behaviour* rather than intervening variables such as anxiety, attitudes, morale and job satisfaction, which may or may not result in behaviour changes. The main problem is to isolate the influence of welfare provision as a factor among the many others which can change behaviour. This is a very difficult problem, but not an insuperable one.

In the absence of research evidence on the economics of welfare one may quote only from experience and the personal conviction which experience has given. It is the conviction that good welfare is good business, that poor welfare is bad business. It is also the conviction that quite apart from any economic advantages which may accrue as by-products, welfare is worth doing well with the best welfare officers one can get, or it is hardly worth doing at all. The experience of others is often the most telling argument for some people who are swayed neither by the humanitarian nor by the economic case. To them one must point out that the use of welfare officers in the modern sense is spreading ever more widely in industry, commerce and elsewhere. Organisations which now have them would not dream of doing with-

---

[1] See also Mullen, 1966, for a more general review of the literature concerning the effects of different 'leadership' styles on morale and productivity.

out. They have penetrated into the B.B.C. and the prison service; the Inner London Education Authority and similar authorities have begun to use them in colleges; they serve deep-sea fishermen, railway and dock workers, civil servants and many others.

Finally, one must anticipate an inevitable question—about staff having direct access to a welfare officer. Will this not lead to 'skiving' —to staff disappearing to the welfare officer for a chat (or even just disappearing, ostensibly to see the welfare officer) without having a real need for his services ? And should this not be prevented by staff having first to explain to line supervisors why they want to go ? We must face the possibility of some skiving, but no supervisor ought to put up with its repetition. He should know his staff well enough to identify the possible malingerers, and if necessary have the courage to refuse permission for time off unless there is a good prima facie case for it. Furthermore, a welfare officer should have such a relationship with supervisors that he could pass the word along informally that so-and-so is bothering him with trivia. But this is a negative point. Our provisions should be positive—directed to the man with a real need. We should not deny him proper facilities just because a few people will inevitably abuse them. The problem of malingerers touches on confidentiality and on the welfare officer's relationships, both of which topics are dealt with in more detail later. But it can be said right away that there should be nothing sloppy or sentimental in good staff welfare. Paternalism, mystique and woolly thinking, the enemies of a clear-sighted and businesslike policy, have done a lot to tarnish the welfare concept; the sooner we can clear them away the better.

2 What Welfare Officers Do

Summary   It is better for the welfare officer to have a purely advisory task than to have executive jobs to do as well. He is provided mainly to help staff solve their own problems, not to take problems out of the individual's hands. His job differs from those of professional social workers, with whom he must liaise, but he is much more than a good 'contact man'. A list of specific duties should be drawn up in consultation with managers and trade unionists.

The main areas of activity are private consultation on any type of personal problem; assistance with problems of health or sickness; special responsibilities with young people, elderly and retired staff; advice on group welfare matters such as accommodation, safety, First Aid, sports and social activities; assistance with training courses and advisory work in staff relations where required.

However, a formal list of duties is only the starting-point. Notice boards, staff handbooks and training courses must all be used as channels of communication to ensure that everybody in the organisation has a clear understanding, according to level, of what welfare officers do. Induction to work is the supervisor's and not the welfare officer's responsibility, but newcomers should meet the welfare officer as early as possible. Different approaches are required in dealing with welfare on training courses for operator supervisor and manager levels.

In the smaller organisation, just big enough to employ a singleton, the welfare officer may, rather regrettably, have a mixed executive and advisory load. He may have to ensure that legislation on physical welfare provision is complied with, and assist in negotiation with the trade unions on provision above the legal minima. He may also have a part-executive, part-advisory role to play in Safety. However, the fewer executive functions the welfare officer has to carry out, the more clearly will his role be defined and the more readily will he be accepted as an adviser by those needing his help. It is not enough to *be* an adviser; one must be seen to be one by having few, if any, executive tasks. A mixed role should, therefore, be avoided if possible. Smaller firms in the same locality might seriously consider sharing the services of a single adviser, rather than each have its own quasi-welfare officer with other executive jobs. It is customary in the larger organisations for one welfare officer to serve several local managers and their staffs, and there is no difference in principle between this arrangement and shared service by independent firms. Joint training schemes are becoming commonplace; why not Joint Welfare Officer Schemes?

The greater the number of staff served by a welfare officer, the bigger will be his load of personal casework; but he should never be forced into the situation of dealing only with personal problems. No man in industry or commerce ought to have to deal exclusively with the seamier side of life. (While the professional social worker may be in a different position in so far as he may be selected and trained to deal only with abnormality, it could be argued with some force, although not properly in this book, that psychiatric social workers, probation officers and the rest need spells of activity with the unworried and 'normal' in their working hours as well as in leisure to keep themselves in perspective.) If the point is reached that personal casework occupies more than three-quarters of the load, there is at least a prima facie case for an increase in the complement. More about this later; the point has been introduced at this early stage to indicate the welfare officer's interest in group welfare. This is still advisory, but time must be found to liaise with secretaries of sports and social clubs, benevolent fund committee members and similar people, to encourage and give advice where it is needed.

Before examining what a welfare officer does or should do, we can begin negatively. A welfare officer service does not seek to provide a welfare state in miniature; it does not seek to duplicate the work of statutory, local authority and voluntary social services; it does not seek to 'stand between management and worker'; it does not seek to abrogate the rights and functions of trade unions and the normal processes of trade union consultation. While not part of line management and having no executive responsibility, welfare officers should be provided to assist managers in discharging their responsibility for the welfare of staff.

Broad Principles

It is sufficient at this stage to offer only the broad principles of personal casework dealt with by a welfare officer. They may differ from those which govern the activities of the statutory social workers (who may none the less be styled 'welfare officer') who may have an executive as well as an advisory job to do. The advisory, occupational welfare officer is there to help the individual to solve his own problems; and, as a corollary, not to stand between the individual and his problem by taking it out of his hands. (There will be emergency exceptions to this rule, which will bear re-examination later.) He is jack of all social welfare trades, but seeks to be master of none but his own. If he has a case which relates to probation, child care, psychiatric social work, or any other highly specialist sphere of professional social work or activity, he will liaise with the appropriate outside expert and not try to do the expert's job for him. He regards outside social workers as his long stops, just as the manager or supervisor, who has the prime responsibility for the welfare of staff under his control, uses the welfare officer as *his* expert adviser on the ever-growing ramifications of the welfare state.

One might almost hear the cry 'enough' at this point. 'You are offering a contact man, a broad shoulder to weep on, an amateur do-gooder who only needs a list of names and addresses of social workers in order to "get by".' At the lowest level of welfare officer work the charge is almost true, but operation at the lowest level in too many places has helped to tarnish the concept of welfare at work. There is a great deal more to it than this 'get by' level, and we can best penetrate beyond superficiality by examining specific duties, and, later, what personal characteristics, knowledge, attitudes and skills are required to carry them out properly.

Agreed Duties

Drawing up a formal list of duties is half the battle; such a list should be agreed between managers, the trade unions and the welfare officer(s) themselves. It need not be exhaustive, only a sketch map of the general pattern. As experience is gained, a finer codification can follow—not in the sense of a 'how-to-do-it' reference book which would seek to establish rigid doctrines on how each type of case should be handled, but simply to ensure that welfare officers serving staff in the same organisation have a common basis of approach and action, a similar attitude. Staff would have every right to object if

Welfare Officer John Jones *invariably* dealt with his debt cases by grants from the petty cash, while Mary Smith *always* advised direct confrontation of hire-purchase firms with a view to offering lower weekly repayments.

The following list is offered as a suggestion, a basis for discussion, a starting-point for finer codification.

1 *General*

To be directly available to *all* members of the staff for private consultation and advice, and where appropriate, practical help, on personal, domestic and other difficulties. To examine all cases of personal difficulty referred to him. To liaise with statutory, local authority and voluntary welfare services and associations and to provide information on these or on any other organisations which may give expert help or assistance with personal or legal difficulties.

2 *Problems of health or sickness*

To cooperate with local managers and their staffs, and with internal or external medical services, on problems arising in connection with sick absence, or retirement or dismissal on medical grounds.

To give information on hospitals, specialist medical services (e.g. radiography, inoculation, cervical tests), convalescent homes, etc., to staff requiring it.

To give help and advice as required, on a friendly basis, to staff frequently on sick absence, where personal, family and/or social causes appear to be involved.

To visit individual members of the staff on prolonged sick absence when an obvious or prima-facie welfare need exists.

Subject to the sick person's wishes, to encourage the arrangement of friendly visits by colleagues in cases of protracted sick absence.

To visit bereaved persons to explain provisions made for dependants and to give any other advice and help required which cannot readily be given by friends or relatives.

To advise on the employment of handicapped or disabled staff.

3 *Young people*

To assist supervisors and training officers where necessary in the friendly follow-up of newcomers in the early years of their service, to ensure settling in and general well-being.

To advise and help newcomers in finding lodgings or hostels.

To cooperate with managers and supervisors, on request, in individual cases where tendencies to bad habits or indiscipline are revealed, especially when the home environment is suspected to be a main or contributory factor.

4 Elderly and retired staff

To advise on preparation for retirement on a personal basis and/or liaison with special training courses.

To keep in touch with retired staff through pensioners' clubs and associations, giving such help and advice as may be required when a welfare need is established.

5 Accommodation and safety

To advise management of any defects in working or welfare accommodation or facilities brought to the welfare officer's attention by members of the staff or coming to his notice in the course of other work.

6 Sports and social activities

To encourage and advise local sports, social and benevolent clubs or societies and to assist in setting them up when a demand exists.

7 First Aid

To encourage and advise local First Aid groups on training, practice, competitions and facilities. To liaise with the external voluntary First Aid associations on these matters. (*Note:* Organisations with premises covered by the Factories Acts, or by the Offices, Shops and Railway Premises Act will frequently employ a full-time First Aid Adviser or First Aid Officer who will take over these functions. The local welfare officer's role in First Aid would then be similar to his duties in connection with accommodation and safety. But it is not unusual for the First Aid Officer to be on the staff of a senior or chief welfare officer having supervisory responsibilities.)

8 Training

To assist with welfare sessions on training courses as required.

9 Joint committees

To serve in an advisory capacity on any joint committees when required to do so by both manager and trade unionists.

10 *Group morale*

To foster good relations between all grades and sections of staff and advise when required on any aspects of group morale.

Welfare Supervisors

When an organisation is big enough to employ a team of welfare officers, the senior or chief welfare officer will take on all or any of the duties listed above, plus the following:

(a) General responsibility for the organisation of the welfare officer service, including oversight and direction of the basic-grade duties.

(b) Induction, field training and direction of day-to-day work of the basic grade, including advice and assistance on more complicated personal cases and group welfare problems.

(c) Advice on welfare matters to higher management.

(d) Liaison with professional bodies and external advisory welfare organisations.

Information about Welfare Officers

The need for knowledge

It is not enough for managers, trade unionists and the welfare officers themselves to agree on a list of duties. It is also necessary to make sure that the staff they serve have a good idea of what welfare officers can and cannot do, who they are and where they are to be found. It is particularly necessary for supervising officers to be even better informed about welfare officer duties than the staff they control. Some attention must therefore be given to publicity methods—staff notice boards, handbooks and training courses. Even when all these channels are used there may still be staff who claim to have no knowledge of the existence of the welfare officer. This may be due in part to some sort of unconscious resistance to the idea of seeking help from another person—or quite simply to the staff notice board being so cluttered with out-of-date information that it has long been abandoned as a possible source of interest. Management cannot do much about the former, but it should be looking after the latter as a matter of course. It is perhaps useful to point out here that although the 'grape-vine' may be a most useful means of communication for other purposes, it should not be relied on to do the manager's job of informing staff of the availability of the welfare officer. Staff may be very reluctant indeed to pass around the fact that they have been to see him. And no welfare officer, nor indeed supervisor, is worth his money if he discusses so-and-so's proposed or actual visit with anyone who is not entitled to know. This is one aspect of the confidentiality problem which can be stated very firmly indeed as a general and un-alterable principle.

Notice boards and staff handbooks

Notice board announcements are usually most effective if they are brief. There should be no need to pin up a list of the welfare officer's duties; it is sufficient to display a small card, replacing it rather than altering it when details are changed, which gives name, location, telephone number and a short statement of time availability:

> *Your welfare officer is* ....
> *who is available for private consultation on any personal or domestic*
> *problem, at* .... [address and telephone]
> *between* .... *and* .... *daily.*

It is also worth adding this 'notice board' information to any other which is sent to a new employee before he reports for duty, particu-larly if it is part of the welfare officer's job to help with lodgings or hostel accommodation. But when the newcomer arrives it should be the supervisor's job to induct him—in the basic sense of showing him the lavatories, canteen, where he can hang his hat and coat, and intro-ducing him to the people he will work with. This task should not be given to the welfare officer—nor, for that matter, to the training officer. Later in the induction process there may well be an introduc-tion to these two specialists, and the training officer may take over initial background or job training. However, the supervisor should be made aware right away that he has the basic responsibility for the well-being of staff under his control; the specialists are there to help him, not to replace him. What better means of gentle insistence has the manager than taking it as a matter of course that the supervisor should be first contact—even if this means meeting the new man or girl at the bus stop or station if necessary? It is only too easy for the welfare officer to get a dogsbody role as the supervisor's messenger boy, and this can be prevented only by clear recognition of roles from top management downwards.

If the welfare officer is geographically remote, personal introduc-tion may have to wait until he is visiting the office or factory for other purposes, or he may meet a group of newcomers at a training course. But the new employee should know early that he can have a welfare officer's services if he needs them, although he should not be bothered with a detailed list of the latter's duties. He has enough to remember without having also to cope with information he may never need. If a staff handbook is issued at recruitment stage, it should contain at least a broad statement. Once again, simplicity rather than detail should be the keynote.

Training courses

Linking training courses with staff notice boards and handbooks as a method of publicising the existence of welfare officers and their duties does not do full justice to training. Indeed, the welfare officer's assistance in welfare sessions on introductory courses for 'operator' level, and on courses for supervisors and managers, is so important a topic that it has been allocated a chapter in its own right.

There are several reasons for this. First, the welfare officer's involvement takes time, and this must be taken into account in his records and returns and subsequently in complementing a welfare officer service. Second, there will be a marked difference in what staff at operator, supervisor and manager level need to know about a welfare officer's duties; the higher the level, the more is necessary, and we cannot assume that supervisors and managers can adequately 'pick it up as they go along'. Third, a welfare officer service can be regarded almost as a group welfare provision in itself—which presents us with a classification problem. Fourth, and most important from a practical point of view, we cannot penetrate into the detail of the welfare content of training courses until we have finished exploring 'scope and limits'. It will therefore be sufficient at this stage to make one or two general points, particularly to show the need for differences in approach at different levels.

When considering the 'operator' level, which will be defined very broadly as all staff who do not have a measure of direct responsibility for the work of others, it is clear that the new employee needs little more than a general appreciation. He needs some detail about physical welfare, for he is a 'user' as soon as he joins the firm. He is an immediate *potential* user of group welfare facilities, and he may well join various clubs and societies within his first week. He is also a potential user of the personal welfare service, but we do not know whether his needs are immediate, nor even whether he will ever be a user at all. He should be made aware of the range of personal help which the welfare officer can offer, but the emphasis should be on the normal—on physical and group welfare provisions.

On the other hand, the supervisor needs to know not only *what* a welfare officer does, but also in some detail *how* he does it. The supervisor is after all a first-line non-specialist welfare officer himself, although this does not deny his own right to be a direct user of the personal welfare service. Staff on other personnel work (e.g. sick absence control) who have close dealings with the welfare officer in a *functional* capacity, but who may have no supervisory responsibilities, are in a similar position. Supervisors will know of the *existence* of physical and group welfare services, but training could deepen their understanding, particularly of the role of volunteers in group welfare. However, their main need will be to know how the welfare officer helps with personal problems.

The 'training in welfare' needs of managers are different again. They must see the welfare officer service in the context of the firm's general staff policy, to the formulation of which they should contribute. They should have an even better appreciation of scope and limits than supervisors, for managers will also be concerned with the selection and training of welfare officers, the flow of information about welfare in the organisation, and with complementing and controlling the service. They are *second-line* non-specialist welfare officers, and will not do this part of their job satisfactorily without a very full appreciation of what the specialist can offer. Clearly we can neither generalise about training courses as a method of publicising the service, nor limit discussion of them to the narrow 'publicity' context.

3 Some Principles

Summary   We start from the axiom that the welfare officer seeks to help the individual in need to solve his own problems, not to solve them for him. This is not a hard-and-fast rule because emergency action is sometimes necessary. Exceptions to the main principle lead to the establishment of subsidiary principles. Further principles emerge from considering *whom* the welfare officer is trying to help, *what* he is trying to do, and how he can do it. The discussion leads to two fundamental problems—the dilemma of 'disengagement versus follow-up' and an analysis of the legal, disciplinary and practical limits of confidentiality.

Duties as Distinct from Capabilities

General duties having been established, the shape of the wood recognised, it is time to have a close look at the trees. Until we know *how* a welfare officer should go about his tasks we cannot begin the detailed job analysis which is an essential preliminary to proper selection, training, continued information, organisation, office methods and complementing. Since personal casework is the main part of a welfare officer's job, and the main reason for his existence, we must first examine some of the principles which should guide him, and see how these can be codified into practice in his dealings with different types of problems. Some of his limits *vis-à-vis* managers and supervisors, trade unionists and outside social workers have already been sketched out and it is important to distinguish between what the welfare officer is *capable* of doing and what he *should* do. For example, in his private life he might be a marriage guidance counsellor of long experience, and thus *capable* of giving highly expert service to people with marriage problems. But it does not follow from this that he should either offer or give such service *in his welfare officer role* to staff in his own organisation. Similarly, he may spend some of his private time in voluntary First Aid or in running a youth club, but it is seriously open to doubt whether he should do these things as an internal expert. In this book we are concerned with those aspects of attitude, knowledge and skill which are essential for the welfare officer working within the limits laid down by his organisation's policy, and not with aspects which policy dictates should be outside his sphere of activity. His job must be delineated as carefully as other jobs in the organisation. The managing director may by chance also be a marriage guidance counsellor, First Aider or youth club leader, but no-one would suggest that he should act as such within his own firm.

Principles and Exceptions

The most important principle of personal casework was stated in the last chapter as *helping the individual to solve his own problems*; and as a corollary to this, not standing between the individual and his problem by taking it out of his hands. But principles are not rules, and even with rules there are usually exceptions. There will be occasions when emergency action is essential, when there may not be time for the individual to fend for himself, even with the best advice, or when he is in such a vulnerable condition that he is simply incapable of action. The welfare officer must then use his own judgment—and if necessary seek the benefit of the experience of his supervisor. Emergencies arising from sheer shortage of time are generally easy to recognise, and examples will be given when we come to look at the handling of different types of cases. The assessment of vulnerability and of capability of action is far more difficult; nice judgment of these can be acquired only through experience. And this means not only years spent actually doing the work, but also *collective* experience and guidance by the welfare supervisor, and condensed experience gained at a training course by discussion and analysis of particular cases.

The exceptions themselves point to a further principle. *Emergency action should be taken in such a way that the individual can later cope with his own difficulties.* This begs a question to which the answer is a very firm Yes; the welfare officer must accept that he has a training or educational role. In common with other trainers and educators he supplies information and he seeks to change attitudes and patterns of thinking. Sometimes—talks at training courses apart—he has to give what amounts to active teaching almost in a classroom sense. In debt cases he will frequently give simple instruction on how to budget income and expenditure, or on how to write to a creditor offering reduced payments. In bereavements he will often 'teach' a relative how to deal with probate or letters of administration. This is his informative role, and it is not a difficult one if he himself knows his facts. His role as attitude changer demands not fact so much as tact—and a great deal of humility. It is only too easy to slip from attitude changer to moral judge, and the temptation can be avoided only if he holds fast to the principle of helping the man to help himself.

There is a different kind of temptation facing the welfare officer who is a little too eager to justify his emergency action. He is prone to take short cuts in the name of efficiency, losing sight of his long-term function for the sake of short-term results, and to by-pass normal channels for the same reason. He lays in several stores of troubles for himself if he does this too often. First, he creates *more* work by allowing the dependent individual to become more dependent on him. Second, if normal channels are not used they become rusty, or hostility is aroused when the by-passing becomes evident; thus good relations are soured and the chances of future cooperation are diminished. (The boot may sometimes be on the other foot. If the 'normal channel' claims that he is too busy and the welfare officer accepts a task for the sake of speed, he is implying that he is underloaded and has all the time in the world to do other people's work for them.) The third store of trouble is in the welfare officer himself. If he makes too big a claim for short-term action, in the name of efficiency, he may be thinking only of himself and his own needs; the individual on whose behalf he claims to act may in fact have taken second place on his priority list. He may argue that he is so busy that only short-term action is possible. If he does, he must accept the consequences—an expert examination of his work load to check whether he is at fault or whether he needs relief.

We may usefully penetrate further into the general principles of personal casework by posing a few questions and trying to answer them in a practical way.

Whom is the welfare officer trying to help?

He is trying to help a person who has a problem caused by:

(a) his *environment*, i.e. the material conditions affecting his everyday life, such as finance, housing, working conditions;

(b) his *relationships* with other persons or organisations—colleagues, relatives, neighbours, landlord, local council, etc.;

(c) his own *personality* or condition. It may be that through poor physical or mental health, lack of intelligence or education, emotional immaturity or instability or other cause the problem is the person himself.

These factors may be almost inextricably blended: if he were more mature, he would not be in debt or having a row with his landlord; with more intelligence or knowledge his housing difficulties would not be so acute; if he were not so temperamentally anxiety-prone, he could cope with his wife's illness—and so forth. It is one of the welfare officer's jobs to analyse and separate out as far as he can, to identify those factors he can help to put right, those which need the attention of a different kind of expert, and those which are just insoluble. There will be many in the last category.

What is he trying to do?

He is trying to help the individual to live his own life as fully and efficiently as possible. He must guard against any tendency to direct the other's life for him, and at all costs should not try to put himself in the other's shoes. There is no more fatuous a piece of advice in our national repertoire of myths and 'things that ain't so' than that we should endeavour to 'put ourselves in the other person's shoes'. Try as we may, it just isn't possible. What *is* possible is to find out in an *objective* fashion how the other person views his own problem. If the welfare officer can do this, he can then set about increasing the self-confidence of the other by one or more of the following:

(a) suggesting practical action or sources of practical advice;

(b) giving facts to help him reorganise his environment;

(c) acting as a mirror to help him see his own attitudes and relationships more clearly or in a different light.

How can he help the individual?

When we ask this question we are beginning to leave principles behind and to examine practice. Precisely how the individual may be helped depends on the individual himself, the nature of his problem, the general ethos of the organisation which employs him—composed of policy, rules, precedents, personalities and many other factors—and even the local conditions and customs of the part of the country concerned. It depends also on the welfare officer—his own attitudes, knowledge and skill. Yet there are genuine principles to be found if one considers how the welfare officer should approach the problem in the face-to-face interviewing situation. To keep these principles in a practical form we may express them as 'hints and tips' to the welfare officer himself.

(a) *Establish an atmosphere of friendly informality*. The individual needing help is already vulnerable. Don't patronise him with your own heartiness, or with offers of cigarettes. A quiet offer of a chair is enough, but certainly not a low armchair looking up at you against the light.

(b) *Be seen to be interested as well as be interested*. No clock watching or premature questioning which is interpreted as interrupting; only full and courteous attention.

(c) *Ask relevant questions*. Ask as many questions as are needed to bring out the *relevant* facts, not the ones you suspect may be interesting. (Another bit of mythology is that we need *all* the facts before we can come to a judgment, decision or conclusion. Nobody ever has them, nor can he expect to get them. We all act on judgment of probabilities.)

(d) *Lead* the discussion towards the *other* person's diagnosis of his problem, and *his* pointers to action.

(e) *Offer* your store of knowledge with the humility that comes from knowing it can never be complete; get the other to add to it if he can.

(f) *Recognise* that many folk come to you not for advice but for confirmation of a decision already taken. Recognise also that some people already know what the decision must be, find it unpalatable, but hope that you can suggest a more acceptable alternative.

(g) *Expect* hostility at times, as well as intimidation and threats— of suicide, leaving home, resigning, reporting you to higher authority and what-not. Turn the other cheek in the milder cases, but put it out of reach in others.

(h) *Avoid* emotional involvement like the plague; it is *his* problem, not yours, and you have plenty of your own.

(i) *Sow the seeds of disengagement* as early as possible in the relationship.

(j) *Follow up* later to check the effectiveness of the first contact and of the action advised. To do this, do not rely on memory, but keep adequate records.

(k) *Above all*, remember that you are there to help and not to make moral judgments. 'There, but for the grace of God . . .' and all that.

Disengagement versus Follow-up

There is an element of contradiction between 'sowing the seeds of disengagement' and 'following up to check effectiveness of action advised'. A tragi-comic example will help to bring out the reality of the dilemma. There was once a very big-hearted welfare officer who tried to help a widowed typist with several children to support. At one stage she became ill; he found that she lived nearby, called in, and in the fashion of a good neighbour offered to get in her week's shopping. He even took home a bit of laundry for his wife to do for her. The next week the good lady was back at work and he popped into the typing room to see how she was getting on. 'Very well, thank you, Mr Bigheart', she said, 'I thought you would call in, so I have got my shopping list ready for you and done up my laundry in a parcel.' To his credit, Mr B told the story against himself.

There is no doubt that, in common with most social workers, the welfare officer has to show by some means, and as early in the relationship as he can possibly contrive, that the link will not be a permanent one. His very attitude should balance on the razor edge between friendliness and, for want of a better word, aloofness. He may even have to say quite deliberately that 'it won't be long before you can manage entirely on your own' or find some other phrase which unmistakably rejects a permanent relationship. The hard cases (so close to the psychiatric borderline that the welfare officer may have to think in terms of getting the individual to expert treatment) may need telling quite bluntly that 'you are now on your own', or 'I am sorry, but I have some other and very urgent problems to deal with'. If he cannot disengage, it is probably because the welfare officer secretly likes the father-figure *in loco parentis* role; he likes to have 'welfare ghosts' in his mind and his room. But if he is of this sort, someone has made a mistake in selection; mental toughness is one of the most important things to look for in would-be welfare officers.

Follow-up does of course bring with it the risk of further cementing a dependent relationship, but there are several very good reasons why it must be done. The individual may have done his best with the advice he received, found that his best was not good enough but be reluctant to go back with an admission of defeat. The welfare officer himself cannot learn from his experience unless he finds out what aspects of his advice led to success and what led to failure. And just as the welfare officer needs 'feed-back' (knowledge of results) to know whether he is on the right lines, so, if the case was first brought to his attention by a line manager, does the manager. Save in very exceptional circumstances, the manager should neither seek nor be given details of a personal case. But, if only as a courtesy, he should be told that Bill Brown has now sorted himself out—or that he still has a problem which might affect his work. If the manager then wants more information, the welfare officer must seek the individual's permission before he gives it. The welfare officer puts his own relationship with the manager at risk if he interprets 'confidentiality' as no feed-back at all. This does not suggest that *all* personal cases affecting a manager's staff should be reported to him in broad terms—only those which the manager initiated, plus the very rare ones brought direct by the individual which may have serious repercussions on his employment.

Confidentiality

A necessary prelude to the codification of personal welfare practice must be to find a route through the very emotional jungle of confidentiality. Some people in the world of welfare like to pretend that such a jungle does not exist; or if it does, it should on no account be explored. 'All must be left to the welfare officer's own discretion', say the ostriches in the sand, but do they really appreciate the very heavy burden they are asking him to carry? And can the welfare officer exercise any discretion at all if he is not well trained in the limits of confidentiality?

Legal limits

One limit can be disposed of fairly quickly, as a point of law. It is another of our cultural myths that, in common with solicitors and counsel, priests, doctors, journalists and welfare officers have the protection of the 'confessional' in respect of information disclosed to them which the man in the street would be bound by law to pass on to the proper authority. Not so long ago the myth was exploded as far as journalists were concerned, when two of them were imprisoned for refusing to divulge information required by the courts. (It is of course fair to comment that in these circumstances the individual may judge the moral law to be above the law of the land; he may decide that just as it is right for the courts to sentence him, it is right for him to refuse to disclose his information. This is not the only field in which thoughtful people may claim that the higher morality stemming from personal integrity must inevitably conflict with a legal system based on the greatest good for the greatest number.)

There is little point in going into legal arguments and precedents here; the task has already been done more expertly (Samuels, 1963). But just one extreme example—not a hypothetical one; it really happened. An individual walks into the welfare officer's room and confesses to murder. What does the welfare officer do? The only thing he *can* do is to persuade him to confess to the police or to a solicitor. If necessary, he can go along with him to give moral support. If he cannot so persuade, possibly in the face of pleas that the welfare officer was told in confidence, he has no alternative whatever to reporting the matter to the police either direct or through management.

The only possible exception is when there are strong reasons to suspect that the 'culprit' is mentally deranged and has confessed to a 'crime' which never happened. If this suspicion is justified, the police should still be informed, but the welfare officer must also get the man to treatment (possibly via the Mental Welfare Officer employed by the local health authority) as soon as possible, with a careful report on the details of the conversation. Save in cases of mental illness, instances of refusal to confess again to the proper authority an offence punishable under the criminal code are rare indeed in the welfare world. None the less, instances have occurred; they are sufficient to show that no welfare officer should offer 100 per cent confidentiality.

Limits imposed by consideration of discipline

A similar limit may be imposed by the existence of a disciplinary code in the organisation which employs both welfare officer and offender; but here the welfare officer has some scope for discretion. In his wisdom he may decide to keep minor breaches to himself, using his knowledge of the individual, the manager and the code itself to draw the line between secrecy on the one hand, and persuasion to confess to the right quarter on the other. In all but the most trivial offences he would be well advised to try persuasion—on the principle of not standing between the man and the problem on his conscience—but there will be occasions when failure to persuade need not be reinforced by hints that disclosure by the welfare officer is inevitable. It is worth pointing out in this connection that the civil service welfare officer and the individual confessing to him are both bound by the Official Secrets Act in matters which in private industry may not be the subject of law. There may for example be differences in passing official civil service information to others not entitled to receive it, and passing information about a firm's practices to its rivals. Civil servants who so indulge are immediately liable to prosecution under the Act, whereas a private firm's only recourse might be a claim for damages. Legal advice should be sought without delay if there is any room for doubt.

Practical limits

Other limits of confidentiality are practical ones. A simple point, although frequently overlooked, is that the problem may be such that the welfare officer needs the technical guidance of his own welfare supervisor. The welfare officer often takes it for granted that confidentiality relates only to the welfare officer organisation as a whole, but it is questionable whether the individual needing help really appreciates this. Even some welfare officers have been known to take the view that what they hear is confidential to *themselves as individuals* and not to their *function*. One even went to the length of burning all his records when he retired, leaving his successor to start from the beginning with all his cases—including those the retiring man was currently dealing with.

The most practical point of all is that when the individual needing help requires the welfare officer to *do* something, and not merely listen to him, third parties must almost always be brought in to a greater or lesser extent. There may be something that the manager or a trade union must do; contact may need to be made with a hospital almoner, children's officer or some other outside social worker or organisation. These people must be given some information, although they need not always know the whole story.

The upshot is that the welfare officer must never offer 100 per cent confidentiality, either orally or by means of a notice board announcement, the proper formula for which is the one already given —'private consultation'. Phrases such as 'in complete confidence', 'in strict (or the strictest) confidence' must therefore be avoided if the welfare officer is not to put himself above the law or deny both himself and the person seeking his help the benefit of more expert guidance or knowledge. If someone comes into his room, looks around somewhat furtively and tests confidence by some such remark as 'It must stay within these four walls', the welfare officer must take his cue and ease himself out of the straitjacket. How he does it depends on himself and his judgment of the situation. Sometimes the light, almost bantering, touch is required—something to the effect that if a crime has been committed he will persuade the offender to confess elsewhere; or, quite coolly, that if he wants something practical done, other people may need to know something of the problem. These approaches work very well in practice, and no welfare officer need fear the confidentiality problem—*as long as he knows its limits.*

Part two

OCCUPATIONAL WELFARE
IN PRACTICE

4 Personal Welfare Problems

Summary   Practice is so much a matter of detail that this summary is inevitably one of purpose rather than content. It is not easy to categorise personal problems. One which starts off as apparently 'domestic' may turn out to be basically 'financial'; a 'sickness' problem becomes one of 'retirement'; and so on. Nevertheless, difficulties do not lessen the need to classify, nor do they make the task impossible; they only make it more important for the welfare officer to analyse his personal casework. The discussion of categories in the chapter on Records and Returns is anticipated by using the same classification of personal problems now.

    This chapter is thus a series of sections dealing with Domestic, Financial, Sickness, Bereavement, Living Accommodation, Employment, Retirement/Resignation, and Miscellaneous problems. One purpose is to show that the principles offered in Chapter 3 are drawn from and based firmly on sound practice. The second is forward-looking: to identify more clearly the attitude, knowledge and skill aspects of the welfare officer job, so that they can be drawn together in a more formal job analysis on which to base selection, training and continued information.

Domestic

Domestic problems cover those which are strictly personal and non-financial, and have nothing to do with the fact that Bill Smith is employed in the Timbuctoo Tea Co. Ltd—or whatever organisation it may be—except that the anxiety and worry they produce may have repercussions on his work. Thus the category covers marital and family problems, unmarried mothers, legal cases, problems of conscience, or any others affecting life at home. In dealing with these the welfare officer is more often than not simply there to give the man a chance to unburden; he may be able to do little more than act as a listener or sounding board. He can of course give names of solicitors for legal cases (and should thoroughly understand the statutory provisions for Legal Aid); he can liaise with the moral welfare worker to help unmarried mothers in their predicament; in marital problems he must know where he stops and where the marriage guidance counsellor takes over.

All this is part of his normal job, but there will be many cases where the problem is quite insoluble and no amount of knowledge of the outside social services will help. How far should the welfare officer go? He should give his time without stinting (unless the stage is reached when it is being abused and others are denied his services) in the knowledge that he may be playing some part in preventing the mental breakdown which could result if the sufferer had no-one to confide in. If his advice is sought, he must give it objectively, not as a suggestion that it would be best to do so-and-so, but by helping to sketch out the alternatives in such a way as to lead the individual himself to make the best decision. Further, he should give it as one who has perhaps a broader knowledge of life and people, and not as an expert in any particular sphere. When highly specialised advice is clearly necessary in the severely personal context, it is the welfare officer's job to see that the individual knows where to get it, and to give him courage to seek it. Thus, he can feed 'higher commonsense' advice and broader knowledge into the individual's thinking about his delinquent son—and the more he knows about delinquency in general, the work of children's officers and probation officers, and about the man himself, the more useful his advice will be. But he must stop short of giving the sort of professional advice which the children's officer or the probation officer can give, no matter how much he knows of their work. Similarly, a problem of conscience might be amenable of solution on the 'trouble shared, trouble halved' principle and thus be within the competence of a welfare officer; but he must judge when he should hand over to priest or psychiatrist.

Marriage guidance has already been mentioned. Here again the line must be drawn between the sort of higher commonsense advice with which a carefully selected and trained welfare officer (himself we hope enjoying a happy and stable home life) can point to the solution of everyday problems; and the superior knowledge of the minister, solicitor, psychiatrist, general practitioner or other expert consultant on the guidance panel. Above all he must not seem to take sides—or to try to appear objective by asking the individual needing help to bring the spouse along to see him. This is a crucial line over which the occupational welfare officer must not step—and for two good reasons. First, he is employed to serve his firm's staff, and not the staff's sisters, cousins and aunts; and second, no matter how amiable a character he may be, he is in the spouse's eyes *his* (or *her*) welfare officer. To the spouse, he has *already* taken sides, as a completely neutral marriage guidance counsellor clearly has not. The obvious exception is when both partners happen to work for the same firm, share the same welfare officer and consult him separately; even in such circumstances the welfare officer would be advised to refer them elsewhere if their problem is complicated. He is in fact in a unique position to help the marriage guidance counsellor, who often finds it difficult to see both partners.

Our consideration of 'domestic' cases has shown that another of the basic skills of the welfare officer is 'counselling'—and this is itself a highly specialised type of interviewing. There are many books about different forms of counselling, and the welfare officer may dip at his leisure to supplement his normal training. He could well start with the chapter on 'The Nature of Counselling' in Wallis' useful book (1961) and then go on to the same author's *Counselling and Social Welfare* (1960). For present purposes we need only quote from the first of these two publications:

> The fact is, he has a unique contribution to make. If the counsellor can give up trying to produce the answer out of a hat, so to speak, give up trying to be an advice-giver, give up trying to be an expert, give up trying to hurry, give up wanting to point out, give up wanting to change people, lecture them or impose his own standards on them or run their lives for them—if the counsellor can really give up all these favourite ways of treating unhappy people, then something very important indeed may happen.
>
> What in fact do any of us want when we are 'steamed up' about something? Do we want advice? Do we want to be bossed? Do we want 'if I were you'? Not if we are really worked up, really angry or frustrated or miserable or jealous or hurt. If we are very lucky, we can go to a friend and pour it all out. If our good friend is in no hurry, can accept all we say, can understand what we are feeling and does not interrupt or butt in or give us any advice at all, but is attentive and helps us to tell our tale of woe and accepts all that we feel without trying to be logical about it or even respectable, what a relief that is. Does it not then become possible

for us to tackle our difficulty afresh, having first 'got it off our chest'? The point is that we can then see it in a better light, we can begin to be sensible, to ask for and take sensible advice. But only because we have got all our feelings out not alone or by kicking the cat, but by sharing them with another person and being accepted.

If the welfare officer can do this for his employer's staff, he will be well worth his salary—and his service to the general community in the mental health field will be a bonus. The cost of a breakdown in absence alone is great; in terms of community care it is greater still.

But what happens if he ignores the principles of casework which we have so far identified? Staff get used to running to the welfare officer, expecting him to see them through. They will unload their burdens, evade personal responsibility, get angry when he cannot get them out of their mess; or, if he can, come back next week with another load of trouble. Dependent spirits get more dependent, stronger ones with real problems soluble after proper advice will sneer at the welfare officer's determination to play God; and worst of all the welfare officer will in fact be encouraged to play God. He will bear the miseries of the whole world on his shoulders, become a martyr or take on an air of omniscience or infallibility. It will not be long before he starts telling managers and supervisors how to do their jobs, and his power over other people's lives will sooner rather than later corrupt him. Exaggerated perhaps? It may be, but the best of welfare officers, the ones with highly developed powers of self-criticism and considerable insight into their own motivation, will be the first to admit the 'ego-inflationary' effects of solving someone else's problem. His intentions may be impeccable, but unless he recognises the road to hell he will find it difficult to resist the temptation to tread it. The same point could be brought out, ad nauseam, in discussion of other types of cases. It is quite fundamental in all the welfare officer's work.

Financial

It is with financial problems that the danger of dependence on the welfare officer is most clearly seen. Staff are obviously on a very easy wicket if, whenever they are in debt, the welfare officer volunteers to take their problems off their hands, either by dealing direct with creditors or by securing a loan from the firm's benevolent fund to concentrate the debt to one point. On the other hand, these cases equally illustrate the danger that the welfare officer may take a moral line and try to impose his own standards.

Neither should he impose his interpretation of 'community' standards, for these will vary considerably in different localities and in different social strata. A young executive sure of his rising salary scale may borrow beyond his present income, carefully weighing interest rates against possible decline in money values. The financier similarly enters into debt on the basis of judgment of future values of stocks and shares. But somehow, in our society, the employee who mortgages his future overtime expectations with a hire purchase washing machine to ease his wife's lot is culpable when overtime is suddenly reduced or he is declared redundant. The welfare officer has to learn to be completely objective, assess the man himself, his character, temperament and ability to learn from his experience, and then, if necessary, do some direct teaching on how to balance a budget and how to get creditors to accept smaller repayments.

Debt is a growing problem in our society. The June 1965 issue of the Consumers' Association journal *Which?* contained a 20-page supplement on 'Borrowing—or how to buy goods without paying cash at the time'. It showed the differences between hire purchase and credit sale, budget accounts and mail-order systems; between finance company personal loans, insurance policy loans, and house mortgage loans; between money-lenders and pawnbrokers; between trading checks and cooperative society mutuality clubs; between tally-men and doorstep salesmen; and it dealt with the possibility of borrowing from one's own savings. There is food for any welfare officer's thought in the existence of a 20-page *summary* of methods of borrowing to buy goods; but there is even more in the knowledge that these represent but a small range of the ways of getting into debt.

We have not yet reached the American stage where the range of debts produces a credit rating which is in turn a measure of social worth; but certainly the opprobrium which the Victorians attached to debt is vanishing under the impact of advertising and salesmanship. The welfare officer is not at all concerned with whether or not this is a good thing (at least *qua* welfare officer, although he may have personal views as a citizen). He only knows that his records show an increasing proportion of debt cases and that he must clarify his mind about how he will help deal with them.

Sometimes he must take emergency action direct instead of through the man himself. If a court order is involved, he may have to find out whether the firm values the man enough to be willing to make a loan (or even a grant) to keep him out of trouble. This must be a *managerial* decision; it cannot and should not be delegated to the welfare officer. Similarly, is the manager prepared to offer evidence of character or present income to the court? If so, it is the manager's role to attend the court and do it—not the welfare officer's. The manager may delegate such a task to a supervisor or to someone else concerned with pay or with 'hire and fire'—but not to the welfare officer. If a welfare officer has information about domestic distress, which the court may wish to take into account, it is his job to see that it is made available to the clerk (in County Court cases) or the probation officer (in cases in the Magistrate's Court) but not necessarily to offer himself as a witness. Indeed, he can only protect his neutrality in the eyes of staff, and make clear his non-involvement in disciplinary matters, by insisting on a subpoena if his direct evidence is required. Even then he must confine himself to the facts of domestic background and of his efforts to help, not taking on the management role of certifying pay, type of work, availability of overtime or similar matters connected with the job itself. Some managers may be only too willing to duck responsibilities when an employee is in trouble with the law; the wise welfare officer will do his best to see that these responsibilities are accepted, and accepted by the right person.

This may seem to many to be an uncompromising point of view, making black and white a matter in which there are many shades of grey. But this is often the case with welfare officer work; unless limits are set and recognised by welfare staff and managers alike, separate areas of responsibility will overlap unnecessarily, confusion will result and the staff's confidence in the welfare officer service will be undermined.

If emergency action is not called for, the welfare officer has to accept that apart from his counselling job he has a clear-cut responsibility to gauge the debtor's ability to learn to fend for himself and then start to 'teach' on this basis. He must first try to make sure that the individual needing help has indeed given him the full facts of his financial state. This may demand far closer questioning than would be possible or admissible in the strictly counselling context; although people in financial difficulties are often better able to 'externalise' the problem in terms of £ s. d. than they could externalise their moral problems or anxieties over members of their family, it often takes a long time to establish the extent of debt. Here the welfare officer is almost an auditor. He must have evidence of incomings and outgoings, of 'capital assets' and the 'liquidity' position, identify the creditors, and above all know what is 'on hire purchase', how long the goods have been held and whether they are—*to the individual*—necessities or luxuries. When the picture is complete, he and the debtor can look at it together to see how it should be altered *by the man's own decision.*

Moral values are bound to be discussed and cannot be avoided—but they must be based on the 'Law of the Situation'[1] which confronts the individual needing help. In a very simple case, the man may be two pounds a week in the red but admit that he spends more than this on cigarettes. He can therefore make the simple decision (simple only in its obviousness!) that he will stop smoking so that his wife may have her spin-dryer. Or what he himself admits is an unreasonable sum goes each week to the pools, the betting shop or the publican. Should this outlay be stopped so that he can continue to run his car or so that he can save enough to take the children on holiday? Cases of this kind are not only simple in content, but it is often plain that the man was already on the point of taking the obvious decision and had called on the welfare officer for confirmation or support. It is far easier to give up a minor vice or extravagance when we have told somebody else that we are going to, than to make such a decision in private; we can easily deceive ourselves and produce first-class reasons why we should not act as we had planned, but it is not so easy to deceive or convince another. The welfare officer will then accept the supportive role into which he has been cast—and make another appointment in a week or two to find out how the other has got on. This is of course precisely what the other wants.

The next stage of difficulty is when there are no obvious things to do about the present budget. He may not smoke, drink or gamble, but overtime has suddenly been withdrawn and his hire-purchase commitments are more than he can now afford. Values come in again. Did he take on the washing machine because his wife is an invalid with young children, or is she healthy and childless with little to do anyway except keep up with the Joneses? How long has he had the machine? How many of the instalments have already been

---

[1] See Mary Parker Follett, 1941. 'No smoking' in an explosives factory is clearly a 'Law of the Situation', but the same notice in the lavatory of a commercial firm clearly is not.

repaid? Should he keep it or send it back and cut his losses? The welfare officer clearly has to know a good deal about hire purchase and in what circumstances goods may be returned. Once again the decision may be simple in principle but difficult in practice. The man may not want to part with the tape-recorder which he started buying only a month ago, and he will lose his deposit and three weeks' instalments if he sends it back. But this may be the best thing to do.

Even if creditors are pressing, they will almost invariably prefer to take smaller weekly repayments than go to the trouble and expense of a court summons (which in any event might result only in an order for smaller weekly repayments). But the individual in need may not know this. He is not used to getting threatening letters—whereas the welfare officer has seen plenty of them and knows that they are often empty. Thus he can reassure, judge what weekly amount would be acceptable and advise the debtor to write offering it. If the man is no more used to writing letters than receiving them, he can even give him a draft to copy.

As a last resort—but only as a last resort if creditors still insist and threaten court action—the welfare officer may even write himself. It is remarkable what a short note on the organisation's headed paper can accomplish, if it is a bald statement to the effect that Jim Jones can no longer make full repayments because he has been taken off overtime (or has been away sick on reduced pay) but is willing to pay at five or ten shillings a week. But unless the man is so physically ill or emotionally disturbed that he really cannot write himself, the welfare officer should show him how to do it rather than do it for him. He is undoubtedly tempted to write himself at the outset, to speed up the case, or because he knows from experience that the particular firm ceases to press when he intervenes, but he has to remember that he is there to help the man in the long term as well as in the here-and-now.

Just as the welfare officer should know something of the law on hire purchase, so he should be aware of the difference (made in the *Which?* supplement) between a normal bank loan and the sort of 'personal loans' offered by firms which describe themselves as 'banking institutions'. It is by no means common knowledge that whereas a bank will frequently make a loan and charge interest only on the amount outstanding, other money-lending institutions will not only charge a fee for initial service but will also charge interest on the whole amount of the loan for the whole period involved. One does not need higher mathematics to work out that this effectively doubles the amount of interest. He can point this out to anyone who comes to seek advice on whether he should ask for such a loan, and find out if there may be other ways of raising money. Perhaps there are National Savings Certificates, insurance policies or other securities which the owner is unwilling to cash for a short-term emergency but which a reputable bank would hold against a loan at a comparatively small rate of interest.

The welfare officer must also know something of the law relating to moneylenders as such (well dealt with by Samuels in the book already quoted), and of the activities of quasi-moneylending organisations which operate by offering 'second mortgages'. In many parts of the country he will have to get wise to the ways of 'tally-men', of loan clubs which frequently penalise their members if they do *not* borrow money, of organisations issuing 'checks' for the purchase of goods (at least one shilling commission for every one pound check) and of ways in which some housewives make money out of their neighbours by selling 'lines' (similar to 'checks') for a commission from district agents. At some stage in the building up of his knowledge of the ramifications of debt-producing and debt-recovery systems he will no doubt begin to point to the utter simplicity of the Post Office or Trustee Savings Bank. This is sound practical advice and he should give it whenever he thinks there is a chance it might be accepted.

Every debt case is different, no matter what the objective situation is, because the debts have been incurred by an *individual in need*, with his own values and weaknesses, his own family background (including his wife—a very important factor in the situation) and his own temperament. It is therefore not possible to lay down hard and fast methods of dealing with them. But, as in all personal casework, the guiding principle of helping the man to help himself will ensure the right approach.

Sickness

Dr H W Ashworth of the Darbishire House Health Centre asks, 'Why bother to go back to work?' (1966). He says that there is no doubt that if unjustified sick absence could be eradicated we would go a long way to increasing production, but . . . 'how to do this in an affluent society, and in a welfare state?' He does not set out to answer the question, but lists certain formulae for sick absence *control* work.

Frequency Rate	Number of periods of sick absence experienced by an employee in one year.
Severity Rate	$\dfrac{\text{Total number of days lost in sick absence}}{\text{Number of periods of sick absence}}$
Disability Rate	$\dfrac{\text{Total days sick absence per year}}{\text{Number of claimants}}$

Ashworth is of course perfectly right about loss of production, and no-one would dissent from his view that, 'We all, as doctors, managers, shop-stewards and workers, have a real need to stand back and take a new look at this problem.' The difficulty of doing anything about it probably lies in the word 'unjustified'. Who is to say whether sick absence is justified or not? How can a manager challenge a medical certificate? How far can sick absence be controlled? What should one do about malingerers?

Questions of this kind sharpen the difference between welfare as approached from the 'social responsibility' philosophy and the 'productivity' philosophy. 'Productivity' tends to take us straight into 'control formulae' in which the individual disappears; and 'social responsibility' straight to the individual, without reference to the possible usefulness of control formulae. We need both; they are complementary and not mutually exclusive. But it must be quite clear that sick absence *control* is no part of a welfare officer's job. He is there to help the individual by sound advice and counselling; control, especially of malingerers, is for the manager.

On the other hand, just as financial cases show up the dangers of dependence, so sickness cases will point to those of woolly-mindedness and sloppy sentimentality. We must first accept that not every individual away on sick leave has a welfare need. He may indeed have broken a leg, be getting full pay (without any travelling or other work expenses) and enjoying himself catching up on his reading, listening to his records or sunning himself in the garden. The pain has long since subsided and he is being well cared for by his wife and quite happy, thanks very much. Or he may be alone in digs or in hospital, without friends or relatives, or at home wondering how he can possibly manage on National Insurance benefits. He may know he is dying from cancer, or that his leg will have to be amputated, or that he will be blind within a year. How is welfare need to be established and who is to do it?

The second thing to accept is that members of the staff on sick absence have as much right to a welfare officer's services—when they need them—as those who are well enough to go to office or factory. Furthermore, they have a right to them via management, via trade union, through an outside organisation, *or direct*.

Unannounced visits

To get an answer to the question of whether a welfare need exists, the novice will probably just go along and find out, more often than not well armed with chocolates, grapes, flowers or what-have-you. And if the man is out, visiting his doctor or hospital or sitting in the park on his doctor's instructions, that's just too bad. Leave a note, call again tomorrow and hope for the best. But if the welfare officer does find him at home, what does the sick man think is the object of the unannounced visit? Should he trust this welfare officer chap, or has he been sent along by the manager to find out if he is really ill or just swinging the lead? A medical certificate in itself is no guarantee that he is not malingering. If a man goes to his doctor and complains of headaches, feeling run down, not able to face work, the doctor has no means whatever—apart from the shrewdness of experience—of finding out if all this is true. He has to take what he is told on trust, and give the patient the benefit of the doubt.

In some localities the chances of wasting time through unannounced visits are small enough to make the risk worth taking. Similarly, when the welfare officer is well known to all members of the staff (or at least to the individual on sick leave) the risk of misinterpretation is also small. There is a delightful true story of the welfare officer who dealt with suspicion by 'instant aplomb'. As he went in the garden gate he found the sick absentee cleaning his bicycle. Not a wit abashed, the welfare officer countered the other's rising flush with, 'Ah, occupational therapy, I see!', only to find out later that the doctor really *had* suggested it. However, instant aplomb apart, the two risks together add up to enough to make the novice think again and find some other way, as a *general* practice, of establishing welfare need, accepting that there will be occasions when general practice should be waived.

When he does his re-thinking he should also take into account who he is, who pays him, for what is he paid and whom he is supposed to be serving. This might lead him to realise that 'I was passing by, so thought I would look you up' is very often a selfish remark—an expression of his own convenience rather than that of the man he is being paid to serve. A further reminder to him: his duties also include 'subject to the sick person's wishes, to encourage the arrangement of friendly visits by colleagues'. It is not his job to take fruit and flowers on their behalf, unless he has to go anyway on his own specialist business, but rather to encourage them to go themselves. Unless there is a real welfare need, most people would far rather have a visit from their workmates. But the sick man may not want anyone at all, and the welfare officer should be the last to drum up a deputation to go and see someone who wants to be left to himself. So, if he must respect a sick person's privacy and feelings in this regard, must he not also respect them himself when he is tempted to 'just drop in' as he is passing by? Furthermore, his personal interest in the man's welfare is the interest which derives from his role, and only rarely (in cases of actual personal friendship carried on outside the firm) his own interest *qua* John Jones. Basically, he, as the welfare officer employed by Fibreglass Dustbins Ltd, wants to know whether another member of the staff of Fibreglass Dustbins Ltd has any need of his help—and he wants to know *on behalf* of Fibreglass Dustbins Ltd.

Of course, we depersonalise the welfare officer in this way only at some peril. If we depersonalise him too much he becomes an automaton, making routine enquiries in a routine spirit, and good welfare dies because its humanitarian root is cut off. Gardening analogies may be dangerous, but a tree will fruit the better after removal of the suckers, and unwanted wood. Good welfare officers must get rid of the suckers of woolliness and sentimentality in order to keep their real purpose firmly in mind; they must cut off the dead wood of nugatory journeys so as to keep and encourage the useful shoots of their effort. In other words, they should not waste their time on social calls which work colleagues could do better and thus remove themselves from those who may have a real need for their services. They should go only when there is at least a prima-facie case to do so.

How to establish welfare need

This digression into analogy has led back to the simple question of how to establish welfare need. One more basic point before the obvious practical answer is offered: whether or not there is a welfare need, a firm which employs a welfare officer should be the sort of firm which wants to be in touch with absent members of the staff. This will be not only because it wants to discharge its moral obligations, but also because it must deal with the practicalities of sick pay, of possible temporary promotion for the man covering the work, and of all the other stresses and strains which absence creates. It is therefore right for line managers/supervisors to make and maintain contact, and not to expect the welfare officer to do it in cases where his expertise is not necessary, nor rely on the man's work colleagues.

Thus the logical and expedient solution is for the manager to write out to sick absentees, express general concern and good wishes for speedy recovery, *and remind the sick man of the availability of the welfare officer*. To preserve the absentee's right to the *direct* approach he could make if he were at work, the manager should go one step further than this and enclose a stamped and addressed envelope so that he can write back to the welfare officer direct, without the knowledge of the manager, if he so wishes. Some managers will want to write and sign their own letters, others will want to sign letters produced by their staff. In the bigger organisations the entire duty might be delegated to someone who deals with sick absence control as a whole-time function. Such letters do not need to be written by specially selected and trained welfare officers; the task is either a personal one for the manager/supervisor of the man concerned, or it is one which can be delegated to clerical level.

If a delegated task, stereotyped letters should be avoided. If Bill Smith gets a duplicated letter with his name filled in, the essential sense of personal interest is lost; he knows that he is just one of many written to in routine fashion, and he may not even value the reminder that the welfare officer is available if he wants him. But a clerk on sick absence work in a large-scale organisation, who may have to send out a score of letters each week, would be hard put to find new forms of words for every individual. In these circumstances there is no harm in having standard drafts duplicated, which may be adapted to individual needs and then sent off to the typist.

A standard practice of this kind will cater for most employees who are away, and the welfare officer may be approached by a proportion of them. But no standard system can possibly meet every need. There will be some people too proud to ask for the welfare officer even though he could help them; others may not be able to write (because they have never learned, or they have never written since they learned, or they are too ill or upset, or a hand is in bandages, or for some other reason). The system *must* incorporate a means by which the welfare officer can himself take the initiative and not wait for the sick man to ask for him. Liaison with sick absence control staff is vital. He must be told immediately of any cases where there is at least a prima-facie reason for him to offer service. For example, the individual may live alone or in lodgings; he may have been taken direct from his work to the hospital; he may be known to be subject to mental illness; office or factory colleagues may have heard through the community grapevine that he is in trouble—or that he is likely to be because his wife has left him and he has young children to look after. While none of these possibilities make a case for unannounced visiting to all and sundry, there will be some occasions when the welfare officer must just put on his hat and coat and go. Indeed, if he does *not* go out to all and sundry, he will be more readily available to meet emergencies of this kind.

Each organisation must decide at what stage in absence the manager should make contact by letter. After one day would be unworkable—the man might be back before the letter had been typed; and after six months would be ludicrous—the man might be long since dead. The choice will be governed partly by staff available to do the work and partly by whether or not the firm has a sick pay scheme, but it should rest mainly on an examination of the sick absence records. Some organisations have found, taking certificated and uncertificated sick absence together, that something like half of the total sick absence in any given year can be accounted for by single days; about ten per cent by two-day spells; and below five per cent each for three-, four-, five-, six- and seven-day spells. Looking at the picture in terms of weeks it may be found that 75 per cent of all sick absence lasts for one week or less, about ten per cent lasts from one to two weeks, and five per cent from two to three weeks, figures for longer periods then dropping very sharply and flattening off for some weeks before dropping to zero.

Whatever the picture for the organisation concerned, the graph will be exponential in character and will suggest times which on the one hand will not involve excessive work but on the other will ensure that the longer absentees are catered for. Organisations with general sick pay schemes will probably find that the choice of two to three weeks as the time to make contact is a sound one, whereas staff whose only benefit is from state provisions may need to be contacted earlier— say at the beginning of the second week.

Visiting is by no means the only task for the welfare officer in the sickness field. He may be able to give straightforward advice or factual information by letter or telephone. He may have to advise managers as well as other staff about specialist medical services. He may be called in by the manager to interview people with poor *cumulative* sick records. In these cases the sick record is such that, although no single spell of absence was long enough for special contact to be made, the *frequency rate* or its reported cause provides an indication that something in the man himself or in his environment needs a welfare officer's attention.

Mental ill-health

Many cases of short but frequent absence will point to the possibility of mental ill-health, particularly if the medical certificates give such clues as 'headache', neurasthenia, sleeplessness or other symptoms of strain. Sometimes there is stress in the environment which can be reduced by increasing the man's knowledge of the social services—the stress of a sick wife, who may need the Home Help service, sleeplessness caused by rowdy neighbours who might respond to a solicitor's letter or police intervention. Such cases are due to be re-classified as 'personal' as soon as the underlying causes have been established. Others may have been *precipitated* by environmental stresses but would not in themselves have led to ill-health had there not been a *predisposing* cause in the man's own genetic make-up. Most of us have a breakdown point somewhere along the line, and predisposition to neurosis is only a matter of a degree; we are all more or less vulnerable.

Mental illness cases are amongst the most difficult for a welfare officer, even when the man may have been seen by his own doctor. Not all G.P.s have been trained in elementary psychiatry, and some are just too busy to do more than treat the symptom; they do not have the time to enquire into home and work background and give the man an hour to talk himself out. This is no slur on the medical profession. Modern medical training *does* include principles of mental health and mental disorder, and G.P.s themselves are increasingly worried by their overload of work. The picture may change in the course of time, but this book is concerned with the facts of present life. Titmuss, 1964, has discussed some of them and the subject is now in open social debate. Most doctors will be only too grateful for the additional information on home and work which the welfare officer can often

supply—with the permission of the man concerned. When they have
it they can decide whether to carry on with treatment themselves or
whether to refer the patient to a psychiatrist.

It is by no means unknown for a man in a disturbed state to with-
hold information from his own doctor—so forcing him to deal only
with the symptom—especially if the same doctor also treats members
of his family. He does not want the doctor to know of his troubles,
either for fear that his wife or mother will get to know, or because he
casts the doctor in a purely medical role and denies his interest in the
man as a whole person. The welfare officer's first task here is to
counsel—to act as a mirror and a repository of information. Once we
have told our troubles to one person we are more prepared to tell
another; thus the individual in need may then accept the welfare
officer's encouragement to repeat it to a doctor. If encouragement is
insufficient, persuasion must be tried, by pointing out the doctor's
need for more information and the confidential nature of his relationship with the patient. If this is not enough he may even have to discuss
with the individual the possibility of transferring to another doctor
(and he can suggest one or two he knows to have special interest in
mental disorder).

What then ? Or what if most of the absence has been uncertificated
and the man refuses to put himself in his doctor's hands ? The welfare
officer often has to try a new tack. People, especially those with paranoid tendencies, may not take kindly to being told bluntly that they
need psychiatric attention; according to them they are quite all right
and it is 'the others' who should be treated. The most fruitful line is
often to concentrate on the physical side and to suggest that a doctor
could 'do something for your nerves' or 'give you a tonic'. To the
average man 'nerves' are *things* and could well go wrong or 'become
frayed'; they can then be 'soothed', perhaps by a bottle of coloured
water. The potential patient may well accept this line of reasoning and
the welfare officer will have achieved his primary object—to get him
under medical care. Subterfuge has its place in welfare work, and this
is one type of case where the end justifies the means. As far as possible
the welfare officer should deal with the doctor only through the
patient, but there will be occasions when he has no alternative but to
see the doctor himself—even without seeking the man's permission.
This may appear to be a breach of confidentiality, but it should be
remembered that rules on confidentiality are drawn up to govern
normality. Here we are dealing with someone who is by definition

abnormal, someone who by definition does not know what his best interests are.

If the welfare officer completely fails to get a mentally disturbed person to medical care he can only pass the responsibility to someone else—to his welfare supervisor, possibly to the manager when there is no welfare supervisor, or, *in extremis*, to the local authority's mental welfare officer. Clearly, he must know a good deal about the Mental Health Act, the statutory duties of mental welfare officers and the role of the psychiatric social worker before he can decide whether he can refer a case in this way. At least he can seek the advice of the mental welfare officer even if the latter is precluded from acting directly.

Especially in mental disorder cases, but generally in all cases he deals with, the welfare officer must know something of transference[1] and how both to use it and avoid it. 'Sowing the seeds of disengagement' has already been mentioned and should always be in the forefront of a welfare officer's mind. But without some degree of transference it is not possible to develop the right relationship. What must be avoided at all costs is the sort of transference situation where the man in need has not only cast the welfare officer into the highly expert role he wants him to take, but the welfare officer has himself accepted it. There was in fact a welfare officer who once got involved in a particularly difficult mental disorder case, where the woman concerned refused absolutely to talk to anyone else. Describing the case to other welfare officers at a training course he suddenly realised that he had said 'my patient'. Although he himself had offered the case for discussion to illustrate the dangers of involvement it was not until he had made the 'Freudian slip' that he became fully aware of how involved he had been. This book cannot deal fully with transference, but there are many written for professional social workers which can be consulted (e.g. Timms, 1964).

To wind up this section we should look ahead to our subsequent job analysis and remind ourselves of what sort of knowledge the welfare officer needs to deal with sickness cases. The Mental Health Act has been mentioned, and the functions of others working in the mental illness field. To this we must add that he must have at his

---

[1] 'Transference' is a technical term in psychotherapy for which we owe a debt to Freud. But it is used here in a much simpler lay sense—the transference of some affection (personal liking) which tends to put the welfare officer on something of a pedestal.

fingertips—or at least in his files—a mass of information about medical insurance schemes (e.g. Hospital Savings Association, Hospital Saturday Fund) as well as state provisions, the location, charges and rules of convalescent homes, the local authority's health services, the Appointed Factory Doctor Service (H.M.S.O., 1966) and a great deal more. He must also be on good terms with G.P.s, hospital doctors and almoners. If his organisation has its own internal medical service he must also know something of the problems of medical etiquette involved in consultation and referral. If he is wise he will deal with local G.P.s and hospitals through the firm's doctor and not direct, except with the firm's doctor's agreement. Attitudes and social skills are just as important for him as factual knowledge.

Bereavements

There can be little doubt that one of the most widely appreciated services of a welfare officer is the friendly advice and help he can give to the relatives of members of the staff who die before retirement. (It may also be the organisation's policy to offer a welfare officer service to *retired* staff and their dependants; more about this later.) Although this help is given to people who are not members of the staff, and is, therefore, strictly outside the normal terms of reference of the welfare officer, it is justified on humanitarian grounds alone. But there are also very good reasons why it should be offered for the sake of 'good morale' and for the good image of the firm in the eyes of the community. The staff will think the more of the sort of management that has an interest in the well-being of those who have been left behind—and their own feelings of security will be reinforced.

This does not imply that without welfare officers bereaved people would be destitute; and in fact the welfare officer does not normally have access to the sort of cash that could lift a needy widow above the poverty line. The state *does* provide; local officers of the Ministry of Pensions and of the National Assistance Board (now Ministry of Social Security) are very helpful and friendly. The gap which the welfare officer can fill, the gap which he so often fills in other cases, is that the scope and operation of statutory bodies are not always apparent to the distressed relative. The welfare officer can frequently help if only by making them known and interpreting them. This should be his primary role. Normally, he will keep to his guiding principle and not stand between the widow and her problem by taking it out of her hands—he should make sure that she knows the various legal and other requirements and get her to make the necessary arrangements herself.

Giving her an active task to do, as long as it is within her competence, is frequently the best welfare measure; the driving force of activity can often dispel depression and tears more effectively than any expressions of sympathy. If the widow clearly cannot cope, because she is too upset, too old, too illiterate, or for any other reason, the welfare officer should try to find another adult member of the family who could take on the work with some help and advice. If no other adult is prepared to act, and if the estate is not of such a size and complexity as would justify calling in a solicitor, the welfare officer should himself give all the direct help he can in making funeral arrangements, clearing the estate and securing the state benefits to which the widow is entitled. But he should do so in such a way as to preserve her independence of mind and action; if he does not, he may well find that she is a 'welfare ghost' for him for the rest of her own life. He must of course also avoid getting personally involved in problems stretching beyond the limits of his powers and responsibility—he should help only in a friendly way and not advise on matters appropriate to a solicitor or to the Probate Office, Ministry of Social Security or local authority welfare officer.

To start right at the beginning, the welfare officer should know something about wills and should actively encourage any member of the staff, coming to him for advice, to make one. He may also tackle this as a group welfare problem and perhaps write a short article for the firm's own magazine or house journal as a propaganda exercise, knowing that the more members of staff who make wills, the less work for himself or his successor in the years ahead. However, he should not give lengthy oral explanations about wills, thus abrogating the solicitor's function. Instead he should encourage folk to go to a solicitor, to have the whole thing done professionally. If such advice is refused (as it often is, through superstition or fear of the cost) he should offer a simply written 'hand-out' which the man may study at leisure. He should on no account actually draw up wills himself; the Law Society would rightly be aggrieved if he did, and he would be liable if anything went wrong.

He must then establish good relationships with staff of the nearest Probate, and Customs and Excise offices. When he does he will frequently find that they are quite willing to act directly with widows without himself as an intermediary. He should also know something of the practices and costs of some of the local funeral directors. He will find that some will do everything and will do it cheaply, while others cater more for Evelyn Waugh's *The Loved One* class. Others may be only too glad if neighbours have offered to 'lay out' the body. In some communities there is always someone who will do this for a small charge, although it is a service properly to be performed by funeral directors.

When he is told of a death, the welfare officer should not necessarily go out right away to offer condolences and to rush in with advice to all and sundry. He should first find out whether someone else has been involved—perhaps the man's colleagues or supervisor. But even if no immediate action on the welfare officer's part seems necessary he should pay a fairly early call to make a superficial assessment of the situation as a guide to his future action. If it is readily apparent that the relatives can well handle their own affairs, he should limit his interest to providing information about what his organisation may need later (e.g. copy of death certificate). Where he finds that further help will be needed it may be sufficient to arrange a meeting *after* the funeral, when relatives are more settled and better able to discuss business matters. However, this should not deter him from making tactful enquiries about the immediate financial position if there is any evidence to suggest that the relatives are short of money to meet the usual needs but are too distressed to talk or think about it. The welfare officer may be able to arrange a short-term loan from the firm or its benevolent fund, pending encashment of savings or insurance policy.

The rest is mainly a matter of technical knowledge. The welfare officer has to know about Widow's Benefit, Widowed Mother's Allowance, National Insurance Death Grant, Grants of Representation, how to claim Post-War Credits (which baffle many widows) and a host of other things. But we must not forget his counselling role. The loss of the family breadwinner usually means a fundamental change in the mode of living of the family, and the welfare officer can often help in the process of rehabilitation. If the widow is able to work he may advise her about the general employment position. He can help her decide the wisdom or otherwise of working if there are children under school age; he can help her cope with her loneliness by putting her in touch with the nearest branch of the 'Cruse Club' (specially for widows) or telling her about various forms of social or other voluntary work. He can in other words help her to get on her feet after one of life's cruellest blows, and then leave her to stand on them, his telephone a lifeline for her if she ever needs it.

Most of the 'action points' in bereavement cases can be put on a tick-sheet for the welfare officer's own use, or for him to hand to any relative capable of direct action. Contrary to the views of some welfare officers who over-fear depersonalisation, this is not a reduction of human misery to the soulless expression of forms and legal requirements; it is merely a sensible precaution in a field where there is so much to remember that memory may fail. Such a tick-sheet can be based on the printed leaflet 'Practical Problems Following the Death of a Relative', obtainable from any Citizens' Advice Bureau or the National Council of Social Service.

Living Accommodation

Many people come to the occupational welfare officer for advice and help about living accommodation, often expecting him to conjure up a council house, twist a landlord's arm or appear for him at a Rent Tribunal. He has to accept that there is usually very little he can do beyond counselling. (If they are unmarried, he may be able to help with lodgings or hostels, which are dealt with later.) He must know something of the law on landlord and tenant, about the Rent Acts and related legislation, and the difference between 'controlled' and 'decontrolled' property, and he may supply such facts. But he may *not* take on the functions of a solicitor, the local court, or the local authority housing officer or of anyone else who has a statutory or legal duty to do. He should certainly not attempt to intercede with the housing authority and use his influence or standing to move his man up the housing list. (This is one of the many reasons why a welfare officer would be wise to resist the temptation to stand for local council election, or should consider resigning when he has been appointed welfare officer. His own probity may not be in doubt, but what if he actually represents the voter who is seeking his help *qua* welfare officer? This seems far-fetched, but it has happened.)

What a welfare officer *can* do, and do most usefully, is to enquire of anyone in accommodation difficulties whether or not he is on the local authority housing list. It is not unknown for a welfare officer to find that this simply has not been considered, in spite of the fact that the applicant would be entitled to so many 'housing points' that he would have prospects of being allocated a house or flat within a measurable time. It is also quite likely that the individual in need has not kept the local authority up-to-date; he may have had two more children since his 'points' were calculated, he may have taken in his own or his wife's widowed mother, his wife may have become invalid, or in some other way his circumstances may have changed to such an extent that if the council's housing department were aware of them something might be done more rapidly. Normally, as with debt cases, the welfare officer should encourage the man himself to call on the local authority or write (perhaps helping him with the drafting), but also as with debt cases there may be occasions when he may do so direct, perhaps enclosing a certificate of employment and income from the manager or wages clerk acting for him.

He should also be knowledgeable about New Towns, expanded towns and similar schemes, and in what circumstances the firm's employees could qualify for rehousing in them. If the firm happens to have a branch office or factory in the new town the welfare officer may already know that managers would be only too willing for the employee to transfer. In other circumstances he will have to discuss the whole case very fully with the manager and get him to decide whether to keep an employee whose accommodation problems may have an effect on his work, or whether to cut losses and encourage him to go. Altruism is not unknown.

Employment

This category covers all cases where the problem originates exclusively from, or can only be solved in the context of the fact that the individual in need works for the particular firm. Thus it includes complaints about supervision, lack of promotion prospects, requests for transfer to another department, office or factory, requests for special duties, or time off, and anything to do with the firm's disciplinary code or rules. The welfare officer will often find that many of the problems should have gone direct to supervisor, manager or trade union officers, and he should do his best to see that they are re-routed. Supervisors should know under what circumstances time off may be granted, and be able to grant it when justified. Complaints about supervisors need very careful handling. They are best taken direct to the one-above level by the man-with-the-moan, or to trade union representatives. But if the welfare officer gets a lot of them, and about the same supervisor, he may well have a quiet word with his own welfare supervisor or the manager: he should only rarely tackle the offending supervisor himself. Requests for transfer are similarly proper to go direct to the supervisor—*even when the applicant claims hardship grounds.*

Transfers

This apparently harsh doctrine on transfers needs a careful explanation, since hardship is the very stuff of life for the welfare officer and the raison d'être of his existence. The point is, whether the applicant is the only one with hardship grounds; and if not, is his hardship any harder than someone else's ? If the welfare officer tries to help a transfer case on its way by *volunteering* a report on domestic or personal circumstances, there is a certain danger that injustice may be done. Another member of the staff may have applied for transfer to the same post and may in fact have a stronger case on hardship grounds—but he may be of a more independent turn of mind and not have brought his problems to the welfare officer. If the welfare officer has already forwarded one case to the manager with his support and the next day has to forward another, he has to decide whether to withdraw his former support or support the second even more strongly. In either event he is making a judgment about the relative merits of the two cases. And this is not his job; it is the manager's.

The only way he can tackle transfers on hardship grounds is first to ask whether the man has put in a formal application through the supervisor. If he has not done so, the welfare officer can show him how to do it. He should get the man to say on his application that he has difficult personal or domestic circumstances which he has disclosed to the welfare officer. The welfare officer can simultaneously report to the manager that Mr X has been to see him and that he can supply a confidential report if required. It is then for the manager to take on the umpire role, calling for the report and taking it into account alongside others—and alongside any operational considerations of which the welfare officer may be unaware. It follows from this that the welfare officer's report must be purely factual. He must give as many background details as possible, offering supporting evidence where it exists but making it quite clear where it does not, and he should not venture his opinion on whether or not Mr X should be transferred. (There is another job analysis point here to take up later. Report writing is one of the essential tools of the welfare officer's trade; and in learning it he has also to learn the value of evidence, the need for cross-checking statements, and the need to differentiate facts and opinions.)

Discipline

Guidance to the welfare officer in dealing with transfer cases is equally applicable to his role in discipline. The welfare officer should have no disciplinary functions whatever. Occasionally he may have to interview a youngster who has been kicking over the traces—but it must be made quite clear that this is something quite outside the normal discipline machine. Such interviews must never be regarded as an *extension* of the disciplinary procedure or a weaker form of it. This is perhaps one of the most important points to be discussed at training courses for managers and supervisors. Only too often is the welfare officer regarded as a 'long stop' to be brought in, in a quasi-disciplinary role, when it is felt that although the full majesty of normal punishment should not be brought to bear, the offender is yet due for a mild ticking-off. The manager or supervisor ought to be able to do this job for himself, and the only cases in which the welfare officer should be involved are those where something in the domestic background is suspected to be a major factor. Managers cannot pry into private life when they already stand in the role of authority, but the listening ear of the welfare officer can be quick to seize on hints of home disturbance and then lead the conversation round to friendly advice on how to cope with it.

Although one normally thinks of young people in this context, the welfare officer may also be able to give friendly hints and warnings to adults who seem to him to be heading for trouble with managerial authority. But managers are markedly less reluctant to throw the disciplinary rule book at the offending adult, on the principle that he is old enough to know better and should accept the consequences of his folly. This is perhaps as it should be—as long as managers do not always equate chronological age with mental age or emotional maturity; there can be no hard and fast line drawn at the age of 21.

Although the first thought of the welfare officer confronted with an 'employment' case is that it should probably be handled by somebody else, he should be warned of the possibility of throwing the baby out with the bathwater. The 'employment' problem may simply be a lead-in story, a testing-out of the welfare officer to see how he reacts. The man must not only be allowed to have his say, he should be encouraged to say it without being hurried. If he asks for a day's leave he must not be told right away to go and see his supervisor; the welfare officer needs to know why. Perhaps it is because the man's wife is sick and there is no-one to get the children off to school, or he wants to go to the Citizens' Advice Bureau. In other words, the 'employment' point may be symptomatic of a deeper problem which really does need the welfare officer's attention.

Rehabilitation

The welfare officer should be consulted by managers as a matter of course in all cases when special duties are being considered for a disabled person, or for a member of staff who may for medical reasons perform only light duties. Some organizations have joint committees with the trade unions, charged with ensuring that 'light duties' go only to those with a real need, to avoid any appearance of favouritism as much as to ensure consultation on a matter which affects the colleagues of the man concerned. If such joint committees do exist the welfare officer should be their *independent* technical adviser—independent of both managers and trade unionists. (If the committee meets formally, the welfare officer should even choose his seat with care; he should not sit with management representatives, nor with trade unionists, on one side of the table, but should be *seen* to be independent. A small point perhaps, but tact over small points is essential in clarifying roles.)

It goes almost without saying that the welfare officer needs a thorough understanding of the work of the Ministry of Labour's Disablement Resettlement Officers and Industrial Rehabilitation Units, as the main sources of his knowledge. He should have visited an I.R.U. and seen what goes on, and not content himself with reading about their work. He can be a very powerful ally for the Ministry, in referring cases which the D.R.O. and/or I.R.U. should be dealing with. He should also be familiar with the principles of design of work for the disabled. A useful booklet (Griew, 1963) has been published by H.M.S.O.

Consideration of disablement or light duties often brings out sentimentality, to which the welfare officer can frequently apply a useful corrective. It is frequently *not* in the man's best interests that he should be given a 'cushy number' and thus made to feel a second-rater, out of the mainstream of things, doing a job (such as manually controlling an automatic lift!) which has been manufactured for him out of misplaced kindness. The *real* kindness lies in trying to establish what he can do, perhaps with extra help, and then increasing his load little by little until he can be declared fully efficient, all the time making him feel that he is playing a worthwhile part in the organisation's activities. This approach is often most clearly apparent with cases of blindness. Instead of turning the man out with a pension or putting him on some lowly-paid telephone-answering job which never existed before, is it not better to get the expert advice of the R.N.I.B. or similar body on how far he could be trained in new skills necessary for him to carry on with his own job? This is the sort of liaison task a welfare officer should do. With his wider knowledge of what blind people have been found capable of doing in the past he will approach the problem with the attitude that anything is possible. On the other hand, the manager, supervisor or the man himself, without such knowledge, will often have a vague notion that the blind are employable only as telephone operators or typists. In practice, many firms have found that with expert help some of their operations can be work-studied and re-designed in such a way as to bring them well within the scope of a blind person. As with the blind, so with the limbless and with others who in a different day and age would have found themselves on the scrap heap, a charge on the community as well as on their own mental resources.

Retirement/Resignation

The term 'exit interview' dropped into the personnel management pool a few years ago and the ripples were appreciable. Those concerned with recruitment and selection started to analyse the cost of newspaper and other advertising, the processes of writing to or interviewing those who were not selected as well as those who were, took into account that agencies were making a fair living out of supplying firms with applicants and then concluded that too much money was being spent in simply *trying* to get staff. Add the cost of training the newcomers and the total was considerable. It was not long before the simple deduction was made that since many of the newcomers were taken on to replace those who had left, money could be saved if the leaving rate could be reduced. Firms became interested in why people were leaving, and exit interviews were laid on to find out. Perhaps one of the most common answers was 'not enough money', which, if taken at its face value, probably led some firms to throw good money after bad and contribute to inflation by raising salaries and wages unnecessarily instead of getting to the heart of the matter.

One might justifiably ask whether people who want to resign always give the real reasons when questioned by someone in authority. The real reason may be the quality (or quantity) of the authority itself—

unlikely to be mentioned except by the boldest spirits in such an interview situation. The boldest spirits would probably have tried to do something about it anyway, before taking such a drastic step. The experienced general personnel officer, provided he has no hire-and-fire function, is more likely to get at real reasons than the line manager or supervisor, but even he is not as likely to be successful as the welfare officer. This is precisely because he is the only person who stands only in a personal and non-authoritarian relationship with the individual; he is the only one with the right, conferred on him by the individual, to deal with personal and domestic problems. There is a very good case indeed for the welfare officer to see anyone who has expressed the wish to leave or has actually 'handed in his cards'.

The case does not rest solely on grounds of economy, although managers clearly have possible cash savings to consider. Again, it is basically humanitarian. For some reason or another the man is dissatisfied with his employment; is there anything about it or about him which could be changed to ensure a better fit? This does not mean that the welfare officer's whole effort should be devoted to persuading him to stay. Nor does it mean that every potential resigner must be forced to go to the welfare officer against his wishes. But it *could* mean that a firm builds up the tradition of stressing to 'resigners' the availability of the welfare officer, and of the welfare officer himself offering his services direct when informed that someone wishes to leave. Most of the reasons given for resignation are probably quite genuine, and in the man's own view are also valid. But they are valid only in the context of the knowledge which the individual has *at the moment*; the fresh knowledge which the welfare officer can help to supply may well make them invalid.

Consider a few random possibilities. Suppose 'not enough money' is offered as a reason for leaving. Does this indicate that the man wants to 'better himself' financially—or in terms of status—or that he is in hire-purchase difficulties to which he can find no other solution? Suppose it is 'too far to travel' or 'awkward hours'? The welfare officer will need to know, and will do his best to find out, why the individual has come to this conclusion—perhaps after years of service in that particular job. Has his domestic life changed? Has his wife left him, perhaps to look after his aged mother alone, so that he thinks he cannot give her enough attention in the early morning or late afternoon? But the welfare officer will know, whether or not the man does, if there is a Home Help or Good Neighbour scheme in the locality which would reduce his problem to manageable size. Or a solution may lie in the job itself if 'too noisy' or 'too dirty' is volunteered as a reason for the grass being greener in the other field. Need it be? Does the supervisor or trade union representative always know that people are leaving because of this? Has the man any other skills to offer which make him a possibility for transfer within the firm? Could he be retrained?

The essential point of exit interviews, which provides justification for the welfare officer's part in them, is that one can never be sure whether one is dealing with an objective complaint (or similar objective and positive reason for leaving—such as better prospects, more responsibility, promotion) or whether there is an underlying grievance or personal problem which could be sorted out with expert counselling or advice. Just as the welfare officer can directly contribute to 'group morale', so he can make an indirect contribution by helping to reduce unnecessary labour turnover; morale in a stable labour force is likely to be better than in one which does not permit the growth of lasting human relationships.

Retirement

Normal-course retirements are superficially quite different from resignations, but there is a link—in so far as many of them are nothing but forced resignations. If the organisation has a firm agreement with the trade unions that employees will be retired at a particular age, that may be almost the end of the matter. *Almost*, because the welfare officer should be very familiar with the literature on ageing and will know that compulsory retirement is not in fact a blessing for many people. *Almost*, because he is entitled to his own opinions as an individual and should not be reluctant to give them when they are sought. In his normal contacts with managers and trade unionists he should not be afraid to voice his doubts and thus do what he can to bring about a change of policy. This book is no place to summarise it, but there is increasing evidence (for example, Heron, 1961) that, except when people really want to go, they and the organisations employing them are better served if they stay. They may not be able to work at the same pressure, they may not be able to do a full day, carry their existing responsibilities or make decisions expected of them in the past. But old dogs *can* be taught new tricks, older workers *are* often more conscientious and reliable, and people *do* frequently die suddenly when all the work and human contacts which have made life worth living are suddenly taken from them. There is now an interdepartmental committee, representing the Ministry of Labour and other Ministries, industry, medical and other research bodies co-ordinating research into the employment of older men and women. Details of the work of this committee, and of relevant literature, may be obtained from the National Old People's Welfare Council. (See also 'Age is Opportunity', 1961, National Council of Social Service.)

The welfare officer will usually be consulted in firms which have a flexible retirement policy—by the men and women if not by managers. He must avoid being drawn too far into any questions of assessment of potential for retraining or for change from paced to other work, or for fitness to do heavy work. These are problems for the joint consideration of training officer, doctor, trade union representative, and occupational psychologist if one is employed. He can, however, supply his usual factual report of personal and domestic circumstances, and those who have to do the assessment will be very glad to have this background information. More often he will be asked by individuals themselves for direct advice on whether to retire or not. These requests draw heavily on his normal counselling expertise and on the fund of knowledge of preparation for retirement which he must accumulate. If he is himself a young man his expertise and knowledge must be that much better; many older people will not take too kindly to advice about retirement, unless it is clearly expert, from younger people.

The first thing the welfare officer will learn is that it is no good preparing to retire one month before one is due to go. By then it is almost too late. Fortunately, the modern welfare officer is not likely to fall into this trap, because he should have attended one of the many courses which are now available on 'Preparation for Retirement'. This is a necessary part of his training; he cannot advise in such a field until he has had the benefit of the more skilled advice which people running these courses can offer. Indeed, it may be his firm's policy to run these courses on their own premises for members of the staff, or to allow them time off, and perhaps some financial assistance, in order to attend them. In these circumstances the welfare officer's job is considerably easier, for even his personal counselling role may be taken over by the tutor (usually from outside the firm) who runs the course.

Almost in parenthesis, it should be mentioned that some of these tutors appear to be very much against personal counselling for retirement inside industry, holding that it is essential for people about to retire to have the *group* experience of active participation in one of their courses. There need not in fact be any dispute over this. One could accept the need for the group experience without any implication that it does not need backing up by personal counselling, whether this is a tutor function or a welfare officer function. Indeed, it may be an important part of the welfare officer's job to encourage those who come to him to seek the wider group experience as well. Otherwise there may be a danger that the groups will consist solely of those who have already been converted to the need to prepare.

Since it is a new and rapidly growing movement, 'Preparation for Retirement' deserves further mention. The number of courses available has increased tenfold in the last few years. (See Pre-Retirement Association, 1964, List of Pre-Retirement Advisory Courses.) It is clearly one of the most important growing points of personal welfare in industry. As so frequently happens in the social field, the National Council of Social Service, through its Preparation for Retirement Committee (now the Pre-Retirement Association), has led the way, admittedly building to some extent on the work of others. A few industrial firms have for many years run special workshops for elderly people; the Americans have developed employment and social schemes for their 'Senior Citizens' (a euphemism which has not caught on in this country); in Britain, certain university Psychology Departments (notably London, Liverpool and Bristol) have pioneered research into the ageing process; and the whole community is increasingly—and somewhat painfully—aware that the proportion of elderly people is going to rise considerably in the next decade. Perhaps the biggest problem is whether the historical trend towards earlier and earlier retirement will be allowed to go on, with automation as its justification, or whether social engineering towards continued employment for the elderly will reverse it. There are good arguments for both, but none at all for allowing circumstances to run away from any sort of social control.

Retirement is, and always should be, a very personal matter. Some people are only too glad to shake the dust of routine and soul-destroying paid employment from their shoes at the first possible moment and free themselves to do whatever they really want to do. To others, routine paid employment is life itself; they have nothing else, and without it they would die. Until we have fully transferable pension rights there must always be a minimum age for retirement for those who are not 'contracted out' of state provisions, but one must question whether there need be any upper limit at all; the only necessary criteria could be personal preference and actual employability (not necessarily always in the same job). We do not as yet follow the logic of 'the right to work' to its conclusion.

But, stay in employment or leave it, there is scope for education. On the one hand, industry must educate itself in the research which is going on and thus accept that age 60 or 65 does not in itself mean decrepitude. It must be prepared to employ older workers, as long as they want to be employed and as long as they are employable. On the other hand, the man himself must seek the knowledge and wisdom he needs to make the right choice. He must learn that continued employment may increase the strain on his health unless he takes sensible precautions; he must learn that his dream of a cottage in Devon might be idyllic during the summer months as long as he can still climb the hill with the shopping and weed his garden—but might be a very different picture in winter, or when he is in an invalid chair or too rheumatic to bend his back. The most important thing he must learn if he is thinking of retiring to a different neighbourhood is that he— and his wife, who is likely to outlive him—will inevitably face the problem of loneliness. And loneliness is an effective killer. Small communities in rural areas do not readily accept new arrivals who are too old to adapt themselves to village ways, and old friends are too far away to drop in as they used to. South Coast seaside resorts may be little better. Some are so full of retired folk that, although there is a chance that a community within a community may form itself, one would imagine the turnover of houses to be so rapid that estate agents there would be by no means penniless. In any event, does an elderly person want to be only one of an aged or ageing group ? Would he not really prefer the companionship of friends and relatives of all ages which he enjoyed during his working life ? There is nothing necessarily wrong about retiring to the country or seaside, as long as one has prepared oneself well for the abrupt change of living, by cultivating interests, stocking the mind. One then goes with the right attitude, knowing what to expect and wearing no rose-coloured spectacles.

Most of this is commonsense, coming within the range of the welfare officer's normal counselling task—but he can encourage the seeking of further and more expert guidance, just as he would if necessary with any other type of personal problem. However, there is one field of knowledge in which his expertise can match that of the Preparation for Retirement tutor. He will know as well as anyone else in the locality what range of voluntary social work or other activity is available to the prospective retirer—because it is part of his normal job to keep in close touch with such organisations. Retiring staff should not be encouraged to take on some form of voluntary work *only in order* to keep loneliness at bay. Motivation should be purer than that; the work should be attractive on its own merits. None the less, voluntary work is one of the best cures for loneliness; we can often serve ourselves best by submerging ourselves in the service of others—a sort of enlightened self-interest. If the welfare officer does not know enough of the vast range of possibilities he can at least read about them and then pass his information on (see Hobman, 1964).

Miscellaneous

It is easy to abuse categories of this sort. They might be dustbins for the lazy-minded, open invitations not to think. But they are usually inevitable, because welfare officer personal casework cannot and should not be shoehorned into tidy compartments. There will always be cases which cannot readily be classified under the headings already given; and there will be others which are so much a mixture of categories that the real classification becomes apparent only long after the case has been dealt with. 'Miscellaneous' can thus often provide a temporary home.

5   The Person and the Group

Summary   This chapter seeks to show the link between personal, group and physical welfare. Although the term 'morale' will often be used as a form of shorthand, the difficulty of defining it is freely accepted. Indeed, many academics seriously question the value of 'morale' as a concept and would prefer to speak only of actual behaviour. Unfortunately, academic theories are not sufficiently developed to displace morale as a term which means something to the layman. In the present context, it means a blend of good relationships and satisfaction in working for the organisation. Although the emphasis will be on what the welfare officer actually does in relation to what other people do, the chapter on Group Welfare Services will deal at some length with activities run mainly by volunteers. The chapter on Physical Welfare Provisions will deal only with those aspects of physical welfare with which the welfare officer may be concerned. These and other aspects outside the scope of this book are much more the *direct* concern of managers.

Classification

The classification of group and physical welfare is so much more straightforward than personal welfare that little time need be spent on it; the headings to be used in the chapter on Records and Returns are a convenient breakdown. However, the borderline between physical, group and personal welfare is by no means as clearly drawn as a record sheet might imply. We cannot be sure whether good group welfare in the 'voluntary' sense is one of the causes or one of the effects of 'good morale'. But if we are right in our assumption that personal problems affect efficiency and morale, we must also accept the converse—that people working in an atmosphere of efficiency and good morale are less likely to be affected by their personal problems. At least, they may not be as weighed down by them as they would be if the working situation itself created anxiety and frustration. Similarly, there is a close link between group and physical welfare provision, and the latter will also have a marked effect on personal welfare; good physical conditions are not simply a matter of legislation, for they depend on people for their smooth running. The most modern canteen can make more problems than it solves if the food is poor and gives rise to resentment of management; hygiene is much more a problem of people than of sterilising systems; a good suite of lavatories is diminished in usefulness if someone has forgotten the soap and paper; vending machines are useless if they are empty; drying rooms are ineffective if the hot air fans await the attention of the electrician. If these things are wrong, group morale may be affected, and when group morale is poor, personal problems may loom larger than they need.

It is essential to bear in mind that just as a firm's *productive* effort can be marred by people with problems, so people with problems can mar its internal physical and group welfare services. The welfare officer may therefore often have a double responsibility—to keep an eye on their smooth running, and help with the personal problems of the people who run them. He must distinguish the two in his records and returns. This may seem an odd thesis, but some examples will illustrate it.

Starting at the extreme—and fortunately rare—end of the scale, the welfare officer has two problems to deal with if the treasurer of the firm's sports and social club confesses dipping into the petty cash. On the one hand he has to realise that if it had not been the club's petty cash it might have been someone else's—he thus has a debt, fraud or embezzlement case (depending on how far it has gone) which originates *in the man himself*. He also has a group welfare problem. What are his responsibilities to the club's other officers and its members, and would they be any different if the money had been taken by an outsider? Or, less extreme, a First Aider comes to him to say that he must be taken off the roster for 'personal reasons'. In conversation, the welfare officer finds that the First Aider has domestic difficulties which worry him so much that he feels he is in no state to give treatment. Once again, he must help with the problem of the man as well as perhaps advise on the group welfare problem of First Aid coverage. Similarly, he is told of a neurotic who is causing difficulties in the working group and work relations are suffering; two problems, not one.

Since legislated physical welfare as such is outside the scope of this book, it is enough to point out where borders meet and sometimes cross, and which aspects of group welfare may be slipping over the border into physical welfare provision. This is clearest in First Aid. The old-style good employer had his First Aid box as a matter of course. The bigger organisations went further and supplied sick bays, to be manned when the need arose by any volunteer, but preferably one who had done some First Aid in the Boy Scouts or Girl Guides. Later, only those who had acquired a recognised adult First Aid certificate were allowed to give treatment. Firms began to pay for training, sometimes during working hours or by time off in lieu. Some firms then paid allowances for First Aid expertise; others employed qualified nursing staff who bridged the gap between the voluntary set-up and the firm's own medical staff. Later, the Factories Acts laid down not only standards of physical provision but also, in certain premises, training and qualification standards for personnel. This was followed by the Offices, Shops and Railway Premises Act which extended legislation virtually to all premises where large groups of staff are employed. The current position is that unless volunteers are forthcoming, whether allowance holders or not, organisations above a certain size will have to employ qualified nurses to comply with the law.

The Volunteer

It is the word *volunteer* which for present purposes provides the demarcation between group and physical welfare. The firm makes provision for the First Aid room, the playing field or the room in which the social club can meet, and this is a matter of physical welfare. But the activities themselves, provided they are run by volunteers, are aspects of group welfare. The full-time nurse would be answerable to the doctor, personnel manager or line manager, as would a full-time sports and social officer or groundsman if either of these were employed by the firm rather than the voluntary organisation. They should not be answerable to the welfare officer. This demarcation clarifies his own role, preserves the voluntary spirit without which the physical provisions would be useless, and incidentally ensures that he is not bogged down by numerous committees—doing jobs which do not need his special training and which restrict his availability to those in need.

The following chapters therefore deal firstly with group welfare arrangements in which volunteers are either essential or at present necessary—First Aid, sports and social clubs, benevolent organisations and retired staff; secondly, with those physical welfare or non-voluntary, managerial arrangements in which the welfare officer will have a close interest—hostels and lodgings, safety, and general physical conditions; finally, with welfare in training courses, which is something of an odd man out but important enough to merit a chapter of its own.

6 · Group Welfare Services

Summary   FIRST AID depends mainly on volunteers, but new legislation emphasises managerial responsibility and points to the need for careful thinking about the voluntary role. One must consider whether allowances should be paid to protect the First Aider's interests if he has an accident on duty which should be registered under Industrial Injuries Act provisions. The organisation of First Aid is also important if the voluntary spirit is to be preserved. A full-time or part-time First Aid adviser to liaise with and control the work of the volunteers is often the best answer.

SPORTS AND SOCIAL CLUBS are often 'laid on' by managers as 'good for morale', but evidence is lacking. Costs are high and may not be justified unless facilities are well-used by the many and not simply by a few activists. Subsidies to match voluntary subscriptions may be the best approach. Youth clubs and youth sections of sports and social clubs may be viable, but some hard thinking is necessary in relationship to general community provision. It is essential to bear in mind legal points affecting the right to audit club's accounts and responsibilities for insurance. Welfare officers must be well informed about clubs so that they can advise and encourage.

BENEVOLENT ORGANISATIONS are peculiarly British institutions and the number in industry and commerce does not decrease with the growth of the welfare state. Trade unions run their own schemes; others range from the unofficial 'kitty' for unfortunate colleagues to the large separate legal entity with the firm's name in its title. Several degrees of management involvement are possible, but whatever the involvement there are problems arising from the distinction to be drawn between distress and benevolence and between loans and grants. The welfare officer has three distinct roles to play: advice to committees as group welfare organisations; advice based on knowledge of outside charities and similar facilities; and personal casework with individuals needing help from benevolent organisations.

RETIRED STAFF are in a special position. Some firms with pension schemes may adopt the policy that they are still on the payroll and thus qualify for full welfare officer service. But it may be better to encourage Veterans' Clubs as a group welfare activity and expect voluntary officers to act as 'first sieve' for personal problems, referring only those they cannot deal with themselves or by direct liaison with outside agencies.

First Aid

Although legislation has put this on a more secure basis, from which more and more specialist First Aid officers will undoubtedly spring, especially in the larger organisations, no one with any knowledge of the world of First Aid will deny that the voluntary spirit keeps it going. The wish to serve colleagues is a good deal more widespread than some of the Jeremiahs of our society would choose to admit, and it is often manifested in First Aid in a purer form than elsewhere. The man who puts his leisure time into the sports club may do so primarily because he is a keen player himself; he whips up some interest partly so that he can get a good game. There are of course the occasional First Aiders who enjoy their position of power, the superiority of their knowledge or the cut of their uniforms; but the majority are motivated only by the sort of social conscience which demands that they must be prepared for an emergency, hoping sincerely that one will never arise.

But even if First Aid provisions were not required by law, firms should regard them as a direct managerial responsibility. The existence of law reinforces the view that First Aid should not be left entirely to volunteers. The firm must provide the stores, equipment and sick bay as matters of physical welfare; the local manager must ensure, through his *direct* line of command, that they are safely kept, sufficient and hygienic. The designated officer must inspect the sickbay log-book from time to time, check that facilities are not being abused and have *executive* power to put things right—and it follows from this that he should not be the welfare officer. There are many advantages in having the First Aid leader, with appropriate time allowance, as the designated officer. One must warn against the easy way out. If the manager knows that one of his men is slightly underloaded and that First Aid would bring the load up to standard he is often tempted to ask for 'one volunteer—Bill Smith'. This is all right as long as Bill Smith is perfectly willing to do First Aid, for his enthusiasm will probably grow with the doing; but the manager must recognise that some folk literally cannot stand the sight of blood. There is no point at all in forcing anyone to take up First Aid if he is unwilling. The manager should therefore think in terms of fitting his complements and duties around the existence of a volunteer, even at some cost of time and trouble, rather than fit First Aid into existing complements and duties.

The manager must also think positively about First Aid and the people who are providing the service. It has not been unknown for some managers to imply—or even say explicitly—'you can't give proper attention to your real job if you keep taking time off for First Aid' and to blight promotion prospects by adverse reports. They will have to accept, however, as the law now insists, that First Aid *is* a real job, just as important as keeping a ledger up-to-date, working a lathe or answering correspondence from customers. Moreover, to do such a job properly requires time and it should not be regarded as something additional to be put on to the willing horse in his tea-break. From this it follows that the volunteer First Aider has something *more* than his non-volunteer colleagues and this should attract a favourable mention in any staff appraisal.

Allowances

Once he has volunteered for First Aid, a member of the staff must accept that by doing so he has made himself answerable to management in a new role, whether or not it carries with it a cash allowance. Some firms insist on a token cash allowance in order to clarify the role as a formal 'condition of service'; others do not. In some organisations the First Aiders themselves feel that allowances kill the voluntary spirit; they seek no reward, but ask only that the firm meets any necessary expenses. For example, they regard it as fair and reasonable that the employer should pay for training and the costs of competitions, giving time off in lieu if these have to be carried out in private time; but beyond the recognition that they are doing something valuable they want no more. This sort of pride and self-respect has to be encouraged, yet the firm has to be sure that pride does not become so stiff-necked that volunteers do not themselves prejudice their rights under Industrial Injuries Acts provisions. For example, a First Aider might slip a disc or injure himself in some other way when lifting a stretcher, patient or box of stores. He may do this while attending a live casualty, in the course of training, or during practice by means of a competition, demonstration, exhibition or otherwise. He may then be off sick for a while, but perhaps be on full pay during sick absence and suffer no apparent long-term injury. But what if the slipped disc resulted in medical trouble in the years ahead? The accident must obviously be registered under the Industrial Injuries Act—if the Ministry of Social Security will allow. The snag is that it may not in fact allow, unless the First Aid activity was clearly carried out under the firm's auspices as part of a recognised condition of service. The irony here is that the ministry acts on behalf of the employer. The employing firm may therefore have to ensure that its member of staff will be able to point to rules or other provisions which make it clear that disciplinary action could have been taken if the man had not carried out the treatment, attended the practice or taken part in the competition, once he had volunteered to do so. The job of the volunteer First Aider should not be attended by difficulties of this kind, but while it is, protective steps must be taken.

If a cash allowance is ruled out, the best protection for the First Aider may be his signature to a statement that he is willing to undertake First Aid duties as laid down by the organisation and to have his name publicised to other members of the staff as being so willing. He will usually accept this as a fair exchange for having his training paid for—knowing that he may have to cope with an emergency at home, on holiday or on the road, apart from at work. In any event, just as he can opt into a First Aid service, so he can opt out if he feels that his firm does not give the backing he needs to carry out First Aid duties alongside the others for which he is mainly employed.

It is possible that the accumulation of precedent case law by the National Insurance Commissioner will render allowances or signatures unnecessary for the protection of the First Aider under the Industrial Injuries Act. A note on the history of this problem may provide useful background for firms wishing to make a decision— or make further enquiries before deciding. The history is given in the January 1966 issue of *State Service* (journal of the Institution of Professional Civil Servants) as follows. In a test case (R (I) 102/53) the Commissioner decided that a railway guard injured in an ambulance competition, organised by his employers, was not covered by the Act because his First Aid training, whilst being encouraged by his

employers, was not essential to his terms of service. His membership of the team was voluntary and non-attendance would not constitute a breach of contract, although he was being paid wages for the
day on which the accident had taken place. However, the Post Office
Engineering Union recently (1965) took a similar case to the National
Insurance Commissioner on which a successful decision was obtained.
It concerned a Sales Representative employed by the G.P.O. who
injured his back while lifting a 'fake casualty' during a First Aid
competition organised by the Post Office. He was a volunteer for
First Aid duties and was taking part in the competition as a volunteer.
The Local Insurance Officer refused to make a declaration that it
was an industrial injury, on the ground that the accident did not
arise out of and in the course of the claimant's employment. The
Local Appeal Tribunal by a majority decision also disallowed his
appeal. The Commissioner directed the Insurance Officer to refer
for determination by the Minister the question whether 'with reference to his First Aid duties or to his training in such duties the
claimant was at the time of his accident employed in insurable employment'. The Minister determined that question in the affirmative
and it necessarily followed that the accident arose out of and in the
course of the claimant's insurable employment. The Commissioner
accordingly made a declaration that the accident in question was an
industrial accident.

Organisation

The pattern of First Aid organisation depends on the size of the
firm and on the way its staff is distributed geographically. In fact,
it will be dictated largely by the requirements of the Factories Acts
and the Offices, Shops and Railway Premises Act. Although the very
small firm may need only two First Aiders to meet the law (if actual
statutory need is for one qualified man or woman, there must be a
second string available to cover meal breaks, holidays and sick
absence), it is always advisable to think in terms of a small team.
There are two reasons for this. First, practices are necessary to keep
up-to-date, and two people get bored with practising on each other;
interest is greater in a small group than one or two in isolation, because
members of a group can be motivated by the twin incentives of
cooperation and competition in their own work. Second, small
teams can compete externally—either with other teams in the same
firm, or with teams from others in the vicinity. Competitions run

or sponsored by one of the voluntary aid societies (St John Ambulance Association, British Red Cross Society, St Andrew's Ambulance Association, etc.) are almost invariably for teams of four, with one reserve, and this suggests that the basic First Aid unit in any office or works should comprise not less than six people. If the firm accepts this as the ideal provision it will be able to ensure that every First Aid box or cupboard is under the charge of a qualified First Aider and not simply 'a responsible person'.

The organisation which needs several teams should think in terms of employing a highly qualified man or woman as First Aid adviser or leader—well qualified in First Aid and also holding a recognised instructor's certificate. This is a job which could well be combined with that of Safety Officer if neither load is a full-time one. There is more than an obvious connection between First Aid and Safety. It is obvious that preventing accidents, and doing something about them when they have happened, are closely linked. But one big organisation has figures to show that trained First Aiders are less accident prone than staff without such training. Of course this does not necessarily mean that training in First Aid *leads* to a reduction in accident proneness—typical *post hoc propter hoc* thinking. It may simply be the case that the responsible person who volunteers for First Aid is also the sort of person who in any case would be less accident prone. There is scope for research on this point. If it were found that training in First Aid itself led to a reduction in accidents, the benefits to the community in general could be considerable— and firms would quickly recoup the cost of the training by direct saving on sick pay, and indirect saving on its consequentials.

The First Aid adviser or leader would occupy himself with laying on training courses in conjunction with the voluntary aid societies, taking the executive responsibility for stores, equipment and sick bays, arranging competitions and maintaining standards by inspection and direct advice. If he were the only person in the organisation fully employed on First Aid (and perhaps kindred duties) he would have to be very careful to run his set-up in as democratic a way as possible, conscious all the time that he relied on volunteers to get the work done. He could best do this by combining his executive role with that of Secretary of the Joe Bloggs and Company First Aid Council or Committee, which may or may not be organisationally linked with one of the voluntary aid societies.

In the really big concerns there may be local First Aid branches with their own secretaries, each branch having power to nominate representatives on the higher-level council. If the firm had a medical officer he could be president, and the chairman should be a senior manager. It is quite essential for the volunteer to know that he has some voice in shaping policy, and that senior managers back his efforts by taking an active part in the work of the voluntary organisation. Even if allowances are paid to First Aiders primarily to protect them for insurance purposes it should be remembered that they are still volunteers. There are admittedly some walks of life, notably in police forces and in the mines, where a First Aid qualification may be a *sine qua non* for employment or promotion, but these are exceptions not affecting the general policy which should apply to industry and commerce. Normally, no person employed primarily for other work can be pressed into First Aid against his will.

Sports and Social Clubs

The 'morale' argument

It is usually claimed that sports and social clubs are 'good for morale', but they may be the effect rather than the cause. Where is the evidence to be found? As far as is known there is no survey of workers' opinions, of job satisfactions or other motivations in the working situation in which such clubs even get a mention, although 'welfare facilities' may find its way on to the list (usually near the bottom). But do staff interpret this blanket term as the canteen, the rest room, the car park, the welfare officer, or something else? Or do they take clubs—as part of 'welfare facilities'—so much for granted that they are more important for morale than survey results would indicate? No one really knows the answers to these questions, but it is perhaps time they were asked—and in a more scientific context than this book will allow. More scope for research here, research in which industry should be very interested for the light it would shed on 'morale' generally and because there is very much more money at stake than may at first be appreciated.

Costs

Just as hard cases may make bad law, so extreme examples may lead to bad general principles; but they can also lead to searching questions. For instance, do firms which have installed a billiard table in a new block in central London realise that the accommodation alone is costing them at least £2,000 a year? Have they also realised that when four people commandeer it for the lunch hour others may resent the loss of a room which could otherwise house 30 or more of them as a lounge? Perhaps the billiard players are key figures on the sports and social council, perhaps the office manager is himself an enthusiast and has put in some special pleading. There may be some vested interest or personal arrogance which in reality is having an *adverse* effect on morale.

Similarly with firms which bought ten acres of playing field on the outskirts of the big city in the less halcyon days of land values. Just what are the economics of a 22-man user for two hours on winter Saturdays in terms of upkeep alone, quite apart from present capital value? (A good social case might be developed for handing over such grounds to local authorities for the use of the community generally, while retaining a lien on some playing time. This would benefit especially school children who may have to be taken by coach to grounds even further afield.) What also are the 'morale economics' of an 80-per-cent sports and social club membership, achieved by managerial persuasion or pressure, which subsidises the eight per cent (or fewer) activists? Staff may have a momentary glow of pride when the office or works team win the local league championship. Conversely, they may think: 'So they jolly well should, considering the amount of time off they have been given for practice.' Whatever the reaction, how long does it last? Is it a major or minor element in general morale? This may imply a cynical view, but at least there are so many unknowns that an objective examination is overdue. Good group welfare should be based on present facts, not on traditions established when the facts may have been different.

The cold facts of the need for sports and social clubs will be related very largely to locality. In very small towns community facilities may scarcely exist, and office or works may be the social focus—it may have the only hall big enough to run a dance or put on a play. If this is so, wise managers will encourage wise officers of the sports and social council to accept as full or affiliated members people who do not actually work for the firm. This is good social welfare in the broad community sense, to which managers should not be oblivious, as well as good public relations. At the other end of the scale, in central London and in other big cities, may it not be better for staff to take part in their local community activities rather than stay on in the evening or travel for miles (at no small cost) to the sports ground at the other end of the city? Staff must decide this for themselves. There should be no hint of a frown if a good goalkeeper prefers to play for Sutton or Penge, where he lives, rather than spend a great deal to get to the firm's ground in Barnet, no matter how much the firm's team needs a good goalkeeper. Who is to say that the firm's team should command first loyalty? Loyalty is a very personal matter, for the conscience of the individual, and it should not be forced by implicit or explicit criticism.

We can redress the balance of cynicism by pointing out that not all sports and social activities demand lavish and expensive provisions by management. The Madrigal Society, Chess Club, Thespians, Pop Group and many others can well meet to play or rehearse in a conference or committee room not needed in the lunch hour or after five o'clock. The cost to the firm is virtually nil and the gain from staff knowing that managers are enlightened, sympathetic and accommodating may be considerable, especially if managers think that madrigals are 'long-haired' and they cannot really abide pop music.

Subsidies

This other end of the sports and social scale points to a quite fundamental difference between those activities which need a special subsidy and those which will proceed under their own steam if they are allowed and even encouraged to meet on the firm's premises. There is in fact a world of difference between facilities, usually classed as fringe benefits, which managers lay on because they *think* that 'the workers' want them (or worse still, think that 'the workers' *ought* to want them), and those which arise quite spontaneously from the real and manifest needs and wishes of the staff themselves. The task of managers should be to encourage spontaneously expressed desires by active assistance and not to go around whipping up spurious enthusiasm for what employees know full well is a dead or dying horse. This is not to say that cash subsidies are never justified. There may be a prestige or public relations angle in the existence of a good soccer or golf team which alone would justify some expenditure; or the staff may be so proud of the record of some of its clubs that they themselves willingly subscribe to help the activists, and expect the firm to match their contribution pound for pound.

The 'pound for pound' approach to subsidies is a useful one. Old-style paternal managers, as well as new-style ones with a woolly view of 'fringe benefits', who lay it all on with a trowel, and then complain of the ingratitude of 'the workers' who do not make use of the facilities, are really taking an authoritarian view which is quite out of place in the context of modern industrial relations. Authoritarianism in the guise of spoon-feeding leads to resentments and to the rapid and early demise of the voluntary spirit. But if the whole thing is tackled in partnership fashion—'we will match any efforts you like to make for yourselves'—staff are very much more likely to respond to the challenge, and later value more the provisions which they themselves have helped to win.

Youth clubs and youth activities

Some organisations run youth clubs for members of staff, but, in line with the thinking of the Albemarle Committee (Cmnd 929, 1960), we may question how far this is sound practice. There is probably no general answer; once again the answer can be found only in the context of locality. If there is a youth club where the boy or girl lives, there is a great deal to be said on general social grounds for encouraging the youngster to belong to it rather than to one run under the firm's auspices. Mixing with potential doctors, dustmen and draughtsmen, social workers, shop assistants and secretaries will probably make better citizens than limiting social life to fellow apprentices or clerks—other things being equal. The most important of the 'other things' are probably quality of leadership, range of activities, whether the clubs are mixed or single-sex, and whether membership is open or restricted. The firm's club should not try to compete with an outside club run by a fully trained youth leader if the firm is not prepared to give one of its own volunteers the opportunity, through suitable courses in the firm's time, to become equally competent. If it has quaint ideas of sex segregation it should not compete with a good mixed club. It cannot offer only table-tennis and darts if the outside club offers facilities for training for the Duke of Edinburgh's Award. Perhaps most important, it should not restrict its youth club membership to members of its own staff (although care should be taken to check the tax position of 'open' clubs). Social grounds are matched by economic ones; quite often, where there is no independent youth club available, a firm may find that an open club run on its premises—provided that it is well run— can be a most useful source of recruitment.

Separately, or in conjunction with its sports and social council and trade unions, a firm may do a great deal to help its younger staff help themselves without thinking in terms of youth clubs. This is an area where welfare overlaps with training, and it is difficult to know whether the training and education department or the higher echelons of welfare organisation should do the executive work. Examples are official encouragement of and release of staff for Outward Bound and similar training courses. It does not really matter *who* should do the work (as long as it is not the basic-grade welfare officer, who should not have an executive commitment) as long as someone does. It is fair to say that all good training is equally good welfare, just as all good welfare should have an education and training component.

A related topic is whether or not sports and social clubs should be encouraged to form youth sections. The answer to this can be found from the experience of those clubs which have done so. The general experience is that no matter how high the initial surge of enthusiasm of the youngsters themselves, such sections rarely last. Youngsters have a habit of growing up, the keen and key figures rapidly find themselves in the adult sections and they are not replaced. When faced with a request of this kind, a sports or social club should really ask itself what is the *cause* of the surge of enthusiasm. Is it genuine and positive, or is it negative, by way of protest? Has the club got into the control of older men who enjoy the rut of their activities, will not extend them or give way to younger blood? However old he may be, the volunteer committee member is to be commended for his interest and for the way he gives up a measure of his private time—but the reverse of the picture may be that he likes the little bit of authority he has managed to build up for himself. He may know and not admit that a younger man could run the show better, but equally he may know and not admit that his own self-respect would diminish with loss of power or prestige. Perhaps it is another myth of our time—and other times as well—that age brings with it wisdom and tolerance. The facts are often otherwise, increasing years bringing selfishness, intolerance and prejudice which prevent the young from expressing themselves and growing up in the exercise of responsibility. (One is reminded of the irony in the situation of the bewigged and begowned judge or learned counsel, who probably runs a luxury car, berating the long-haired young offender because he seems to have nothing better to do than rush around the countryside in outlandish clothes on a motor cycle.)

This roundabout answer is not necessarily of universal application. Youth sections can be, and often are, viable in large clubs, especially in localities where junior leagues exist, young people and adults working hand in hand for the common good of all the members. But one usually finds that a large and *active* adult membership is necessary to sustain separate divisions; there must be a good supply of officers at both junior and senior levels, and a firm age limit must ensure that the junior section does not grow with the years while the senior club declines.

Retired staff

Sports and social clubs can often provide the focus of interest and contact with the firm for retired staff, although there is a certain danger that these people—willing horses with time on their hands—may effectively take over all the officerships and hog the facilities. There is of course more danger of this with social clubs than with sports clubs, but even some of these (such as golf) may be very actively supported by the retired. This raises the question of whether there should also be 'Veterans' Sections', and by and large the answer must again be negative. In thinking out the problem of age-group divisions we should avoid getting side-tracked on secondary issues at the expense of the main one. The main one is surely that *people* have banded themselves together to further a common interest or activity— chess, soccer, tennis, music or whatever it is—and not because they are young, old or middle-aged. The activity is primary, age is secondary. Competence and willingness to play should be the only criteria for selecting a team; competence and willingness to serve should be the only proper criteria for holding office. Age or youth should not be a factor, except that the old should have the courage to see that the young have their opportunity. Members of the drama club will know this from often bitter experience. Their common complaint is 'not enough men', and they are equally put out when the juvenile leads have to be taken by people whose fast-approaching senility cannot be disguised by the resources of the make-up box. Drama reflects and interprets life, and life is the prerogative of young and old, men and women alike. There can be Veterans' Clubs, and we shall discuss them later, but here the common and primary interest is in age and retirement; the activities may be secondary.

Legal points

There are two quasi-legal points which managers and volunteers alike have to watch. The first is that if the firm's name is used in the title of the sports or social club, managers may fairly claim an auditing responsibility for whatever finances are involved. They, in the ultimate, are responsible for the good name of the concern and for the welfare of its members; they therefore must vet the constitution and rules and, especially but not only if they have made a subsidy, claim the right to audit the accounts. For example, the club could not have the right, except by agreement of managers, to make contributions or donations to outside organisations (affiliation fees, etc.) from money part of which came from the firm's own coffers. And if the treasurer should abscond with the money, whether or not the matter was taken to court, managers must retain a measure of responsibility. They can safeguard their own interest and be answerable to their shareholders only if they have the right to audit.

The second point relates to insurance. Managers must accept that once they have given authority for their premises to be used for meetings of a sports or social club they also accept liability for any accidents directly attributable to the condition of those premises (e.g. a falling electric light fitting, an uneven floor surface, a loose handrail). On the other hand, the club itself must accept liability for any accidents arising directly from the nature of its own activities—the arrow wound of a member of the archery club, the slipped disc of a cavorting member of the pop group or the dislocated shoulder of the wing three-quarter. Clubs must decide for themselves whether they wish to insure against such risks on behalf of their own members or visiting teams; it is not a managerial responsibility. The degree of risk will of course vary with the nature of the activity, but the most innocuous of recreations are not entirely without them. There is indeed the story (probably apocryphal) of the international chess player who broke his leg by twisting it round his chair!

If he wishes to, the welfare officer will be a member of certain sports or social clubs in his own right, as a member of Bloggs and Sons' staff. He may find his way on to the executive committee or other governing body, but if he does accept office he must make it clear that he accepts it *qua* John Jones and not *qua* welfare officer. To avoid any misunderstanding about his role and function he would be much better advised not to hold office at all, but to stay in the background as an ordinary member and take the opportunity of relaxing. But *qua* welfare officer he must be on good terms with the officers of the club, know its rules, know about auditing and insurance and be able to advise or encourage when advice is sought or encouragement is necessary.

Benevolent Organisations

It can almost be said of British society that whenever two or more are gathered together they will start a benevolent fund, loan club, holiday fund or similar institution. Whether this is the result of nineteenth-century exploitation or the depression of the '30s—the expression of a basic insecurity—or whether it is community-mindedness, clubbability, unwillingness to save by more orthodox methods or the oft-quoted British sympathy for the underdog and the unfortunate, is open to question. It may be significant that the growth of the welfare state seems to have made little difference to the number of charities and other voluntary organisations which spring up everywhere and every year. By all accounts the Charity Commissioners had a difficult time in registering those which are registrable—and these are a very small proportion of the whole. (Maurice, 1961, gives a useful account of the requirements of the Charities Act, 1960, under which certain 'charities' have to be registered. The Chief Charity Commissioner is reported by the *Guardian* (4 May 1964) as saying that the commissioners had completed at that stage a classified index of 50,000 welfare charities.)

The old National Assistance Board made it quite clear in the Foreword of its general leaflet (*Help for Those in Need*) that 'It is quite wrong and unnecessary that anyone in Britain today should be in serious financial need.' Why then do benevolent and similar organisations spring up in every quarter of industry and commerce? This question must remain rhetorical; we are concerned with the fact of their existence rather than with the reason. We must leave it to the sociologists to provide an answer, meanwhile hazarding the guess that people at work like to help their fellows in a direct personal way—and being thankful that this is so. Indeed, the N.A.B. fully recognised the need for and value of benevolence, by allowing the income of those receiving its financial assistance to be 'topped-up' to a certain extent by independent charities, etc., before its own grants were reduced.

Our interest in the existence of benevolent organisations can be broken down into several areas. First, we want to know what is their range—what types of organisation exist; second, how far should managers accept them and/or support them; third, where voluntary activity begins and ends; and fourth, where the welfare officer fits into the picture.

Trade union schemes

Before we look at these questions it is necessary to make an important general point. It is that trade unions, either nationally, in areas, or in branches within firms or within individual offices, works and factories, frequently run their own benevolent funds, holiday or loan clubs or other schemes which can be classed generally as 'benevolent organisations'. There is no reason why they should not do so; they have every right, indeed a responsibility, to look after the interests of their members in this way. But managers and welfare officers alike are concerned with general facilities for all staff, and not only with particular facilities for trade union members; welfare knows no closed shop. And just as it would be wrong for trade unions to raise objections to the setting up of schemes for staff as a whole, it would be equally wrong for managers to take the initiative about such schemes without proper consultation with elected representatives. Wise trade unionists will probably bless general schemes in parallel with or in default of their own 'members only' arrangements and will not seek the sort of 'double representation' which would result from having union people in their union roles on general committees. They would prefer to leave this task to individual volunteers who may or may not be active trade unionists. But this is a matter which can only be worked out in particular local settings. Many organisations work perfectly satisfactorily under committees composed equally of management and union representatives—especially where there are several unions in the same firm which cooperate in joint consultative bodies in other fields. If non-union staff, or staff who may belong to small unions outside the general joint consultation machinery, are happy with this arrangement—all well and good.

Range of schemes

The range of benevolent schemes is truly astonishing. At one end we have a dozen or so staff 'whipping round' for a close colleague who finds himself in a jam, and then deciding to keep something in a more permanent kitty to meet future needs. All this is quite informal—no savings account, no auditors, no officers, rules or constitution. At the other end of the range we have the separate legal entity which has the firm's name in its title, permanent paid staff with pension schemes, a membership counted in thousands and assets which may be counted in hundreds of thousands. An example of the latter is the Post Office Fellowship of Remembrance Ltd, which was set up after the last war as a permanent memorial to staff killed in the two world wars. Its purpose is to 'provide and maintain residential centres to which those who now comprise the movement may, subject to certain medical certificate requirements, go for free convalescent rest and, insofar as the requirements of convalescents and the availability of accommodation permit, for holidays at specific rates'.

Between these two extremes there are mutual aid funds, which in spite of their title may not necessarily restrict benefit to members; funds run on an entirely voluntary basis; funds supported by managers on the basis of 'pound-for-pound' matching of voluntary contributions; funds entirely management-controlled; and outside organisations with branches within a firm. Some funds have as primary object the collection of money for outside charities; others exist only for internal benevolent purposes; some combine both. Sometimes managerial help is given in the form of facilities for the deduction of subscriptions from pay, by provision of accommodation for the permanent staff of the fund, by appeals for new members through house journals and posters on the firm's notice boards—by all of these, by some, or by financial aid only. Almost every permutation and combination exists somewhere.

Types of scheme

If we allow ourselves to stretch the definition of benevolence to its limit, there are broadly four types of benevolent organisation:

(a) Those which offer *quasi-insurance facilities* to members only (sometimes also members' dependants as affiliated members or at special rates). These may be internal, such as the Post Office Fellowship of Remembrance quoted above, the Civil Service Nursing Aid Association or the Civil Service (formerly Post Office) Sanatorium Society; or they may be external, with recognised branches within individual firms, such as the Hospital Saturday Fund or the Hospital Savings Association.

(b) *Special-purpose organisations* which usually cater more for the welfare of dependants of *ex-staff*—the Timbuctoo Tin Co. Ltd Orphans' Fund, the Fibre Glass Dustbins Co. Widows' Benevolent Fund, or whatever its official title may be.

(c) *Management-supported* funds which serve existing staff as well as retired staff and dependants. In large firms with considerable geographical spread these are usually 'national' in scope, but much of the work is done by local volunteer enquiry agents or committees.

(d) Purely *local funds*, many of which command the first loyalty of staff. These are rarely big enough to offer help of a continuing kind, and it is not uncommon for them to pass their longer-term cases on to the 'national' body (if one exists in the firm) or to ensure that outside sources of help are called in.

Managerial involvement

How far should managers go in accepting or supporting the possible multiplicity of funds? Should they, for example, forbid loan clubs, holiday funds and other informal arrangements for which the firm can have no legal liability and for which it has no auditing responsibility? There is really little point in taking a repressive view, since the very informality of organisation defies any sanctions which the firm might hope to impose. More important, the liberty of the individual is at issue. If the individual chooses to risk his savings at the hands of someone who may abscond or use the money for his own purposes, there is nothing that managers could or should do about it. Even the compromise of forbidding the collection of dues during the firm's time is very difficult to enforce; managers would be better advised to tackle the problem in a more positive way. It should be possible for staff to save through schemes which are not so open to abuse. There are many ways of doing this: by encouraging a National Saving Group; by suggesting the formation of a properly constituted fund (for which managers would accept ultimate responsibility in return for the right of audit); by allowing 'official' loans or advances of pay. There is of course some slight risk of bad debts if loans or advances are allowed, although these can readily be recovered by later stoppage of pay or reduction of pension if staff are on long-term contract or take part in pension schemes. This raises the question of whether there should be any differentiation between 'staff' in the old-fashioned sense of the monthly and weekly paid who have some security of tenure, and those on hourly or day rates who have not. The answer depends on one's views on industrial relations. Those who have followed the general tenor of the welfare argument so far will guess that they lead to a very firm NO!

However managers decide to encourage properly organised savings schemes, the encouragement will not be effective unless backed up by facilities for deduction of subscription from pay. Admittedly, this gives extra work to wages clerks; unless marginal clerical time is available direct management costs will thus be increased. But these direct charges must be set against the indirect ones which would otherwise result from loss of time caused by collecting cash during working hours.

Managers must consider very carefully their policy regarding the purely benevolent funds described in groups (c) and (d) above, and it is essential that this policy should be evolved from full consultation with members or their representatives. For managers to impose their own predilections about benevolent funds and their organisation, on a 'take it or leave it' basis, is the quickest way of effectively killing the voluntary spirit. However little managers may wish to be in- volved, they have one clear moral responsibility. They must see that the officers of the fund are aware of the requirements of the Charities Act, 1960. Strictly, the Act places the onus of checking whether the fund is registrable on the officers themselves; but, particularly when the name of the firm is used in the title of the fund, managers should satisfy themselves on this score. It is doubtful whether the funds described in this chapter are in fact registrable unless they own land or have income from investments, but Maurice (1961) should be con- sulted, and enquiries made of the Charity Commission in cases of doubt.

Several degrees of management involvement are possible. It may be argued that the 'good employer' role should go no further than the deduction-from-pay facility, combined with ultimate responsibility and the right of audit. This would leave the day-to-day work of the fund—the assessment of individual welfare need and the disbursement of money to meet it—entirely in the hands of the committee of volunteer staff, and their local agents if the fund is national in scope. The committee is in turn responsible to the whole membership at annual general meetings. The firm may or may not decide to make occasional or regular donations to support what it considers to be a worthy cause, but at this level of involvement donations should be without strings, demonstrating faith that the volunteers will use the money wisely.

The next step after 'no-strings' donations is the principle of matching staff contributions on a percentage basis, or, more fully, pound-for-pound. If the firm thus becomes an equal partner it may exact the very fair price of having some of its managers as repre-

sentatives on the committee, in which case many details of organisation and control will have to be worked out in joint consultation.
For example, will managers have the right to nominate the chairman?
Will they have any power of vote? Will cases for grants or loans to
individuals go up from the committee to management for approval
or modification? Only joint consulation based on the facts of local
circumstances can answer these questions—but it is essential that
the questions are not left hanging in the air. They should be answered,
and the answers written into the constitution of the fund.

Distress and benevolence

Whatever the degree of managerial involvement, the fund must
very early decide whether to draw a distinction between distress and
benevolence. There is a world of difference between making a grant
or loan to a member of staff, orphan or widow to meet an emergency
which the State cannot provide for, and spending money to send
flowers or fruit to someone in hospital or making a donation to some
recognised outside charity (such as the Lifeboat Fund or the Society
for the Aid of Thalidomide Children). The membership may decide
to give the committee an entirely free hand in this matter, basing
disbursement on income and whatever is in the kitty at the end of the
financial year.

But there is another way of looking at the problem. Managers,
after due consultation, may decide that it is the firm's duty as a good
employer to make some of the firm's resources available to staff in
financial trouble, irrespective of what the State may or may not
provide. It is reasonable to argue that whereas staff are fully entitled
to band together to make gifts to the sick or donations to charity—
and indeed should be encouraged to do so—it is for the firm itself to
see that no member of staff or dependant of a deceased member is in
acute financial distress which the State cannot immediately alleviate.

This pattern of thinking opens up two possibilities concerning the
limits of voluntary activity. First, the firm may make its contribution
to the general benevolent society, but earmark it for the sole use of
that society's subsidiary distress fund (to which staff may also contribute if they so wish). Or it may set up a parallel distress fund from
which the local manager may make immediate loans or grants in
emergencies with such staff consultation as may be possible or
necessary. Indeed, if staff do not want a benevolent society, with
or without a distress fund as subsidiary, there is nothing to stop the

firm from 'going it alone' with its own arrangements for emergencies. Unless the shareholders agree (and this presents the nationalised industries and the civil service with certain problems!) it is very difficult for managers to justify using money for outside charities or for social-type gifts for staff who are sick. An emergency grant to alleviate distress can be justified on the same grounds that welfare officers can be justified—humanitarian, plus the cost to the firm of worry and absence. But gifts of flowers and fruit, *unless from friendly colleagues*, smack too much of the woolly sentimentality which is the enemy of good welfare.

Local and immediate help

Whatever measures are taken to relieve distress, it must be remembered that if help is to be given at all it must be given locally and immediately. One cannot wait for next month's meeting of the benevolent club committee, or, if the fund has a national function for geographically dispersed units of the firm, for 'head office' to make up its mind at *its* next meeting. The national fund could well devolve emergency powers to a local committee or to the local manager; the local fund could authorise its secretary to act within certain financial limits and seek covering authority later. Perhaps most important, the local distress fund or the local agent of the national fund should deal only with 'one-off' emergencies. If there is a *continuing* need, the Ministry of Social Security or an external charitable organisation should be brought in, bearing also in mind the possibility of a wealthy fund 'topping-up' when M.S.S. are already making a contribution.

Loans or grants?

Every benevolent organisation has to work out a policy on the loans versus grants issue. While the only safe generalisation is that the decision to make a loan or an outright grant can only be taken in the light of individual circumstances, a fund should be guided by the general welfare principle of trying to help a man to help himself. Thus the approach most strongly to be commended is 'loans whenever *possible*, and grants whenever *necessary*'. A few examples can show how this works out in practice.

If a well-paid employee loses his purse or wallet or has it stolen just after going to the bank at the beginning of the month, the fund's committee may decide that there is a good case for a loan to tide him over until next pay day, or to be repaid over several months by in-increased subscriptions deducted from pay, depending on the amount lost. A fund committee could not be expected to make an outright grant of a sum which would be a major item in its balance sheet, but which over a period might be small to the individual concerned. On the other hand, a much smaller amount lost by a junior employee who has to budget in pence, and has nothing left to pay for fares or meals, may merit a grant. But the lad who has spent all his money on luxuries and then has nothing to pay his landlady is in a quite different position; he cannot expect more than a loan. (This is the sort of case in which the welfare officer should be involved, for he has an educational role to play. There is no reason at all for him to come into the problem of the more senior member who has been plain careless; the latter is more capable of educating himself.)

Although grants are usually more appropriate than loans for re-tired staff or their dependants, who cannot reimburse by deduction from pay or increased subscriptions, there are often circumstances when financial need is clearly temporary. Thus a widow may be virtually penniless immediately after the death of her husband but may have good and sufficient capital or income once the estate has been cleared. In this case a loan is appropriate, a grant is not. These examples are simple to the point of naivety, but it is surprising how many benevolent funds take the view that only grants should be made. They have the somewhat odd idea that loans create resentment and that charity should always be without strings. However, it is the experience of most welfare officers that paternal-type charity may lead not only to greater resentment amongst those who would be willing to repay, but also to increasing dependence in those who could otherwise be helped to stand on their own feet. If these funds are entirely voluntary and self-supporting it is up to the members to decide their policy, but they should do so only after careful discussion with the welfare officer to ensure that their policy does not make his work more difficult. They should also consider the practical point that loans preserve capital, the interest from which can be used for grants.

Assistance in kind

Benevolent funds which cater for retired staff are becoming in-creasingly aware that assistance in kind rather than in cash may be better for many old people. This approach might seem to take us back full circle to the days of Lady Bountiful who lived at the Manor, but interest in it has been stimulated by the publicity given to the condition known as 'hypothermia'. This is in essence excessively low bodily temperature caused by insufficient external warmth and/or inadequate diet and exercise. Most clinical thermometers do not register very low body temperatures, and the condition is not easily diagnosed unless special thermometers are used. Old people are often too parsimonious with fuel (not always through economic necessity) and gradually get accustomed to room temperatures which are lower than they require to maintain proper metabolism. Or they may accustom themselves to an inadequate diet, take insufficient exercise and in these ways also lower their metabolic rate and so sink into hypothermia.

Benevolent organisations considering how best to help an elderly person should be fully alive to this possibility. Grants of cash may be hoarded unnecessarily, or not used to create the warm atmosphere which is essential to full health. Fund committees could therefore think in terms of making grants of fuel, extra blankets, warm clothing or nourishing food—not forgetting the wall thermometer which would give the recipient the cue to call for more help in severe weather. If cash grants are made to elderly people known to live alone, local representatives of the benevolent fund may need to satisfy themselves that the money is being spent wisely to reduce the risk of hypothermia.

Role of the welfare officer

We have already introduced the role of the welfare officer vis-à-vis benevolent organisations, in connection with debtors who may need the services of both. However, there is a great deal more to it than this. He really has three distinct roles. In the first place he discharges his normal group welfare responsibility towards them as voluntary organisations, whether or not they are management-supported. As with sports and social clubs he must know their officers and their rules and be prepared to give all the advice they might need, or know where it can be found. This advisory task is connected with his second sphere of responsibility—to know a great deal about *external* charitable and benevolent organisations, how they operate and what their limits are; a copy of the *Annual Charities Register and Digest* (Family Welfare Association and Butterworth, London) will be on his bookshelf. He then uses these two areas of knowledge in his third, personal casework, function. When an individual seeks his help he has to decide whether such help should come from resources within the firm or outside it. Equally, individuals may go direct to the internal benevolent fund and be referred by that fund to the welfare officer, either because financial aid is only part of the story or because the fund's constitution does not allow it to give the sort of help more appropriately sought from an outside body.

It follows from this that the members of internal committees must be very well versed in what a welfare officer can and cannot do. Ideally he should be co-opted on to the committee as an *adviser*. This word must be stressed. He should *not* be expected to take the chair, be secretary or treasurer or in any other way have an executive responsibility. His expert advice in the discussion of cases will be invaluable, but the expertise of a welfare officer is not required to look after accounts or correspondence or to keep a meeting in order. And if his advisory role is clearly understood by one group welfare committee he will be better able to advise other committees in a like manner. If on the other hand he becomes part of the machinery of management of one particular committee he cannot in all honesty and fairness reject requests for his management services on another. The welfare officer foolish enough to accept an executive role may end up an excellent committee man but more certainly a poor welfare officer, so bogged down with paper work on behalf of pseudo-volunteers that he can never do his own job properly.

This uncompromising argument applies equally to welfare officers at supervisory level. The senior or chief welfare officer must make it abundantly clear to managers, trade unions and voluntary bodies themselves that his prime function is to supervise the work of his staff and not to take group welfare out of the hands of others by running all the committees. The supervisory welfare officer job will be discussed later, but this is something which can and must be said while we are looking at benevolent funds, which are often prone to think that welfare officers should provide the mainspring of their efforts.

Welfare officers' expenses

Benevolent fund committees will often authorise a welfare officer to make *ad hoc* emergency grants or loans, up to certain limits. They may also provide him with a 'social' fund which he can use to buy small comforts when he is visiting staff away sick at home or in hospital. They may go further than either, and make him an allowance to use in his work at his sole discretion. This is a matter entirely for the committees, answerable as they are to their memberships. However, even if the benevolent organisation is management-supported, managers should not allow all the welfare officer's incidental expenses to be met in this way. There must be a distinction drawn between those expenses he incurs in the course of his official duties and those which arise from his liaison with a benevolent fund to further *its* objectives. The former *must* be paid by the firm, and the latter *can* be paid by the fund if it so wishes. Welfare officers must resist the temptation to dip into their own pockets to meet needs which they wrongly think cannot otherwise be met. The firm's resources, benevolent funds and statutory provisions should be adequate to meet all financial emergencies; if they are not, it is infinitely preferable to try to seek changes in them than rely on an approach which sets up a wrong relationship between the welfare officer, the firm which employs him and the individual he seeks to serve.

The firm should be prepared to meet the following incidental expenses:

Hospitality (tea, coffee, light refreshments—but not, for obvious health reasons, cigarettes) during a private interview or in the course of a joint visit, with a member of staff or dependant in need, to an outside social service or similar agency.

Fares to enable a distant member of staff or dependant in need of help to visit the welfare officer, where such a visit will save the latter's time.

Small short-term loans to staff temporarily without money for fares, lunches and similar essentials (this could include small loans for advance payment of hostel or lodging charges).

Small grants to meet essential and immediate needs only, to staff or dependants for whom assistance is being sought from a benevolent fund.

How far the welfare officer should be asked to account for small sums in detail, whether he should get an advance payment to cover an expected quarter's or year's outlay or should claim actual expenses in retrospect, are minor matters to be decided by firms, which might have widely different accounting systems. Whatever the system, this should be a separate payment quite unrelated to salary. It would be easy to increase the welfare officer's pay to *allow* for incidentals, but this is not the same. He would still be dipping into his own pocket and

risking confusion about his role as a private individual and his role
as a welfare officer. This must be avoided, even if the incidental payment system is an irritant to both welfare officer and accountant.

Retired Staff

The personal welfare job of counselling those who have retired or are
beginning to think about the problems of retirement has already been
discussed. In the chapter on Personal Welfare Problems it was also
suggested that firms must decide as a matter of policy whether to
extend full welfare coverage to the retired and their dependants.
There is undoubtedly a good case for such an extension on simple
humanitarian grounds. There is an equally good one on the grounds
of 'morale', the area where humanitarianism joins forces with economics and cost-consciousness. In brief, it is that those at present
serving in the firm have the security of knowing that they too will not
be forgotten when they go on the retired list—and this is something
which adds to the social satisfaction of work and should thus reduce
manpower turnover. The 'good employer' image is also affected;
better-quality people are attracted as recruits if the firm is manifestly
concerned with them as individuals in the long as well as the short
term.

The logic of such thinking will lead the best firms to the most
advanced policy of all—'These people are still on our payroll and we
give them service just as we give service to the sick absentees who are
also on the payroll but are similarly non-productive.' Firms at this
stage of development of personnel policy will already have sick pay
and pension schemes over and above what the State provides, and it
is a simple step to put everyone on the payroll under the welfare
officer's umbrella. More power to the elbows of those which take this
step; but before this policy is declared it would be wise to consider
two major reservations. They both take us back to the first principles
governing the initial acceptance of the welfare officer function.

The first is that the prime purpose of a welfare officer service in
industry is to contain as many of *industry's* personal problems as
possible. At the present stage in the development of national social
welfare policy, one cannot argue very convincingly that the problems
of retired staff are the problems of industry; they are much more the
problems of the community as a whole, of which industry is an in-
tegral part. The productivity of industry *pays* for community service
to older people, just as it pays for every other community service from

the cradle to the grave; but it does so through rates and taxes, via national and local government, and to a very small extent through corporate and individual subscriptions to the voluntary organisations. At present it does not pay *directly*, but there may be future scope for direct involvement, in the same way that direct involvement in recruitment abroad, or in the joint use of hostels or recreational facilities, can be discerned.

The second reservation relates to one of the supporting practical arguments for an occupational welfare officer service: working staff find it difficult, sometimes even impossible, to take their problems to the Citizens' Advice Bureaux or similar outside agencies which might not be open in the evenings. Clearly this argument does not apply with equal force to retired people, many of whom have time on their hands. It is true that not every locality has its c.a.b., and that pensioners cannot afford to travel many miles to the nearest one. However, in cases of real distress, there are always agencies operating during the day-time which can send someone out to more remote areas or otherwise fill in the vacuum caused by the absence of a c.a.b. In any event, there are hopeful signs that the number of c.a.b.s will increase as a result of the stimulus afforded by the subsidy the organisation now enjoys to enable it to extend the part it plays in the solution of consumer problems.

The group welfare approach

These two reservations in no sense point to the rejection of the policy of extending service to retired staff; but they do point to the most useful way of doing it. The approach is through *group* welfare. Since many retired staff will be comparatively active (some will even seek full-time or part-time jobs), cannot some of the 'time on their hands' be utilised for the benefit of their older and less active colleagues? There is room for many more firms' veterans' clubs than exist at present.

Veterans' clubs usually have a dual purpose. The main emphasis is normally on the generation and organisation of social activities which help to cope with the major problem of loneliness; but many of them also have the specific objective of looking after the personal welfare of members and their dependants. Given these aims, it is therefore possible for the firm's welfare officer to take precisely the same interest in them as he does in a group of working staff, because the veterans' voluntary officers should be capable of sifting out as many minor problems as the local manager sifts out amongst staff in his care.

Indeed, since these voluntary officers do not have the same 'authority relationship' with ex-staff as the manager has with serving staff, more problems are likely to come their way. Thus, if veterans' clubs act as an intermediary, the 'welfare officer service for all on the payroll' policy is most unlikely to create demands for more welfare officers, except in marginal cases where the load already indicates that the shoe is pinching excessively.

Clubs may even go a step further and appoint their own welfare officer (they would doubtless be overjoyed to have the services of the firm's welfare officer when *he* retires!). In this case the sieve can be even finer; the well-trained and experienced man will cope by himself with a minimum of help from the firm's officer. However, such ideal arrangements will be rare. Even without a 'welfare officer', the voluntary officers will quickly build up some expertise in dealing with the minor problems of the membership. More difficult cases can be referred to the firm's officer or direct to the community agencies which exist for the purpose. These may be specifically old people's welfare committees, or more generally the local authority welfare officer, or, mainly but not exclusively where financial hardship is involved, the Ministry of Social Security.

If the veterans are to be treated as just one of many group welfare bodies run by volunteers, how far should managers go in giving support? Some firms provide money for all running costs, membership is automatic and free for all retired staff; others may adopt the 'pound for pound' policy of financial support; others give no money, but only help in kind. Help in kind is perhaps the minimum; the firm should at least allow the veterans to meet on its premises and give as much publicity support through house journals and leaflets in pension envelopes as it can. It may also allow its solicitor and accountant to give free advice (to the body, not to individual members), for example on investment of funds. The firm may supply an office and stationery and meet postage and telephone costs. Some firms go even further, along the road pioneered by Unilever, meeting the full costs of the veterans and additionally laying on schemes for providing birthday presents, gifts for the sick and a series of regular visists. But there is the danger that if the firm does it all, albeit using expenses-paid voluntary effort, the voluntary spirit is gradually eroded and the veterans' organisation just becomes another part of the personnel department. And the erosion of the voluntary spirit affects not only the veterans themselves but also the serving members of staff who 'in the old days' helped to run Christmas parties, outings and other entertainments for the retired. The same danger is present if the welfare officer takes every veterans' personal welfare case without questioning how far the veterans have gone to help themselves as a cohesive social and mutual aid group.

7   Physical Welfare Provisions

Summary   There are three aspects of physical welfare in which the welfare officer will have a close interest but no executive role. Rightly or wrongly he will often be brought into problems affecting or arising from *general physical conditions and provisions*, frequently as 'presenting problems' which disguise the real nature of the call on his services. He will have something to do with *safety*, particularly when no safety officer is employed. He will usually have a lot to do with *hostels and lodgings* as an adviser, and in respect of any group welfare activities connected with them. He may have a special responsibility for the maintenance of lodgings registers, although this work does not need his particular expertise. In particular, the problem of 'vetting' lodgings has to be considered.

General Physical Conditions and Provisions

If we accept the principle that general physical conditions and provisions should be largely a matter of minimum statutory standards or such improvements on these as are agreed with the trade unions, it is not easy to see where the welfare officer fits in. He should certainly have no executive role in their control. If he is given one, he will be embroiled in committees which discuss standards; and committee work reduces his availability for the expert work which only he can do. He would also be drawn into the control of staff (e.g. cleaning and other maintenance people) and would thus have a disciplinary job which would chime ill with his neutral role in the organisation. Attention to physical conditions must be seen as a statutory obligation of managers, and managers must provide appropriate staff in the normal line of supervision to discharge it. Larger organisations may centre all this work on a full-time accommodation officer or even in a buildings section; in smaller ones the office manager may be responsible.

The welfare officer's interest will be limited to the impact of general physical conditions on groups and individuals. In theory, only a small amount of his time should be devoted to it. In practice, things may be rather different. He is likely to be consulted by many folk who do not clearly appreciate the limits of his job.

Even managers who have a full-time or part-time internal accommodation officer on their staff have been known to send the welfare officer a brisk note asking why there is no paper in the lavatory; and staff complain to the welfare officer that the standard of cleaning is not all that it should be. Complaints and criticisms of this sort are acceptable if they come from newcomers who have not yet attended the training course where the welfare officer will disclaim executive responsibility; but if they come from those who *should* know his limits he has to ask himself what has gone wrong and why. There are three practical possibilities: the training in which he took part was ineffective; the designated accommodation officer is not doing his job properly; or the criticisms are really grievances—symptomatic of a bad morale state in which the welfare officer should be interested as a matter of group welfare. Whatever the cause, there is action he must take.

If training is at fault, the welfare officer has to discuss content and technique with the training officer. Was the point just missed out or were the trainees so bored and uninterested that it didn't register? If the accommodation officer is slacking (or has been so overloaded with other things that he has no time for his inspectorial job), the welfare officer has a duty to make sure the manager knows of the complaints. In no circumstances should he make good the deficiency himself (except by acting as a fellow human being in an emergency) and then forget to tell the manager. If general bad morale is the cause of complaints and criticisms about physical conditions, it is usually because the 'proper channels' are either clogged up or have been allowed to fall into disuse. Sometimes the welfare officer can put them in working order by a few informal words here and there; sometimes he will have to show managers the need to take the drains up completely. Whatever form his intervention takes he must never allow himself to be drawn into any dispute between management and trade unions as a sort of umpire, referee or court of appeal and thus play the undertaker in the funeral of joint consultation.

But the welfare officer will always remember that complaints and criticisms about cleaning, hygiene, drying rooms, canteens and similar physical amenities may often come to him for precisely the same reason that he gets other complaints and enquiries which ought to be routed elsewhere. They may be 'probes', 'tests', 'conversation gambits' or other means of giving the enquirer or complainer the chance of meeting the welfare officer and assessing whether he can be trusted with the *real* personal problem which is the unstated reason for making the contact. Such a 'probe' is often called the 'presenting problem' in social welfare circles. Tired though the welfare officer may be of enquiries about replacement light bulbs, the price or quality of meals in the canteen or the shortage of soap, brusque treatment not only loses the confidence of the enquirer (and gets around the grapevine very rapidly) but often means that the welfare officer is not consulted on something else where his expertise is really wanted. The complainant must be heard out, courteously and patiently, the welfare officer checking at the end of the story whether there is something else on his mind. If there is not, he encourages the individual to take his story to the man with executive responsibility.

To be able to play his part to the full, the welfare officer must have a sound general knowledge of the statutory obligations laid down by the Factories Acts and by the Offices, Shops and Railway Premises Act, and of the higher standards achieved by joint consultation. He must also thoroughly understand the responsibilities of others in the physical welfare field. But he should not be expected to become an expert in such matters. This expertise belongs to those who exercise executive responsibility, and these people in turn have the higher-level experts (H.M. Inspectors of Factories, Appointed Factory Doctors, Public Health Inspectors, architects, lawyers) to go to if they are unsure of themselves. These outsiders should be consulted direct if consultation is required; there is no need at all for the welfare officer to act as an intermediary.

This clear delineation of responsibility and function should be extended down to even the petty things in which welfare officers are known sometimes to be involved. Thus, canteens and luncheon vouchers are matters of physical welfare; supervisors and not welfare officers should therefore hand out vouchers and tickets. Welfare officers who do this chore often accept it on the grounds that it provides a means for them to keep in touch with staff—especially youngsters. The argument is that this day-to-day contact makes them known and thus makes the youngsters more willing to confide in them if they are in trouble. However, a much more convincing argument, and one which does more for welfare in the long run, is that it is the business of supervisors to make these contacts as a way of improving *their* relations with staff. If these relationships are good, confidence will grow and the supervisor can bring in the welfare officer when he suspects the existence of a personal problem with which he may not be equipped to deal. Similarly, supervisors rather than welfare officers have the prime responsibility for seeing that their staff work in good light, that lavatories are clean, clothes-drying facilities are in working order, and temperatures and ventilation are satisfactory. As a very minimum, leaving humanitarianism out of it, this is no more than enlightened self-interest. Supervisors are responsible for getting work done through others; hindrances, which may even result in sick absence, must be cleared away so that work may be done effectively.

Safety

Although safety officers have been with us for a considerable time, it is only in comparatively recent years that progress has been made towards recognising the safety function as one for the expert. Safety, Health and Welfare are linked together in a single Department in the Ministry of Labour, where the main emphasis is on physical welfare in the broad sense. But it is a happy enough combination from the personnel point of view, and some large organisations adopt it. In dealing with First Aid, it was also pointed out that safety has close links with group welfare—safety being concerned largely with the prevention of accidents, and First Aid with doing something about them if preventive work has failed. When one also takes into account the very marked personal welfare element of safety, it is clear that it makes a very comfortable bed-fellow with welfare as it is conceptualised in this book.

However, even personnel people writing about personnel and welfare do not necessarily accept that safety is a personnel function. For example, Hopkins (1955) lists the main areas of safety work as accident prevention; investigation; notifications and records, liaison with H.M. Factory Inspectorate; maintenance of guards, safety devices and lifting gear; and possibly safety training, leaflets and posters. He goes on to say that the nature of the job is such that the man holding the responsibility must fully understand all the processes involved in the factory, i.e. the safety officer in an engineering concern should be an engineer. Analysing the responsibility for safety on the shop floor, he adds that this can only be laid on the foreman or manager in charge; the safety officer must be advisory. But he later admits the reasonableness of the safety officer's being empowered to take executive action—for example, shutting down a machine—where necessary.

Assuming that Hopkins' list of the areas of safety work is sufficient —and it is certainly a useful starting point—we ought to look at them and decide whether they are all proper to a full-time or part-time safety officer. His point on safety *responsibility* should be the real start, for it is no use identifying the functions unless responsibility for carrying them out is also made clear. We must therefore criticise his statement in so far as it does not mention the responsibility of the *individual himself*, without which no safety policy is worth anything at all. He might have taken this for granted, but it is the one thing which should *never* be taken for granted. It must be emphasised time and time again and kept in the forefront of all safety thinking. If we do this we see that accident prevention is basically the individual's own responsibility and that he himself must report hazards which may arise from the improper use or maintenance of equipment. Above the individual, the supervisor has responsibility for prevention of accidents by keeping an eye on unsafe attitudes, practices or equipment. He has thus a share in the training responsibility. He also should have the responsibility for investigation, notification and records— and this leaves only liaison with H.M.F.I. to cover. Where then does the expert role come in ? H.M.F.I. liaison does not of itself warrant one, for H.M.F.I. will hold the *manager* responsible if the law is not complied with, and the supervisor can attend a Training within Industry Job Safety course.

One can make many 'personnel' functions disappear in this way, by a sort of sleight of hand. In fact, conjuring with responsibilities so that they vanish into supervision and management is one of the best ways of testing whether there is an advisory 'personnel' function to identify at all. If they do so vanish, and all that is left is a supervisory or managerial cry that 'we don't have time' or 'we don't know enough about it', it is a pretty sure sign that there is enough work demanding enough specialised knowledge to warrant someone being selected and trained for it. The vanishing trick also tends to show up for what it is worth the idea (increasingly recognised as a fallacy) that only engineers can act as safety officers in an engineering works.

What is clearly wanted is a *safety* expert and not an *engineering* expert. This is not to say that engineers, other things being equal, will not make good safety officers. One could no more say that an engineer would not make a good welfare officer or training officer if he were well selected and had the right training for his new job. But there might be a good deal of truth in an emergent school of thought which says that the last person one wants as safety officer *in an engineering works* is an engineer. The argument runs on the lines that he has grown so used to engineering practices, customs, design and attitudes that he just cannot see what may be wrong with them; only the man coming in with a fresh mind can do so. This is very likely to be true, although it is difficult to find real evidence either way.

Looked at as an aspect of personnel work, the safety officer's job is really a curious blend of physical welfare (knowledge of legislation), training and publicity. He may not necessarily train directly himself, unless he has adequate training experience, but he will certainly be responsible for advising the training officer on the content of safety courses or of safety elements in more general courses. Similarly he may not be a dab hand at poster and leaflet design, but he should be able to advise the designers on content. On the other hand, he gets from others what he needs in the way of information about the firm's processes; he will go to work-study officers as well as to engineers, physicists, chemists and any other technical specialists the firm might employ.

This analysis is admittedly brief and superficial, but it is necessary to sketch in some of the background of safety before considering to what extent it may be considered as an aspect of occupational welfare. If the firm cannot justify a safety officer, and the welfare officer's load is light, then it may be quite reasonable to expect him to double up— *provided* that the firm is willing to spare him long enough for him to be properly trained. And, because he is now wearing two hats, management should go to any lengths necessary to ensure that he has no executive responsibility for safety which might tend to smudge his neutral image as a welfare officer; he must be well qualified to give advice, but responsibility must rest firmly with management and supervision.

Whether or not there is a safety officer, there will remain a hard core of interest for the welfare officer. In his travels around office, factory or stores he must always be on the look-out for any situations which offer a hazard, bringing them as quickly as possible to the attention of the individual, the supervisor, safety officer or manager. His choice will be governed mainly by knowledge of the level of authority required to put the matter right with all speed. Any active complaints about hazards must be dealt with in just the same way. Naturally, the welfare officer must be prepared to act in an emergency as any responsible citizen would act—cordon off the broken stairway, put sand on the patch of oil, take out the fuses, turn off the gas, or do whatever else needs to be done. No-one stands by and says that he has no executive responsibility when human life may be at stake. But acting in an emergency does not itself give the welfare officer the right to be regarded as second-line safety officer. The first-line safety officer must always be the man-at-work, the second-line the supervisor. The welfare officer is a very useful adjunct to the team, because he gets around a good deal and because he can be trusted by all members of the staff to put the well-being of others first on his list of priorities. He must also have safety in mind in his personal welfare work. To take an extreme case as an example, he *must* inform management if he suspects anxiety or depression in someone he knows to have access to cyanide in the plating shop. Extreme perhaps, but the connection has been pointed out more than once; and less extreme cases of accident proneness aggravated by personal anxieties abound in the welfare officer's case notes.

Housing, Hostels and Lodgings

Urbanisation, rural depopulation and the 'drift to the South' have been going on for many years, but it is only since the war that we have really taken notice, and only in the last few years that notice has been translated into scientific study and pressure for action. We now enjoy full employment on the one hand and suffer from manpower shortage on the other. But 'full employment' is in many areas a statistical artefact; national statistics obscure regional differences; regional statistics obscure local variations; local statistics obscure individual preferences, qualifications and ambitions. At the individual level, men and women from the less affluent and developed areas seek outlets for their talents and tastes; firms in districts where manpower demand outstrips local supply actively seek to recruit some of their staff, especially young people, from districts where supply exceeds demand. This two-way process has been going on for centuries on a world-wide scale and we have called it emigration and immigration between countries. But more recently large organisations have become directly involved—recruitment teams operate in Ireland, Malta, the West Indies and elsewhere abroad, as well as in underdeveloped areas in the United Kingdom.

We are at last beginning to accept the idea that wherever possible work should be taken to where there are people wanting to do it—an idea very much in line with the premise that work exists for the satisfaction of human needs. It is fortunate that in this instance economic necessity backs up the requirements of ethics and morals. The Fleming Report led to the adoption of a firm policy of dispersal of Government Departments to the provinces, and the Location of Offices Bureau endeavours to persuade industry and commerce to do likewise. The process is speeding up.

Meanwhile the problem of balancing manpower and work is with us, and managers inevitably ask whether provision of houses, hostels or lodgings will help solve it. All three possibilities come within the scope of 'welfare' in its broadest sense, as all personnel policies must come within its scope. But the main responsibility for the formulation of policy affecting recruitment lies with those parts of the organisation which handle recruitment for operational needs. They alone can make forecasts of staff requirements and, with the accountants, assess the degree of financial subsidy which the firm can pay to ensure that staff recruited from a distance are adequately housed. Naturally, the occupational welfare side of the organisation should be consulted at every stage, for it can give expert *advice* in the formulation of policy; but it alone should not be expected to determine what that policy should be.

Housing

If the final decision is that assistance should be restricted to loans or advances of salary for house purchase, the *welfare officer* interest is minimal. In this context the individual fends for himself with such financial help as the firm thinks appropriate and justified; the welfare officer offers to him the services he offers to all other members of staff as individuals. The welfare officer interest is stronger when the firm decides to build an estate for a *group* of staff, or reaches agreement with the local housing authority to do so. These are both possibilities when the firm is dispersing from the city, sometimes but not always to 'new' or 'expanded' towns. Local authority provision is at present the general rule and provision by firms the exception, but as dispersal becomes more attractive and its benefits more widely accepted, firms may take an increasingly direct part. In this context the welfare officer will play a major group welfare role. He will find out about local sports and social facilities, help to create new ones externally or internally (in the firm) to fill gaps, and he will assist with individuals—particularly hardship cases—who do not fit into the pattern of agreement reached with staff through their trade unions and with the local authority.

Yet he still acts as an adviser; he does not concern himself with the financial and other planning detail which is properly the province of managers, or the accountants and recruitment officers acting on management's behalf. Similarly, he should not be expected to act as the sole channel through which staff are kept informed. He has a supplementary, individual, role to play; but the proper channels of communication are the normal ones of management and trade unions. Excepting welfare information channels, communication channels are not in the province of this book; but in passing, one may point out how rarely managers actively accept the role of communicator. If a trade union can put up on its notice boards the results of a joint meeting a few hours after the event there is no reason why managers should not be able to do so as well—or even more quickly. It is quite wrong for managers to rely on union channels; they should operate their own, efficiently and speedily. (Brown and Jaques, 1965, carry this argument a step further by rejecting the practice of communicating proposals to the 'workers' representatives'. They point out that representatives are not responsible to managers but to their constituents; thus, accuracy of communication concerning managers' intentions is very much at a discount. They say that for a manager to rely on the representative system as an accurate means of communicating his proposals to 'the worker' (my quotes) is unrealistic.)

The welfare officer acts as a member of a team, providing knowledge of the social services which managers and trade unionists may lack, when general policy on dispersal is being worked out. If this policy includes the provision of hostels and lodgings in place of or as substitutes for normal housing he will have a better-defined function. Hostels and lodgings differ from housing far more than may appear at first sight. Housing is the *permanent* solution, basically for families, couples, and unmarried adults who prefer to live alone; hostels are a *temporary* solution, basically for young unmarried people who welcome a community life; lodgings lie somewhere in between, catering for younger and older transients and for the unmarried adults who either want to be with a family or do not wish to be bothered with the housekeeping involved in setting up their own establishments. These differences are psychological and social rather than physical, and introduce personal and group welfare factors well within the welfare officer's normal sphere of activity. Hostels and lodgings are far more likely to be required in the big city than in dispersal to new or expanded towns, since one of the main justifications for dispersal—apart from permanent housing for married staff—is the availability of local manpower which has no need of temporary accommodation.

Special needs of training centres

Hostels and lodgings may also be required in association with a training centre which may be located well within or at the periphery of the city, or quite away from it in a rural area. If the centre is big enough, a full-time welfare officer may be needed, for its transient population may throw up many personal and group problems; smaller centres may need him for two or three days a week. Whatever his load, his position should be exactly the same as his colleague in office, works or factory. He should advise according to the list of duties sketched out for welfare officers in general, but he should not be part of management. Nor should he be the chairman, secretary or council member for the sports and social clubs which are so specially necessary in an isolated area. These tasks are better carried out by executive and teaching staff who must be closely involved in all the social provisions which help to relieve anxiety and stimulate interest, thus speeding the learning process. Above all, he should have no disciplinary responsibility. This belongs to the head of the centre and cannot be delegated to a person whose main raison d'être lies in his 'neutral' advisory role.

There is no ready answer to the question whether hostels or lodgings are to be preferred for training centres set up by industry. The general opinion in university and teacher-training circles seems to be that community life is an essential ingredient in the educational process; and this usually leads to preference for hostels and arrangements for hostel life for at least part of the three- or four-year spell if they cannot be provided for the whole period. Although industrial training should have a marked educational component, it is open to doubt whether there is any real analogy between the full-time professional education and training at college and the much shorter courses provided in the industrial setting. It could be argued equally that college life should be closer to the community for which the college product is destined to provide leadership; and that industry should move a little away from the basic skill and knowledge approach towards fuller education for living. If the first argument is true, the implication is that there is more value in lodgings than the educationalists seem to think. Correspondingly, industry should be considering whether the closed community of a hostel can make a contribution to the educational processes within industrial training which are now recognised by the Industrial Training Act, 1964, as essential. In any event, at least for many years, what is possible and practical will take precedence over what is considered desirable. Hostels—or halls of residence in college circles—are very expensive; lodgings are very much cheaper. Location is also important, and so is the pattern of women's employment in the area: hostels are essential in rural areas where there are no lodgings available, or in areas where married women of all ages tend to work outside the home.

Hostels

If the firm decides to provide a hostel or hostels, it normally goes straight on to a decision to manage directly. Even if the firm were competent to run hostels there are several good reasons why it should not do so. First and foremost, it seems quite wrong for young people to be under the disciplinary control of their employer for 24 hours of the day. The only exception is the armed forces (and perhaps we assume too readily that these should be an exception) where conditions of service and 'contracts of employment' are quite different. Industry employs staff for working hours, whatever these hours may be, and as part of the bargain can lay down a disciplinary code which governs conduct in working hours. It should recognise this by accepting quite unambiguously that control should not extend into private time. Secondly, very few industrial organisations are in a position to offer hostel staff reasonable career prospects—the opportunity to move from small hostels to larger ones, climbing a salary scale en route. They cannot train their own staff from scratch except by inefficient job exposure, and they have to compete for the trained people in the open market. And the trained people are in short supply; they do not stay long if they have better opportunities elsewhere. Thirdly, only the very wealthiest organisations can provide the sort of hostel which is now necessary for the well-being of young people.

PHYSICAL WELFARE PROVISIONS

The good modern hostel must be big enough to include a sports hall, rooms for clubs and societies of various kinds, and the leaders who can stimulate group activities in them.

Whether at a training school on the periphery, or in the large town or city where the firm has its factories, offices or shops, it is usually better to think in terms of putting the hostel in the hands of an expert body, leaving day-to-day management and discipline to those who have long experience in their exercise. Organisations such as the Y.M.C.A. and Y.W.C.A. run their own internal training schemes for hostel staff; they can offer career prospects. They know young people and what young people want, and they know how to provide it. They know what firm, fair and sympathetic discipline means in hostel life and how to get it. Most important, they can run the hostel as a centre for their *whole* membership in the area, and from this stable membership they can produce the leaders to stimulate group welfare activities in the hostel. The staff of the firm providing the residential core will inevitably be in transit—whether short-term at a training centre or longer-term at factory, shop of office. These transient residentials cannot provide the continuity which group welfare activities need, even if numbers are big enough to throw up a few folk with the necessary expertise and interest in applying it. Residents may number up to 200, but the area membership of the hostel management organisation (Y.M.C.A., Y.W.C.A. or other similar body) may be 2,000. A great many of these members will be in the area for some years.

There is also a social advantage in bring the firm's youngsters into direct contact with local residents from many different walks of life. Friendships are made, young people in transit are invited to homes, gaining some family life and being able to leave the 'school' or 'hostel' atmosphere occasionally without having to pay for outside entertainment. Even the best communal living does not suit all of the people for all of the time. Finally, parents are reassured if they know that their children are under the general eye of an organisation with the sort of reputation which Y.M.C.A. and Y.W.C.A. enjoy. They know, for example, that although religion will not be stuffed down unwilling necks the opportunities will be there, along with other social facilities and means of following hobby interests and active sports.

A firm wanting a hostel for an isolated training school will probably have to start from scratch with the hostel-management organisation, which may have little or nothing in the district. It may have to bear the whole capital cost; or it may come to some arrangement to provide capital for its own needs, the managing body adding what is required to extend facilities to its area members. The picture may be similar in the big towns; or it is possible that the hostel-management organisation may already have a hostel which it is wanting to rebuild or extend but cannot for lack of capital. There is scope for imaginative partnership. A firm could offer to buy residential places for the whole of the estimated life of the buildings, or for a shorter period, or agree to make a capital contribution in exchange for a lien on a given number of places which the hostel-management organisation could use for its own members when not required by the firm. Such partnership between industry and what can fairly be called a voluntary social service is very similar to the idea of sharing sports facilities with other firms or with local authorities, mentioned earlier. It equally illustrates how industry and commerce could be much more closely integrated with the social services, to the mutual benefit of both sides of the partnership.

Lodgings

No matter how large it may be (and there are psychological and social, as well as physical limits to size) it will be clear that a single hostel cannot do much to solve a major recruitment problem if staff stay in it until they marry or leave the firm. There will of course be a certain amount of natural 'wastage', since hostel life does not appeal to everybody; but firms should consider using a hostel for purely short-term transit purposes. They can either set a limit on stay and actively encourage staff to look around for lodgings or flats themselves, or go a step further and set up a lodgings register. There is another possibility by means of which hostels can be dispensed with entirely. This is to offer new recruits a special subsistence grant to stay in a small hotel for the first few weeks while looking for permanent accommodation. Such an arrangement could also be backed up by a lodgings register run by the firm. Subsistence grants are a matter of recruitment and pay policy, outside the scope of welfare as sketched in this book; but the welfare side of the organisation may still be involved in helping to find the permanent private accommodation necessary to make such a scheme effective.

It is not essential to use a specially selected and trained welfare officer in the task of seeking and vetting lodgings. On the other hand, if this work does not take too much of his time it is reasonable to accept the arguments that the welfare officer is used to dealing with all classes; that his title makes him *persona grata* with landladies; and that his experience of people enables him to judge the adequacy of lodgings for different levels of staff. But where a small firm has a big lodgings problem, or where in a larger firm there are several welfare officers each with a little finger in the lodgings pie (each of them unable to give the job the time it needs to do it properly), there is a case for a specially appointed lodgings officer who will quickly develop his own particular expertise and make his own personal contacts.

Whoever may have the job of looking for them, lodgings are becoming increasingly difficult to find. The social dice are loaded against a system which served the community well in the past. The trend is to smaller and smaller houses; fewer rooms are thus available. Especially in the small modern house, mechanisation frees the housewife to go out to work if she wants to; and she is encouraged to do so by manpower shortage and the rising costs of living the sort of life the advertising men claim she should live. In fact she would probably prefer to go out to work, gaining in companionship and interest as well as income, than 'take in a lodger' in the sense of supplying services (food, laundry, cleaning, etc.) as well as accommodation. If she has a room or rooms to spare she can get the best of both worlds by supplying cooker and sink and 'letting furnished'. The trend is also towards a higher proportion of local authority housing, and some local authorities forbid their tenants to sub-let in any way whatever—furnished, unfurnished or by lodgings.

The lodgings officer may well find that there are more possibilities of help from those sections of the community which have well-developed social consciences than where the profit motive is uppermost. Putting advertisements in local papers or on postcards in newsagents' windows (and, conversely, studying papers and postcard advertisements) may have some result; but there are likely to be richer rewards for time spent in making direct contact with Women's Institutes, w.v.s. branches, church and chapel 'Young Wives' Clubs' and 'Women's Bright Hours', and similar organisations which attract the housebound housewife. (The 'Housebound Housewives' is itself an organisation of this sort!) It is not enough simply to write to the local vicar and ask him to invite his congregation to get in touch with the lodgings officer. The man has plenty of other things to do; he may forget; members of his congregation may be momentarily stimulated but omit to write down the address or phone number. The goodwill may be there, but it may not result in action. The personal touch is essential. Most women's organisations are only too eager to receive suggestions about possible speakers for their meetings. Cannot the lodgings officer volunteer his services to talk about the firm and its place in the community, and use the opportunity to put in his plea for help with lodgings, either during his talk or later when the tea cups are passed round? If he does so, he should remember that his main purpose is to *give* information, rather than get it. He must accept that *his* need is secondary to theirs.

The firm's house magazine may be another useful source of help. While staff may not be stirred into offering lodgings to the community generally, by advertising themselves or by answering the advertisements of others, they may indeed find a home for newcomers to their own organisation—especially young people who may become almost part of the family. For preference, the youngster's own supervisor should not also be his landlord; but this will depend largely on the pattern of human relations in the firm, and beggars cannot always be choosers.

Whether the appeal is to staff or to outsiders, the lodgings officer should not imply that the help is one-sided. Financial gain apart, there is some social and psychological benefit to the landlady. There was at least one old lady in the community, who right up to her seventy-fifth birthday kept fresh as a daisy and well in touch with life by taking in two students as lodgers—usually from abroad because she knew their needs may be greater. She had been doing it for years; she had been 'Mum' to dozens, apart from her own children; she got letters from all over the world and was no mean correspondent and conversationalist herself. She did the washing in her machine, mended clothes as necessary—but she never had to hump coal, pay to have a tap-washer replaced or climb up a ladder to change an electric light bulb. 'The boys' would never dream of letting her. It was a two-way business. In her quiet way she broke down some racial prejudice, increased international understanding and added a great deal to the pool of human happiness—including her own. To cap it, she had an assisted pension; but the kindly N.A.B. did not bother much about the very small increase of net income from her lodgers. They knew that she put far more into the community than she took out, and that she was unlikely to be a charge on the state as an occupant of a ward for the senile. There must be many like her, and there could be many more.

A final word about 'vetting'. A firm which employs a lodgings officer, or in which the welfare officer helps with lodgings, has a responsibility to ensure that they are adequate, and that youngsters especially are not unwittingly put into quite unsuitable homes. But this responsibility is a moral one, and there can be no question of any legal liability. The contract, written or otherwise, must be between the landlady and lodger alone; if the two do not get on together they must sort their troubles out for themselves (with or without advice) or part company. The firm cannot be held liable if the lodger defaults with his rent, nor if the landlady does not provide the services she promised. The firm's neutrality must be made quite clear to both parties from the outset, both of whom must have no sense of obligation to the firm. The lodgings or welfare officer therefore should not vet the accommodation *on behalf* of the prospective lodger—it is up to the latter to satisfy himself when he first goes to see it. Nor is the lodger vetted *on behalf* of the landlady, for this would take something away from her right not to accept an individual she did not like.

Strictly, the firm 'vets' (when it decides to do so at all) only to apply a coarse-meshed sieve to reject the obvious non-starters and to discharge its own sense of responsibility, satisfying itself that there are no obvious dangers to physical or mental health and well-being. 'Vetting' should never be a formal affair, preceded by a stuffy official letter to the effect that so-and-so will call at such-and-such a time to 'inspect the premises'. This would be quite the best way of deterring potential landladies. It must be done quite informally by a social call to exchange information, during which the landlady will quite naturally show the caller around and proudly point to the general cleanliness and comfort of her home. And the visitor should never forget that he is looking at somebody's *home*, and not at a hotel or commercial boarding house. While he is doing it, he has one important judgment to make. Is the general atmosphere and level of the home something near what the potential lodger has been used to? He must be realistic enough to see that suggesting a near-illiterate labourer as lodger in a home where the signs of culture are unmistakable may be asking for trouble and unhappiness on both sides; equally the new recruit at Advanced G.C.E. or graduate level from a cultured background is less likely to settle down in the labourer's home. Class barriers are breaking down, and we are glad of it; the graduate may be a labourer's son, and the converse may even be true. But there is no point at all in pretending that barriers and the tensions which go with them do not exist; desire for classlessness does not of itself bring it about. There must be as much realism in the lodgings sphere as in any other in welfare. The lodgings officer or welfare officer thus makes the first rough judgment and matches lodgers and landladies as far as he is able. But lodger and landlady themselves must have the final say.

8 Welfare in Training Courses

Summary   Staff in the organisation must be trained to use a welfare officer service if it is to function properly. Their training needs will differ according to whether they are simply users in the personal sense, users in the sense of having some responsibility for the well-being of staff they control, or managers who make a direct contribution to welfare policy. For purposes of illustration, staff are therefore categorised in three broad levels: operators, supervisors and managers. Operators need background knowledge of group and physical welfare and the availability of the welfare officer for personal help. Supervisors will still be personal users of the service, but they also need to know *how* a welfare officer approaches various types of personal problem. Managers need in addition an appreciation of the service as part of general personnel policy, for they will also have a share in running the service as such.

When talking about 'What Welfare Officers Do', it was taken as axiomatic that internal training programmes for each of the three broad bands of staff—operator, supervisor and manager—should include something on the welfare officer function. However, this was really a statement of the ideal, and the ideal is still a long way off. It is only in the best (not necessarily the biggest) firms that we shall find anything approaching it. Yet the reality can be improved only if the ideal has been stated as the goal. We must make the assumption for present purposes that a firm which is sufficiently 'welfare-conscious' to employ a welfare officer with the kind of duties which have been outlined will also be sufficiently 'training-conscious' to run in-service training schemes.

The best firms have been training-conscious for a long while;

departments of government, the nationalised industries and the armed services have an even longer history of training and have built up an expertise which few other organisations can match. But the modern concept of training was quite foreign to some sectors of industry and commerce until the Industrial Training Act set up the twin stick-and-carrot incentives of levy and grant. Where there was training at all it was 'sitting by Nelly', and Nelly was not necessarily expert in her own work, and only rarely trained to instruct others.

Initially, the Act swung the pendulum in the opposite direction—some people felt that only 'off-the-job' training merited the title. However, it must not swing so far as to knock poor Nelly and her male equivalent right out of the picture. Sometimes a well-informed and well-trained instructor can do just as efficiently, more humanly and certainly less expensively what would otherwise have to be done by a simulator. We shall see later, for example, that a considerable proportion of the training of the new welfare officer himself can only be achieved by exposure to the demands of the job and training at the hands of an assortment of Nellies. The modern concept of training rests on the careful identification of training needs, which will almost in themselves dictate the type, location and method of training within the limits set by circumstances. This doctrine of the identification of needs can be applied to the welfare content of training courses designed for the three broad bands of staff which have been mentioned.

Operators

This word has been chosen as a shorthand term to describe all at the basic grade—the people who do the ground-level work of producing goods or services, whether these are services to the customer or internal services for others in the organisation (as for example in many clerical, wages, maintenance and similar activities). In a sense, all who do any form of work are operators in so far as they operate materials or systems; but it is difficult to think of a better term which will take in clerks, drivers, packers, porters, salesmen and technicians along with production people who operate directly and have no supervision responsibilities. The lack of responsibility for *control* of the work of others is the criterion.

Provided that the organisation's general paper publicity for its welfare officer service is adequate, it is by no means essential for all at the operator level to be given the same material again at a training course, orally and by the welfare officer himself. It is sufficient if the operator knows that he has access to such a service if he needs it. There is certainly scope for sessions on *group and physical* welfare in all newcomers' training programmes, and induction or 'company background' courses provide the best opportunity. Or sessions may often usefully be fitted in as change of activity between spells of practical work (e.g. practical 'stamina training' to reach Qualified Worker Standard). But they should be regarded as *changes of* activity, and never as *rests from* activity—the latter attitude stems from belief in welfare only as a non-essential, albeit accepted, frill.

It is useful for the welfare officer to be introduced at this time and in this context, most appropriately as an 'expert witness' for the instructor or chairman who has charge of the group. The instructor must be fully briefed. He should himself know far more about physical and group welfare than his group of trainees will need, so that he would be quite capable of running the session by himself if the welfare officer were busy with an urgent problem. The main purpose is to introduce the welfare officer as a neutral in the organisation, lacking even the tinge of formal status authority which inevitably attaches to the instructor's role. Although his willingness to help with personal problems must be covered, particularly the range of his knowledge of the social services, he should be introduced essentially as one who deals with the normal, rather than stress his dealing with the seamier side of life. Any instructor introducing the welfare officer as 'our head-shrinker' or as 'the biggest and dampest shoulder in the factory', or similar descriptions resulting from a combination of misplaced humour and lack of understanding of the welfare officer role, should be taken out of circuit immediately. Something has gone wrong with his selection, his training, or his supply of information— most likely all three. Neither instructor nor welfare officer should regale newcomers with the details of the difficult personal welfare cases which have arisen or might arise in the organisation. This is merely indirect or direct 'god-playing', a boost to the ego and a way of displaying superiority of knowledge or function, which can do a great deal of harm to trainer and learner alike. In other words he should not *invite* people to seek his services, but show that he will be around if ever he is needed. He should also make it clear that questions on conditions of service or problems of the work itself are proper to be answered by supervisors. If he does not, he risks being pestered by enquiries he should not have to answer, and this limits his availability to staff with problems needing his help in their solution.

Supervisors

'Supervisor' covers a very broad band of people, from the individual with a single assistant through the chargehand or foreman up to the second or even third-line supervisor who is still not regarded as part of management. The line between supervision and management is a very wavy or tenuous one and there will be anomalies even within organisations, let alone between them. The line might not exist at all in firms which not only *say* that supervision is part of management but actually *treat* supervisors as such. For present purposes we may regard a supervisor as one who is responsible for the work and well-being of others but lacks overall control of the shop, factory or office as a local unit. It is possible that courses for supervisors will be run for particular levels, according to the size and organisation of the undertaking. If so, the general principles below may be applied with different shades of emphasis—but they are still applicable. They are also applicable to staff on other personnel work (e.g. sick absence control) who have close dealings with the welfare officer in a functional capacity.

There are two distinct purposes of sessions on welfare for supervisors. They may be personal users of the welfare officer service, but they are more often users *qua* supervisor rather than *qua* Henry Brown or Henrietta Black. Especially in the lower levels of supervision, the element of personal use should not be underestimated. Personal problems do not disappear when one has a responsibility for the work of others; they may even loom larger. On the other hand, there is a saying in welfare officer circles—'The Higher the Fewer' (to which the experienced add ... 'but what stinkers the few can be'!). This is as it should be. The further up the hierarchy, the higher should be the levels of intelligence and general background knowledge; the higher these levels, the more problems the individual can cope with himself... and the more difficult are the few which still need the expert assistance of the welfare officer.

Supervisors *qua* supervisors must have a closer and more perfect understanding of the scope and limits of the welfare officer function than they require to use in their personal capacities. This is axiomatic if they are going to make the best possible use of it in discharging their own responsibilities for the well-being of staff in their care. One must hope that this axiom will be accepted by the firm so thoroughly that it also accepts the logical inference—that it points to a training need which should be met by the most appropriate training method. In this case 'exposure training' is not enough. Supervisors may gradually reach perfect understanding in the process of consulting the welfare officer about their people and the problems of those people; but this is the hard way which may result in the poor handling of cases dealt with before perfect understanding is reached. Short cuts, by way of 'concentrated experience', must be found.

There is a sound case for ensuring that every supervisor training course has at least one session devoted to staff welfare. Supervisors must be made aware, without being encouraged into laisser-faire softness and sloppiness, of the fact that they control the activities of human beings with hopes and anxieties and not simply pairs of hands. And if the firm employs welfare officers, it follows that supervisors must have a detailed appreciation of what they do and of how they should and should not be used. As a minimum, the newly-appointed supervisor should be given a full list of duties of the welfare officer, with any exegeses which have been written about them, and early in his new career should have an opportunity to talk with the welfare officer and come to an understanding about how the two can work together in the interests of the staff and the organisation. This minimum is probably sufficient for the supervisor who recognises his chargeship, who has the basic personality and interest in people to make him *want* to do his best for them, although even he would benefit from the insight that comes from discussion of difficult human problems. Unfortunately, there are other supervisors who are either apathetic about their human responsibilities or outright antipathetic to people and their needs. One is tempted to say that such folk should not be supervisors anyway, that one of the most important selection criteria should be human awareness. However, in considering welfare officers and their duties, we are concerned with life as we find it and not as we think it should be. We have them *because* people are imperfect; we cannot seek perfection in supervisor selection in order to ease the lives of welfare officers who are provided to help cope with an imperfect world.

This is not the place to discuss supervisor training in great detail. But it is worth making the point that far too many training courses are so heavily weighted on work processes and work knowledge that insufficient time is given to people—how to induct them, train them, appraise them, get their confidence and help them give of their best. Yet a supervisor is there to overlook *people doing work*, not work in the abstract; his task is to get work done through and by *people*, not just to inspect and criticise the finished products, whether goods or services.

Membership of a supervisor training course will range from the eager, through the apathetic to the antipathetic. One of the purposes of a session on staff welfare will be to identify who is who, and if possible why. Increased knowledge alone can change attitudes, and the prime job of the instructor or training officer (prime in the sense of first as well as in the sense of most important) is to present information about personal, group and physical welfare in such a way that none can say they 'did not know'. But the attitude of the instructor himself is equally important. It would be quite easy for him to have the factual knowledge and to reel off the list of welfare officer's duties from memory. The training group would very soon assess whether this knowledge was backed up by a sincere belief in the usefulness of a welfare officer's work. If it were not, then attitude would certainly change with increased knowledge, but in the wrong direction.

If selection of the instructor has not been at fault, we must assume that his attitude is right, and we can thus give a little attention to the teaching techniques he will employ. A useful guide will be found in Frank (1964). No one technique is the right one for every instructor; his own training and predilections come into the picture, as do the techniques employed on other material in the course.

Generally, the best first step is to establish the basic knowledge of the welfare officer's job, probably by issuing a handout for private study and subsequent discussion, the instructor chairing the session and guiding the discussion around the questions asked of the welfare officer—as expert witness—by members of the training group. However, while it is still more appropriate for the welfare officer to attend sessions on supervisor training courses as 'expert witness' rather than as direct instructor or trainer, much more time must be given to personal welfare than to his more limited group welfare and physical welfare roles. Case discussion is almost certainly the best approach, using a case or cases in which the problem centred around the welfare officer/supervisor/individual-in-need relationship. Naturally, the welfare officer should mention no names, and he should leave out any other characteristics which would identify the individual; but in other respects the case should be a real one. Just as they are quick to spot insincerity, so training groups also have keen eyes and ears for the fictitious case. Even if they had not, penetration of the case would force the welfare officer to invent background details. Fiction, like truth, will out.

One may first deal with the 'single case' approach to the whole course, during which welfare aspects may be picked out and accumulated for more thorough treatment in the presence of the welfare officer. He can then illuminate them with his more expert knowledge or draw parallels from the store of his experience to help the group to reach the most useful conclusions. The single-case method is a very advanced form of supervisor training which can be entrusted only to trainers of high calibre, themselves well trained in the task of disentangling a complicated problem with a group, giving direct teaching when it is required and calling in subject experts for aspects which only they can deal with adequately.

However, few supervisor courses are built round the single-case approach. Where case study is used at all it is generally in the sense of presenting specific cases to illustrate particular aspects—cases to deal with production or service difficulties, with the layout of work, with cost-consciousness, with training responsibility, with work relations or any other aspect of the supervisor's job. If this is the pattern, there is no reason why special cases to illustrate welfare responsibility and the best use of the welfare officer service should not be presented, as long as it is made quite clear that there is no 'separateness' about welfare but that it is inextricably part of the working situation as a whole.

Cases may be presented in many ways. Case presentation and discussion is a subject which demands a whole book to itself. Presentation can be by the oral 'critical incident' presented by the trainer or member of the group or issued on paper in advance for preliminary thinking and leaderless group discussion; by the fully detailed written case for analysis as a syndicate project; by tape-recorded conversations, films or filmstrips or by many combinations and permutations of these methods. Whichever method is chosen, in the context of the course as a whole, the purpose of the welfare officer's visit and his participation in discussion about human problems is to illuminate his list of duties with the insights which come from face-to-face communication. To know *how* the welfare officer approaches debt or sick-absence problems is worth very much more to a supervisor than to know *that* he takes them on. An essential point is that the instructor himself must know a great deal about personal welfare, as well as group and physical welfare, yet recognise his limits—knowing when to hand over to the welfare officer as expert. And the expertise of the welfare officer must be matched to the level of the group. The experienced basic grade welfare officer will be able to deal with first-line supervisor groups, of most levels, but there is a strong case for *his* supervisor to assist the instructor for the higher grades.

Managers

All that has been said about higher reaches of supervisors applies with equal force to managers; as remarked earlier, there is often little to distinguish the two levels. If a distinguishing mark must be found, it is that welfare sessions in the training of managers must be related to the firm's personnel policy as a whole. They must be able to see the thing in the round. They must know how welfare officers are selected and trained, for they will have a part to play in these processes. They must know how they are kept informed and how their work can be recorded and controlled. Managers must share responsibility for formulating the policy which decides whether or not to have a welfare officer service at all and, if so, what shape it should take. In short, the training of managers in welfare will cover broadly the ground which this book also attempts to cover. Indeed, one of the main reasons for making the attempt is to assist them in thinking about policy so that its formulation in particular organisations can be based on the adaptation of general considerations to meet specific needs.

Manager training need not be done in precisely the same way as for supervisors, and pressures of other topics may lead to some streamlining. This does not matter as long as the welfare sessions are not streamlined right out of the course programme because its designer feels that operational research, cost or stock control, manpower budgeting, critical path analysis or his other favourite hobby-horse is more important than people and their problems. We cannot continually go back to our basic philosophy at 'square one', but there is certainly a danger that the more remote the manager is from humanity on the shop floor or office, the more those who purport to teach him will forget that if he had no staff he would have nothing to manage anyway.

Because of the need to put welfare policy in perspective, it goes almost without saying that sessions on welfare in 'in-service' manager training courses should be attended by the top welfare specialist in the organisation, for he is basically responsible for making recommendations on policy which managers and directors consider and pronounce on. On balance, the best rule in the larger organisations about attendance at training courses in an expert witness capacity is to match the level of the specialist to the level of the trainees where it is possible to do so. When it is not, the specialist may go 'one up'. In smaller organisations where the welfare officer is a singleton he must clearly act for all levels—but it is doubtful whether *formal* in-service training for higher supervisors and managers in small organisations is a viable proposition. Informal discussions and conferences are likely to be far more used; and the fact that everybody already knows everybody else probably means that they will be far more effective.

Part three

THE WELFARE OFFICER
HIMSELF

9 Analysing the Job

Summary Pointers to the aspects of attitude, knowledge and skill required in a welfare officer have been found in the discussion of Scope and Limits, and Occupational Welfare in Practice. While a work-study type of job analysis is inappropriate for looking at jobs of a 'social' character, a great deal can be achieved by analysing them in terms of subdivisions of the N.I.I.P. seven-point plan. From this breakdown a rating scale can be constructed on which to base a consensus of opinion. There is a need for research on the 'criteria of success' of occupational welfare officers and their colleagues in the social welfare and 'personnel' spheres.

In looking at why welfare officers should be provided, what formal list of duties could be drawn up, what basic principles should guide their work, and how the practice of personal, group and physical welfare may be codified, we have achieved a very broad kind of job synthesis. We have a rough idea of what sort of person we want, what knowledge he requires to do his job, the attitudes which should inform the translation of this knowledge into practical skills. It is now time to break this synthesis down again to provide a 'model man' for the guidance of those who have to recruit, select and train. In other words, we need a job analysis—to decide what essential characteristics must be looked for at the selection stage and what we can reasonably expect to add or develop by suitable training.

In supporting an early definition of job analysis ('the scientific study and statement of all the facts about a job which reveal its content and all the modifying factors which surround it'), Roff and Watson, 1961, comment that much work we now accept as 'job analysis' is not particularly scientific. However, these authors were not deterred from producing their booklet, which, although it may not be regarded as 'scientific', introduced some clear thinking and commonsense principles into a previously somewhat foggy area.

We must accept at the outset that the welfare officer's job does not lend itself to scientific analysis in a 'work-study' way, timing elements of the task with a stopwatch in order to lay down Qualified Worker Standards. The language of the *Work Study Glossary*, 1959, is singularly inappropriate for any job which is based primarily on social skills. Similarly, concepts of the measurement of responsibility and 'time span of discretion' (Jaques, 1956, 1961) are also difficult to apply. We can rarely watch the welfare officer at work. If we do, we are a new factor in the human situation—one which he does not normally have to contend with. If we tried the work-study technique of activity sampling (getting the welfare officer to fill in a schedule describing his activity at random times) we should probably finish up with a list of the basic 'doing' things which fill his day—telephoning, writing a report, making a visit, interviewing an individual needing help, talking to a manager, looking up a reference book, etc.—but it would tell us nothing about the purpose or quality of his effort. For complementing, we need to know how many cases he deals with, what proportion of his time is spent on personal and group welfare, and what is 'lost' by travelling; but this analysis of work *load* is different from job analysis for selection and training.

What we *can* do is to talk to him off the job, discuss his cases and what knowledge he needed to deal with them, find out where he went wrong and why, what his past and present difficulties are, and what are his own views of his needs. But we cannot stop there. We must also talk to those who have selected him, and find out their assessment of his past potential and their prognosis of his performance. We must question those who train him and keep him up-to-date, supervise and employ him—and we should not be chary of augmenting this information by the views of the 'customers', as represented by managers and by appropriate trade unions. We thus fill out the detail of the picture which previous chapters have been concerned to sketch.

Attitude, Knowledge and Skill

So far we have talked in terms of attitude, knowledge and skill, a type of analysis used by Fryer, 1951, in the context of evaluation of training. (See also McGehee and Thayer, 1961, and Martin, 1957.) Fryer pointed out that 'Most training programs have grown like Topsy, out of industrial development. They are as they are because someone says some particular content should be included or not included in the training.' Much the same sort of criticism could be levelled at many so-called 'job-specifications'. Someone in authority says: 'We must have a graduate', 'We must have a man and not a woman', 'We must have someone under 40.' Juniors whose judgment may be sounder because they are in closer contact with the real needs of the job do not dare to challenge. But neither selection nor training can be realistic if no-one has gone to the trouble to make a thorough job analysis, as scientific as the circumstances will allow.

Fryer goes on to say that training courses should be based carefully on the pattern of behaviour required in the actual job for which the person is being trained. He identifies this behaviour as 'the attitude to perform, the knowledge required to take the right attitude and the skills necessary to do it—the "attitude/knowledge/skill pattern"'. All jobs can be analysed in relation to the pattern as a whole, but the emphasis will vary. Some courses will aim mainly at knowledge (e.g. stores clerks and enquiry staff), others at manual skill (e.g. typists, hosiery linkers, transistor assemblers) and others at social skill and attitude (e.g. interviewers, salesmen and some types of supervisors). Yet it is important to keep the whole pattern in mind, since all training must be a blend, in varying proportion, of all three of these aspects.

Attitude

It will already be clear that the welfare officer's *attitude* to his job and to those needing his help will be of fundamental importance. No matter how good the training laid on for him it will be of no avail unless he has the right basic attitudes, rooted largely in temperament and constitution. He must have a genuine and sincere interest in people and their problems and a desire to help find solutions. He must be sympathetic (but unsentimental, and able to take a very tough line indeed when the situation demands), approachable, friendly, frank and straightforward in his dealings. His integrity must be beyond question, his zeal must be kept in proportion, and his motives for doing welfare officer work must be sound and not based on neurosis. His health and constitution must be rugged enough to take a good deal of strain. The basic constitutional qualities cannot be taught: silk purses cannot be made from sows' ears, although the exploration of his own attitudes and motives will be an essential part of the welfare officer's training.

Knowledge

It is clear also that his knowledge must be wide, and that he must have a good memory to store it. He must know where to find more knowledge and find it quickly, when he needs it. As well as a good memory, he will also need a good level of intelligence; he must learn rapidly, and see the point quickly, reading between the lines of what he sees and hears without falling into the snare of over-hasty judgment based on insufficient evidence. He must know his way around his own organisation and around the outside social services. He must be able to distinguish the malingerer from the genuine hardship case, know when he is being taken for a ride and have the firmness to get off when he is. He must know a good deal about people, in sickness and in health, and why they behave as they do. Knowledge of individual differences (the best safeguard from thinking in terms of 'types'), of prejudices (his own included), and of behaviour in groups, must be part of his stock-in-trade.

Skill

We can also identify particular skills, bearing in mind the whole time that they are part and parcel of the 'attitude/knowledge/skill pattern'. The welfare officer must be a skilful interviewer and counsellor. He must develop insight, differentiating the way in which he sees a problem from the 'emotional logic' used by the individual needing help. He must be able to talk with confidence to all manner of people, and even more important, listen to them with concentration. He must learn the skills of forming objective judgments, of avoiding emotional involvement, and of not trying to 'put himself in the other man's shoes'. He must have the potential (which can be developed by training) to write clear and concise reports. These are not only of prime importance in their own right, but they are also part of the evidence by which the quality of his effort will be judged. Also at the basic skill level, he should for preference be able to type (or be willing to learn), or dictate concisely when he has the services of a confidential audio-typist. His working methods must be businesslike and he must be able to plan his day, particularly his travelling, to make the best use of his time. He must be a skilled persuader, but never an insincere manipulator of people, and he must develop his sensitivity to the reactions of others. Finally, he must be able to criticise himself without morbid introspection or the inverted arrogance which displays itself in self-abasement.

All this seems to call for a paragon, the sort of man who will also be in demand as a training officer, manager, or almost any other type of 'working with people' job one could think of. But we don't want perfection at all. We don't want the man who feels he has a call from the Almighty (of whatever sect) to put the world to rights. We want an ordinary, stable, intelligent and mature human being with wide experience of life and his fellows, who knows his limits, whose feet are firmly on the ground, who is basically tough and earthy, who wants to do the work, and who feels he could do it as successfully as the next man if given proper training.

Job Evaluation

A natural question at this stage is: How much is such a man worth? While to a certain extent an answer must be related to the organisation's decision on whether to recruit professionally qualified social workers or to select from its own ranks (a problem discussed a little later) the question takes us into job *evaluation* rather than job analysis and job specification.[1] This is somewhat outside the scope of this book. It could be examined further in the light of such publications as C. W. Lytle, *Job Evaluation Methods*, Ronald Press, New York, 1954; Elliott Jaques, *Measurement of Responsibility*, Tavistock, 1956; Joseph Tiffin and Ernest McCormick, *Industrial Psychology*, Prentice-Hall, 1965; and *Job Evaluation, a Practical Guide*, British Institute of Management, 1961. The most that will be said at this stage is that the welfare officer in the basic grade should be on a par with the training officer in the basic grade, or the safety officer, selection officer, or any other of what might be called first-line personnel officers. Supervisory welfare officers will thus be at the same level in the organisation as other personnel officers with supervisory responsibilities.

The Seven Point Plan

While a broad analysis in terms of attitude, knowledge and skill may be sufficient to give selectors a good idea of what they should be look-

---

[1] These subjects may themselves be taken further by reference to O.E.C.D. Project Number 231, *Job Analysis—A Tool of Productivity*, European Productivity Agency, 1956, available from H.M.S.O. See also G. W. Howells, 'A Scientific Approach to Job Specification', *Scientific Business*, August 1964.

ing for, and to indicate the training which will be required, it is better to take it to finer detail. The bigger organisations will no doubt have their own systems of analysis, within which the detailed differences between various jobs can be accommodated. Many of them will use the Seven Point Plan (Rodger, 1951), which is perhaps the best of its kind. Not only does it provide a framework for selection, but it is the most useful tool available for the essential complement of selection—vocational guidance. It can also clarify thoughts on training needs, distinguishing these from basic qualities which cannot be modified by training.

On first looking into the merits of a job analysis scheme such as the Seven Point Plan, an organisation is tempted to adapt it immediately in an effort to make it more appropriate to its own needs. The best schemes may in fact be those which have been so adapted—but only if the changes are based firmly on research and not on the personal predilections of the adapter. But as Roff and Watson (1961) have pointed out, there is value in using the Plan without modification unless there are compelling reasons for making changes. In this way it is possible to derive the maximum benefit from published research and to collect data for further research. For example, there is a need for those concerned with the training of various kinds of social worker to sponsor research into the criteria of success of each group, including occupational welfare officers. If both vocational guidance and selection of would-be social workers were universally based on the Seven Point Plan such comparative studies would be very much easier to carry out. As a contribution to such future research, the Plan as it stands will be used below for the finer analysis of the occupational welfare officer's job.

The main headings of the Plan are as follows:

1. *Physical Make-up*—covering health and physique, including appearance, bearing and speech.
2. *Attainments*—including educational and occupational attainments.
3. *General Intelligence*—the ability to reason quickly and accurately, to learn quickly, and to handle complex ideas.
4. *Special Aptitudes*—including manual dexterity, mechanical aptitude, verbal facility, numerical facility, and artistic aptitudes.
5. *Interests*—divided into five classes and their combinations: (a) intellectual; (b) practical and constructional; (c) physically active; (d) social; (e) artistic.

6. *Disposition*—qualities of temperament and characteristics of an individual shown in his relationships with other people and his work: his steadiness, self-reliance, acceptability to others and his influence over others.

7. *Circumstances*—these may be mainly domestic circumstances to be considered, for example in vocational guidance and selection for jobs involving travelling or awkward shifts; or may be concerned with the physical, etc., environment of the job (e.g. paced, dirty, hot, cold or noisy work, and similar features).

The vocational guidance counsellor's or selection officer's use of the Seven Point Plan for an individual will be different from that of the job analyst's. When an individual is being appraised for a specific job, or for a range of jobs against which he can be matched, the assessor must measure each characteristic as carefully as he can, using objective tests or other quantified items of behaviour as far as possible. The aim is to assess the *individual*. But in the present context the job analyst is more concerned with identifying the demands of the *job*. This involves ascertaining the *range* of the characteristics shown by people doing the same job in different places. To do this, he must also know whether they are doing it well or badly. He wants to know, for example, whether the welfare officers' job demands an I.Q. of 110, or 140; whether the more successful welfare officers cluster closely around the 120 level—or whatever it may be; how far the 'right' I.Q. level is crucial to success. When he has identified the range and shown *what* characteristics, and at what *level*, are most important for success, he has provided the vocational guidance counsellor and selection officer with limits within which they know they should work.

Need for Research

In spite of the earlier categorical statements, that the welfare officer 'must be of good intelligence', 'must have a good memory', and must have this or that skill, the brutal truth is that these are subjective assessments based only on the experience of selecting, training and following the careers of a considerable number of welfare officers. They are not based on a scientific 'criteria of success' study. This is a research task which needs to be done, so that subjective assessments may be corrected by established fact. The same sort of research is needed for other jobs in the personnel sphere and elsewhere. The question: 'What makes a good welfare officer ?', is the same in prin-

ciple as: 'What makes a good selection officer, training officer or
safety officer?' Many people can answer these questions subjectively
from within their own experience, but none can point to any general
surveys designed to find out even the consensus of *opinion*, let alone
the results of objective measures. Full-scale 'criteria of success'
research is still in the future; but it need not be difficult for large-
scale organisations, which employ several personnel supervisors in
charge of teams doing virtually identical jobs, to get a consensus of
informed opinion on a reasonably scientific basis.

Use of a Rating Scale

It is suggested that this can be done by converting the Seven Point
Plan into a rating scale and asking each supervisor (the welfare supervisors in this case) to complete it for the 'best' and the 'weakest'
member in his team. A simple analysis of the ratings on each characteristic will then reveal which of them differentiate most clearly
between 'best' and 'weakest'. This technique has been used in a
pilot study (Martin, 1965) designed to start answering the question:
What makes a good instructor?

The procedure begins by listing under the main headings of the
Seven Point Plan all the questions about the man which may be
relevant to his job. These are then converted into statements of
extremes of behaviour and other descriptions at each end of a six-
point scale, labelled X and Y. Thus, to take as a random example one
of the customary sub-headings of the Plan—artistic interest—we place
at the X end of the scale something like 'Strong artistic interests, e.g.
painting, music, literature', and at the Y end the converse: 'No
artistic interests at all; dislikes or is quite indifferent to painting,
music, literature, etc.' The points of the scale are then:

A = X applies
B = Strong tendency to X
C = Slight tendency to X
D = Slight tendency to Y
E = Strong tendency to Y
F = Y applies.

This rating-scale development of the Seven Point Plan can be seen
readily in Table 1. Three points may be noted in passing.

First, no 'average' or middle assessment is allowed. The assessor
has to make up his mind and is not given the chance of taking refuge

Assessment of Welfare Officers

X	X applies	Strong tendency to X	Slight tendency to X	Slight tendency to Y	Strong tendency to Y	Y applies
	A	B	C	D	E	F

1 Physical Make-up

   (i) Health excellent; good sickness record
  (ii) Robust constitution; strong and hardy
 (iii) Appearance clean, neat and tidy, well dressed but not over-dressed
 (iv) Bearing excellent; moves, sits and stands well
  (v) Voice pleasant and well modulated; variety in pitch, power and pace

2 Attainments

   (i) Type of education (A = University
                      B = Grammar)
  (ii) Educational achievement excellent considering type of education
 (iii) Has continued his education and retained his interest
 (iv) Occupational training good—has made full use of opportunities
  (v) Occupational experience wide; has benefited fully from occupational changes
 (vi) Knowledge of work both wide and detailed
(vii) Has benefited fully from recent experience (e.g. training course, probation)

3 General Intelligence

   (i) *Capable* of displaying great intelligence and insight: imaginative, original
  (ii) *Normally* very alert, quick on the uptake

4 Special Aptitudes

   (i) Has a strong mechanical bent
  (ii) Manually very dexterous; quick and sure with hands
 (iii) Good facility with words; easily makes himself understood in conversation, discussion and explanation
 (iv) Writes clear and concise reports

Y	NAME (Mr, Mrs, Miss) Age LOCATION

Physical Make-up

(i) Health very poor; bad sickness record

(ii) Poor constitution; weak; soon collapses under strain

iii) Slovenly in appearance or over-dressed

iv) Moves, sits and stands very badly

(v) Voice unattractive (harsh, dull, monotonous, squeaky or heavily accented)

GENERAL REMARKS
(Please use this space to amplify your markings if necessary and write a brief pen-picture)

Attainments

(i) C = Technical, D = 'Elementary' or 'Secondary Modern' types of education

(ii) Educational achievement very poor considering type of education

iii) No interest in furthering his education and content to vegetate mentally

iv) No occupational training; no use made of opportunities

(v) Occupational experience narrow; no benefit from changes of occupation. Bad employment record

vi) Narrow and superficial knowledge of work

vii) Has not benefited at all from recent experience

General Intelligence

(i) *Incapable* of displaying much intelligence and insight: no imagination or originality

(ii) *Normally* dull: slow to see the point

Special Aptitudes

(i) No mechanical bent whatsoever

(ii) Slow and clumsy with hands

iii) No facility with words; cannot make himself understood in conversation, discussion and explanation. Verbose, muddled

iv) Very poor at report writing (e.g. bad style, punctuation, grammar; poor layout; verbosity, etc.)

continued

Table one (continued)

	X	A x applies	B Strong tendency to x	C Slight tendency to x	D Slight tendency to Y	E Strong tendency to Y	F Y applies

5 Interests

  (i) Strongly intellectual; likes abstract ideas, theories

 (ii) Strongly practical; an excellent constructor and craftsman

(iii) Strongly physically active; fond of sports and outdoor activities

 (iv) Strongly social interests; likes companionship, parties, dances, entertainments

  (v) Strongly artistic interests, e.g. paintings, music, literature

6 Disposition

  (i) Readily acceptable to other people; popular; a good listener

 (ii) Has a strong influence on others; accepted as a leader; holds opinions firmly but rationally

(iii) Steady, dependable, fully reliable

 (iv) Completely self-reliant and confident without 'bounce'

  (v) Ambitious: anxious for more scope

 (vi) Sensitive and insightful; unaggressive and sympathetic; always willing to learn

(vii) Zealous without being immoderate. Always rises to the occasion. Plenty of drive

7 Circumstances

  (i) Free from domestic worries; stable home life

 (ii) Fully mobile; could move on promotion

(iii) Married with children (A)
     Married without children (B)

Y

Interests

(i) No intellectual interests at all; dislikes abstract ideas; no time for theory

(ii) No practical interests at all; no use at making things

(iii) No interests of a physically active nature; does not engage in any sports or outdoor activities

(iv) Dislikes social contacts and companionship; prefers to be alone; a solitary individual

(v) No artistic interests at all; dislikes or is indifferent to painting, music, literature

Disposition

(i) Does not get on well with people; unpopular; cannot listen

(ii) No influence at all on other people; a 'follower' or 'yes-man'. Easily swayed

(iii) Erratic and unpredictable; unreliable

(iv) Lacks confidence; always looking to others for support; over-confident and 'bouncy'

(v) Quite unambitious: does not want to change present way of life

(vi) Lacks sensitivity and insight; aggressive; unsympathetic; thinks he knows it all

(vii) Lacks zeal or is immoderately zealous. Always appears over-pressed. Lacks drive

Circumstances

(i) Unsettled or unstable domestic life

(ii) Cannot leave present home; not interested in promotion

(iii) Widowed or divorced, with children (C); single, widowed or divorced, without children (D)

Please tick appropriate box according to the stage at which the assessment is being made

1 Basic Training Course

2 Probationary Period*

3 Follow-up

Date of assessment

Signed:

* Enter date of appointment here

in an 'average' funkhole.[1] Two jobs, or two men, may indeed be 'average' if taken in the round, but it would be remarkable if every characteristic were really 'average'. Second, a six-point scale is probably preferable to a four-point scale (X applies, tendency to X, tendency to Y, Y applies), to differentiate more finely. Third, it will be apparent that a scaled Seven Point Plan is not only useful in its own right for job analysis, selection and vocational guidance purposes. It can also lead to the design of an instrument for the annual appraisal of (in our case) the welfare officer once he is in post, or more frequently during the probation period. Ideally, the selector's assessment of him before appointment should be compared with his trainer's assessment during the basic training course and the subsequent assessments of the welfare supervisor. And if the organisation employs a sufficient number of welfare officers (involving different supervisors doing the assessments) appraisements can be compared and balanced for the guidance of promotion boards. All the data can then be treated statistically to improve the design of the form.

A word of caution is necessary at this point. If the form developed from the rating scale survey is to be used exclusively for work-appraisement purposes, only the items which differentiate most clearly between the 'best' and the 'weakest' need be incorporated. But in the study of instructors quoted above, some items, although attracting high ratings, did not differentiate at all—for the very obvious reason that the selectors had done their job well and had rejected those applicants who did not measure up. For example, good health, reasonable appearance and bearing, freedom from domestic worry, and dependability, did not differentiate the 'best' from the 'weakest'. Applicants who had failed to satisfy the selectors in these respects never became instructors at all. But if the form is also to be

---

[1] Rowe, 1964, found that managers were very reluctant to appraise at all. When they did, analysis of rating scales showed the 'well-known phenomenon of skewed central tendency'. That is to say, they tended to go for an average, but the average came out above the mid-point of the scale and not at the mid-point itself. Elliott, 1955, puts this in a less technical fashion: 'It is a safe bet that in 90 per cent of industrial rating schemes the average mark awarded is above the mid-point of the scale used.' Finding reluctance to appraise, Rowe suggests that 'no attempt should be made to classify or categorise performance in terms of grades'. She feels that concrete statements should be made instead. My own view is that the six-point X and Y technique offers a way of putting such concrete statements on a rating scale.

used at the selection stage, such items must be included; they may be highly critical factors in occupational success even though they may not distinguish at the *post*-selection stage.

Summary   In the absence of research on the criteria of success of welfare officers, one can offer only personal opinions on the main characteristics to be looked for at the selection stage. The sex of the welfare officer is rarely important; 'he' must enjoy good health and be both mentally and physically robust; firms selecting from their own staffs may not find a specific social-science qualification necessary, but should encourage welfare officers to further their specialist education and training after appointment; a good level of intelligence is necessary; interests and disposition are of great importance; other things being equal, the married applicant is to be preferred.

Strictly, in the absence of research, we should assume that all the positive characteristics and qualities set out on the X side of Table 1 *may* be relevant to the success of an occupational welfare officer. Nevertheless, without prejudicing such research too far, clearly some are prima facie more relevant than others. These have already been highlighted in the discussion of duties and in subsequent chapters, have found their way into the initial attitude/knowledge/skill analysis. But only proper research could establish which are *most* important, and those which selectors must rate as essential rather than merely desirable—and only proper research can identify other items which are not on the list. It is also possible that some characteristics may be more desirable in some posts than in others. For example, one could argue that strong practical interests may be an advantage for a welfare officer serving the staff of an engineering firm, in so far as these will give him a better understanding of the work done, and of the attitudes of staff to it. Domestic mobility may be quite irrelevant in a firm with only one geographical location—although it might be important to the man himself if he has to look elsewhere for promotion. Some accents of speech may be more acceptable than others in certain parts of the country; although the usual experience is that accent is unimportant as long as it is not so marked that it leads to difficulties in communication.

We can now run briefly through the list, picking out a few items of particular interest, before moving on to selection and probation.

Sex

This is not mentioned at all in the Seven Point Plan. Walker, 1961, has said, though without firm evidence to support the statement, that women are the natural confidantes of both sexes and are therefore more likely than men to be welfare officers. One has to question this point of view. It is certainly not the experience of at least one large organisation which employs about 100 welfare staff, the larger proportion of whom are in fact men and are found to be perfectly acceptable to both sexes. This organisation's women welfare officers are also equally acceptable to both sexes; sex differences just do not arise, save in very exceptional circumstances. If *all* the staff are women, or *all* the staff are men, there may just be a case to employ only one or the other—but it is a very reluctant 'may'. If the welfare officer happens to be single and is accommodated in a men's or women's hostel, perhaps the sex should match—but it would be far better to have a mixed hostel!

Organisations big enough to employ more than one welfare officer are fortunate. They should have one of each; or if there is a team, make sure that it is mixed, so that the few staff who may be reluctant to confide in someone of the opposite sex do not have to go without. People are becoming more and more accustomed to going to both men and women doctors, to be cared for by both men and women nurses, to have men or women listen to their troubles at the Citizens' Advice Bureau, and so on. They only rarely reject the services of a welfare officer of the other sex. Writers on social work are now beginning to drop the invariable 'she' and are adopting the normal convention of 'he' to mean either sex (see Timms, 1964). Selectors should therefore examine their own prejudices very carefully indeed, and pick out the best-qualified applicants irrespective of sex, unless there are really compelling reasons for doing otherwise—for example, to secure a mixed team.

Physical Make-up

Good health and a robust constitution are essential. The welfare officer's job is full of stresses and strains, and he is very little use to anyone if he is frequently off sick. The health record of the applicant must be examined carefully, especially if it mentions spells of 'neurasthenia' or other medical euphemisms and synonyms for instability or neurosis. This does not mean that the selectors should reject someone who has had months off after a serious accident, who may have had psychiatric treatment many years ago, or is minus an arm or leg. Such people may have had their understanding deepened by their own disability or suffering; they know what it is to be afraid, to lie in pain and perhaps be gushed over by well-meaning but incompetent 'do-gooders'. If they are of the right basic quality they will have gained in stature from their experience.

Normality is called for in the other aspects of physical make-up. People who are neat and tidy without being over-dressed, who carry themselves well without having 'sergeant-major' written all over them, who speak pleasantly without being suspected of having taken elocution lessons, are usually more acceptable than those whose unusualness sticks out like a sore thumb.

Attainments

It is rather curious that there seems to be little interchange between industry and the statutory social services in the employment of welfare officers. Industry has little experience of the type of man who comes straight to occupational welfare (as distinct from general personnel work) after taking a degree in the social sciences or similar training. Conversely, apart from very welcome moves in such directions as the recruitment of older non-graduates to the Probation Service, the statutory social services do not seem to have much experience of the occupational welfare officer who wants to specialise after his general experience. This is not the place to discuss the qualifications and training of statutory social workers: interested readers should begin with the *Younghusband Report*, 1959, on this. One wonders, though, whether recent emphasis on training has resulted in too little attention to the selection which should precede it. Naturally, if an industrial organisation had the opportunity of employing a *mature* person with good social work training and experience who filled the bill in all other respects as well, it would be wise to take him—as long as he was destined later for a welfare supervisory role. He might be employed below his capacity at the first-line level, and it would be better for him to be extended in the more general service of the community, as one of the 'professional' long-stops with whom the occupational welfare officer should be in close contact.

There are two main arguments *against* employing a new young graduate as an occupational welfare officer. First, his job is purely advisory. His authority comes only from his knowledge, attitude and skill. The youngster has to be very good indeed before older people will go to him *voluntarily* and spill out their troubles; whereas the statutory social worker, no matter how young, gains some authority, and thus some security, from the statute under which he is employed. The children's officer, or probation officer, or almost any other statutory worker, has certain *powers* which would be quite out of place in industry, where the welfare officer's only instruments are persuasion and advice. Second, the young graduate has had little, if any, experience of people at work. Whereas the statutory worker deals mainly with people in the context of their homes and private lives, the welfare officer is *initially* concerned with the 'man-at-work' context, although this will promptly lead back into the home and private area in many cases. Those who train the statutory workers sometimes give the impression that knowledge of working, industrial and commercial man, as distinct from private and domestic man, is irrelevant. Or, if not considered irrelevant, this knowledge does not occupy a central place in the textbooks designed to inform the statutory worker. This curious omission might itself be responsible for the overemphasis on the psychology of Freud (and of his followers and dissentients of the general psychodynamic schools) which appears in some of these texts. Thus the young graduate may come into industry well versed in Egos, Superegos and Ids, and knowing how Klein differs from Freud and both differ from Jung, but completely uninformed about job satisfaction, staff consultation, bonus schemes and similar subjects which should be part of the background of the occupational welfare officer. He may have to unlearn his Freud and start learning material which is far more important to his job.

This must not be construed as an anti-psychodynamic diatribe, nor as criticism of the way in which statutory social workers are trained. There is a good deal of ferment going on in the field of social work theory, and the flag of 'commonsense' as an antidote to an excess of psychodynamics has been nailed firmly to the mast by Barbara

Wootton, 1959.[1] The 'professionals' must fight it out amongst themselves, but one hopes they will remember that although man does not live by bread alone, he spends a considerable part of his waking life in earning it. They could also bear in mind that there is a total lack of evidence on the relative efficacy of casework as practised by those trained in the various psychodynamic schools.

The purpose of this digression has been to show that a social science qualification is not a *sine qua non* for a basic-grade occupational welfare officer at the selection stage. If the applicant has one, and is acceptable in other respects, so much the better. People learn about welfare in different ways after their primary training. Some may be helped most by textbooks, by W.E.A. or extra-mural courses which do not lead to formal examination, by meeting social workers at local discussions, by insights about people from novels, by severe self-criticism of their face-to-face dealings with people needing help, and in countless other ways. Willingness to learn and the acceptance of some discipline in doing it are essential; the method of doing so is secondary.

[1] The core of the argument is to be found in the chapter on 'Contemporary Attitudes in Social Work'. Lady Wootton begins by pointing out how psychiatry rushed into the vacuum created by the loss of the social worker's function of relieving poverty. '... In a very few years practically the whole profession has succeeded in exchanging the garments of charity for a uniform borrowed from the practitioners of psychological medicine.' Although some good has resulted from this, 'the price of these advances has been the erection of a fantastically pretentious façade. . . .' She gives examples of pretentiousness from many countries, finishing up with Eileen Younghusband's now celebrated statement of aims and relationships. Lady Wootton's beautifully apt and elegantly acid comment on this breathtaking statement is that 'It might well be thought that the social worker's best, indeed perhaps her only, chance of achieving aims at once so intimate and so ambitious would be to marry her client.'

Miss Younghusband distinguishes very carefully between the trained caseworker and the 'good, sensible person with an all-round experience of life' who is widely, though not in her view wisely, believed to be just as, if not more valuable than the specialised social worker. But this was in 1952. In 1965 we are told by a psychiatrist ('Kind Hearts and Competence', *New Society*, Vol. 5, No. 135, 29 April) that the amateur has much to give to social work and that the 'professional' can learn from him. One might well ask how much more could be offered by good sensible people with an all-round experience of life who are *also* carefully selected, and trained in a practical way to help with the real problems of everyday life. Social workers who seek 'professional' status by insisting that they should be trained as quasi-psychiatrists may do more harm than good.

The best welfare officers, particularly those who hope to rise to supervisory positions, will go out of their way to extend their knowledge. They will usually be helped most by undertaking the discipline of a formal course which leads to a recognised diploma, such as the four-year Diploma in Sociology of the Extra-Mural Department of London University, and paralleled elsewhere. When they work in parts of the country which do not offer these facilities they will somehow find others, such as residential courses in adult education centres, and summer schools of various kinds. Employing organisations should encourage them to do so in every possible way—by paying fees, allowing paid leave, and by laying down the firm policy that training is a continuous process. They must appreciate that continued training for the welfare officer is investment in the welfare of all the staff with whom he has dealings.

An organisation which is big enough to 'grow its own' welfare supervisors, and is prepared to help to the maximum in offering facilities for continued training, is entitled to look for such qualifications and attendances at the promotion stage—but only if all welfare staff in range for promotion have equal facilities. Formal qualifications are in themselves no complete guarantee of the qualities necessary in a good welfare supervisor; but the man with an academic edge over his juniors is more likely to be respected by them than the man without it. If continued study is as worthwhile as the organisation's training policy implies, then the man who has taken advantage of it should in any event be a better man. As a minimum, he has taken the trouble to gain relevant and objective evidence of his merit; and this is something the promotion authority must take into account.

It has been necessary to digress into training, in order to highlight the standards of attainment which the selectors must have in mind. They should look for a good standard of educational achievement, *bearing in mind* the man's opportunities. If he attended a secondary modern school and yet gained some G.C.E.s, he might be a better bet than the man who did not appear to profit much from the grammar or technical school. Similarly, has he made full use of his opportunities in occupational training? If his background is technical, did he chase his certificates, and if so, with what success? Has he been around on different jobs—and was this to gain experience or because he could not settle down? Is he good at his present work, or does he view welfare work simply as a means of change, or a way to a higher salary?

Attainments and motives for seeking them will clearly shade into the 'disposition' area of the Seven Point Plan.

General Intelligence

Properly constructed and validated intelligence tests should be used unless there are major political considerations which rule them out—and they should be administered and scored by someone who has been trained to do so. The sooner we do away with home-made tests administered by self-styled experts the better.

Organisations such as the National Institute of Industrial Psychology and the National Foundation for Educational Research have tests for a wide variety of purposes. Training in their use is offered by the N.I.I.P. and some other institutions. These facilities are remarkably under-used by industry and commerce, especially in contrast with the U.S.A., and industry and commerce could learn a great deal from them and make far better use of manpower in the process. It is now more customary to think in terms of actual test scores rather than in terms of 'Intelligence Quotients', but I.Q. is a concept now fairly well understood by the layman and will serve as a form of shorthand in the present context. By definition, the average I.Q. of the population as a whole is 100. By personal guess, in the absence of objective research, the best range of I.Q. for welfare officers is probably around 120. They must be bright enough to cope with the thought processes of most of those requiring their help, and the average I.Q. of these people will be *above* 100. The explanation of this is that industry and commerce do not employ the very low levels of intelligence—e.g. those in institutions and others who are virtually unemployable—which contribute to the *national* average of 100. On the other hand, the highly intelligent employees are more likely to sort out their own problems, providing that factors of mental disturbance do not intervene. Welfare officers should not be so near the genius end of the I.Q. scale that they cannot readily communicate with lower intelligence levels, but there is little possibility of this. Nowadays, the very highly intelligent have a 'through route' to university and will be pre-selected for other work unless they have a very strong desire to be occupational welfare officers. Other things being equal, welfare officers in the upper part of the range are the best candidates for senior or chief welfare officers.

It should be emphasised that the Seven Point Plan draws the distinction between basic or innate intelligence as measured by objective tests, and the use to which it has been put. The best measures of use of intelligence are educational and job training qualifications and the assessments of previous employers (or supervisors in the same firm). Selectors must bear this distinction in mind. If there is a marked discrepancy they should carefully examine motivational factors—disposition and interests—and domestic history and any other relevant evidence to find out as accurately as they can how it has arisen. If a flaw in character such as laziness or lack of determination is at the root, a warning is sounded. But if interests are firmly non-intellectual or domestic circumstances have inhibited opportunity the judgment of the selectors may be quite different.

Special Aptitudes

Aptitudes must be differentiated from *interests*. Some may be dormant, or rusty from lack of use. The aptitudes listed in Table 1 can all be assessed on the basis of more or less objective evidence from tests, references, reports and interviews. The value of specific aptitude tests in selecting welfare officers is doubtful, but selectors should be capable of making sound judgments of oral and report-writing ability. They should bear in mind, however, that the more than averagely sensitive person they are looking for might be more than averagely shy, and therefore orally stilted, in the formal interview board situation. And while evidence of attainment in report writing is valuable, it has to be remembered that this facility is trainable if the potential is there—good intelligence and well-constructed oral responses are the best guides to such potential.

Interests

We are clearly looking for the man who leans towards extraversion rather than introversion, but both extremes should be avoided. The cheery backslapper who calls everybody in the office or factory 'Charlie' is usually so insensitive that he is just as poor a welfare officer as the introvert who would really prefer to live with books than people. Social interests are essential, but there is a good case for looking also for the sort of man who can put the cares of people aside in his spare time and do something else which is a complete relaxation. The man who has nothing in his life but welfare, in private as well as at work, who cannot be happy unless he is helping people all of the time, may be just as much a menace to staff as he is to himself. Without doubt, he must have a real and genuine interest in people, but he will return to them refreshed if he can also relax away from them.

Disposition

It is in the disposition area that we reach one of the crucial points in selection (others will be recognised as health, intelligence and motivation). Firmly as one may believe in the perfectibility of the human species by the long process of evolution and the adoption of better value systems by succeeding generations, temperament is mainly inborn, a matter largely of the endocrine glands. We cannot teach or exhort welfare officers to be acceptable, dependable, self-reliant and unsentimentally sympathetic. We can only select them for these basic qualities and bring out in training courses the need for their higher development. Attitudes can be and are changed by training; a flash of insight into how he is regarded by his fellows can change a person overnight. But there is no point in a selection board thinking that training can put right the wrong basic personality, or that the most self-centred applicant can hope for conversion on the road to Damascus. Most of us can only learn gradually from our experience, and even this presupposes the basic humility which enables us to do so. Whether or not they use the more orthodox objective personality tests which are available (such as the Eysenck Personality Inventory), the selectors will have a most interesting time in exploring and penetrating the attitudes of welfare officer applicants. To get at prejudice and willingness to accept evidence they may try out such test pieces as the colour bar, capital punishment, homosexuality and the like. They may find it equally worthwhile to outline a personal case to the applicant to see how he approaches it. Attitudes may then be examined by judicious use of 'Why?' questions. They may also be judged on the basis of the applicant's past or current voluntary welfare interests; evidence of these is one of the best guides to motive.

Circumstances

Notwithstanding the point of view which has already been expressed about the sex of the welfare officer, one might reasonably ask whether the unmarried welfare officer can be as effective as his or her married colleague. Can anyone who is keeping lasting heterosexual relationships at bay really begin to understand the anxieties and inadequacies which may have their roots in sex life or lack of it? Can he or she really know of the love-hate, tenderness-aggression, companionship-loneliness polarities which are inherent in many marriages? Or the 'talking through the children' one-upmanship which often takes the place of real man-and-wife communication? Can he know of the temptations to debt facing a couple with two or three young children, living on a very low wage? In other words, should all welfare officers be or have been married themselves?

There is no ready answer to this. There are plenty of married people around who live at such a vegetative level that they lack the imagination to think that others can live differently. They never argue, always budget to the last penny, would never dream of hire purchase, and would regard any other sort of behaviour with stern moral disapproval. On the other hand, the single person may have vivid memories of the hustle and bustle of family life from his own childhood; his intended spouse may have died; or he (more often she) may have given up any idea of marriage because the needs of aged parents came first in the list of priorities. We cannot say Yes to the married and No to the single; for if we do we may take on somebody we shouldn't really have, or reject someone we should have. We can only say that marriage, like sex, is a balancing factor to be taken into account when other things are equal. If they *are* equal, then we should choose the married rather than the single, for marriage is the norm of adult life.

Whether married or single, the welfare officer needs a stable and well-adjusted home life. He should not need a welfare officer himself. He needs to be reasonably free from the stresses which make other people seek his help, but not too far removed from them to be out of touch with other people's realities.

11 Selection and Probation

Summary   The organisation has first to decide whether to recruit a trained specialist from outside, or to select from within. The qualifications and experience required will depend to a large extent on the firm's own internal training facilities. The use of specialist selection agencies can be considered by those firms which are unfamiliar with appropriate journals for advertisement and with the design of special application forms. Interview panels, supplemented with objective tests, are recommended, and the group selection method is to be preferred. If the selection is from internal candidates, the whole of the advertisement, application, selection and training process should be seen as part of probation, which can ensure that no misfits are kept on. A change of location is essential for the welfare officer selected from within.

Selection

A full account of selection techniques would fill another book. Indeed, Mandell, 1964, has recently written it for the American Management Association. There are naturally cultural differences between Britain and the U.S.A., especially in the use of personality tests (see Vernon, 1964), but most of the lessons in it are valid for the U.K. The National Institute of Industrial Psychology is the best source of British information on the subject for those who want more detail. For present purposes it is necessary only to look briefly at a few essential points.

Source

The organisation first has to decide whether to look within at its own potential talent, or to look outside. This depends largely on its size and on the types of staff it employs. The big organisation which also reckons to do most of its own training can decide to select only internally, or it may augment internal sources by open advertisement. This should be a matter of joint consultation and not an arbitrary managerial decision. The compromise might be to advertise both within and without, but giving first preference to an internal recruit— *as long as, and only as long as, he is well up to the required standard.* The rejection of a slightly superior outsider may be a small price to pay for good staff relations, but no management should allow itself to be stampeded or persuaded into taking somebody from within who is simply not good enough for the job, when there are others outside who are.

Qualifications/experience

The next decision must be on the degree of previous experience or level of formal qualifications to be asked for. Once again, the big organisation with good training resources is able to ask for nothing but potential. If this is the case, the selectors will be even more careful in finding out whether the individual's welfare interest has ever manifested itself in some sort of voluntary work, or whether it is merely hiding the desire for a change. People who have helped in a C.A.B., run a youth club, served on a local Old People's Welfare Committee, read to the blind, or done something else which shows a *real* interest, are the ones the selectors should be looking for. The smaller firm which decides at the outset to look outside, can reasonably ask for a Diploma in Sociology or Social Studies, social work certificate or certificate of attendance at various courses, associateship of the Institute of Welfare Officers, or other firm evidence of qualification beyond personal characteristics.

Use of an agency

There is a third preparatory decision to be made. Even big organisations with expert personnel departments often use consultants for selecting higher-level staff, or at least for producing short-lists. As long as it is remembered that personal acceptability is an important key to success as an occupational welfare officer, and that this can be judged only by the employers, the practice has much to commend it. However, the choice of agency must be made with care. An 'office staff' bureau clearly will not do; only those consultant agencies which can offer professional help in selecting *professional* people should be considered. If the employing firm finds it cannot reach the standards suggested in the next few pages, the use of an expert agency is a better approach.

Advertisement

If outsiders are to be considered, care must be taken to see that the advertisement goes into the type of journal which will be read by the sort of people who are likely to be interested. The weekly *New Society* is rapidly gaining a reputation in this connection, and it has the useful advantage of frequency of publication. It will also prove fruitful to advertise in the journals of the Institute of Welfare Officers and the Institute of Personnel Management, the National Council of Social Service's *Social Service Quarterly* or the journals of the Association of Social Workers and the Family Welfare Association. A tiny advertisement in the 'Personal' or 'Sits. Vac.' column of one of the dailies is no use at all.

Application forms

Firms with good personnel departments know the usefulness of well-designed application forms. They can save administrative time by making it clear that certain applicants do not warrant an interview at all, and they can save interview time which would otherwise have to be spent in the collection of factual information. The time of a good interviewer is very expensive and a few hours invested in designing a proper application form can pay a handsome dividend in the first year of its use.

Ideally, the form should reflect the job analysis or selection schema, and aim to collect at the time of application all the factual material which the applicant can himself supply. For present purposes this schema should be the Seven Point Plan but there is no need for it slavishly to follow and explicitly to present the main and subsidiary headings. For example, the applicant is rarely able to supply a health record and the other items of 'Physical Make-up' are matters for the selectors' judgment and not the applicant's. Similarly, he cannot be expected to rate himself on intelligence or disposition. The form will therefore concentrate on attainments, aptitudes, interests, and circumstances—and it should contain plenty of space for the applicant to spread himself if he wants to, with a clear invitation to do so. The quality of a prose statement (as distinct from ticked answers to a questionnaire list) will be one of the measures of writing ability.

One small point is not to give the applicant the drudgery of filling in more than one copy of the form. If the organisation does not have a photocopying machine it should think twice before employing a welfare officer. And a potentially good applicant will think twice before wanting to go to a firm which stuffily insists on duplicates or triplicates. It is perhaps sad that these things have still to be said, but personnel selection in this country is by no means all that it could be. Firms forget to state a closing date, to say whether all applicants or only short-listed people will be seen, whether travelling expenses will be paid—even forget to include with the application form a statement of the duties, salary, to whom the successful applicant will be responsible, whether there is a pension scheme and so forth. What such firms have really forgotten is that, in the present era of full employment, applicants are as much vetting the potential employer as firms are vetting the potential employee. If they remembered this basic point the rest would follow; they would then supply information more generously.

Interviews

It is unwise for a firm to place the whole responsibility for personnel selection on its own personnel department, particularly in selecting a welfare officer who must be acceptable to line managers. Indeed, selection work should be as advisory as welfare work itself. Thus, the personnel selection man should never be more than the technical expert who *assists* line managers in their selection responsibilities. He should design application forms, perhaps do the paper sifting of applications, look after the arrangements for objective personality and intelligence testing, and do everything else a specialist can do to save a line manager's time—*short of making the actual decision*. It is the *firm* which employs the welfare officers, and not the personnel officer; and only the firm, represented by line management, can take the responsibility for any wrong decision which has been made. It follows from this that a line manager should be on the interview panel with the personnel man.

The other interested party is the welfare supervisor—the man who will train, guide and bring the welfare officer to account for his activities. If this party happens to be the personnel manager, someone else will have to be brought in to make up the triumvirate—perhaps the medical officer, or where joint consultation is well-advanced, a trade union representative. But three there should be; two may not come to agreement, but a two-to-one majority is usually acceptable. If the personnel manager is not in the welfare officer's line of command, he can well act as neutral chairman of the three-man panel, with welfare supervisor and line manager as the other two. If he is in the line of command, it would be better for the line manager to chair.

The existence of a selection panel or board should not be taken to imply that a formal 'board' layout should be adopted—three judge-and-jury men at one side of a vast width of polished mahogany and the candidate (usually supplied with carafe and glass, pencil and paper, blotting pad, ash-tray and other things he never uses) at the other. It is possible to be businesslike without excessive formality, but above all it is the attitude of the interviewers which is important, and this may well overcome the barriers of physical layout. Clock-watching is an important factor here. Put the clock *behind* the appli-cant, where the interviewers can see it easily and do not have to put their wristwatches on the table in front of them, and where the candi-date cannot see his time running out. And give him *enough* time—an hour is not too long to interview a welfare officer who may be able to make a significant contribution to the smooth running of the organisa-tion over a period of years. The 20-minute sausage-machine approach, with two applicants in the waiting room because of the inevitable over-running of time, is definitely 'out'.

Group selection

If four or more applicants are to be seen, the group selection method can be used to great advantage. The total time required need be no greater than for the applicants taken separately. The main point of using this method for welfare officers is that personal acceptability and the ability to discuss with peers and colleagues are of unusual importance. These qualities are to be observed much more accurately in group discussion than in the formal situation where they may not be displayed at all. It may be argued that the group situation favours the orally aggressive at the expense of the sound but reticent—but the 'board' situation does just the same, and the interviewers are more likely objectively to assess aggression and reticence in a social peer group setting than with individuals.

However, the group discussion (usually of an anonymous welfare case or point of recent social controversy) should be part of the inter-viewing procedure, and not the whole of it. It will be backed up by shorter individual personal interviews with members of the selection panel and may be augmented further by a short formal panel interview for each applicant. The great advantage of this is that members of the interviewing team will be forced to come to *independent written* conclusions on which to compare notes later. (Many who have taken part in the work of selection panels will know how often the first opinion ventured after the candidate has left the room sways the subsequent discussion. If they do not know, they should try it some time—be purposely glowing or disparaging and see how reluctant the others are to challenge!)

Thus, if a whole day is set aside for up to eight candidates (this is a very good day's work indeed), and there are three in the interviewing team, there are up to 24 manhours available. Of these, a two-hour discussion will account for 6 manhours; each interviewer can have up to half an hour with each candidate (12 manhours); and there will still be time for short joint formal boards (say 15 minutes each) if required. Lunch shared by all interviewers and applicants provides another opportunity for observation, and itself can break the ice for the candidates to meet informally before going into discussion.

Finally, an advantage of the group method is that it may be possible to inform candidates of their success or failure before they leave the premises. If the whole process can be wrapped up in one day, so much the better. If this is not possible, selectors should take care to give this information as soon as they can, always bearing in mind that the good man they want may have other offers to consider. He may take up one of them long before slothful selectors get round to making their decision and informing him about it.

Many will have had the group interview experience in the armed services and since. Whether they have or have not, it would be as well to contact the National Institute of Industrial Psychology for further information and guidance about using it as a selection tool. Like all tools, it will get good results only when properly used.

Probation

Only the very large organisation selecting and training its welfare officers internally can afford the luxury of a formal probation period. Such an organisation can come to agreement with its trade union interests to specify a one- or two-year probation period in its advertisements of welfare officer posts, and can in fact make probation a tripartite business. The man has to prove acceptable to managers and to staff as represented by the trade unions; and, just as important, the job has to prove acceptable to the man. Smaller firms without internal training facilities will almost invariably have to advertise for an experienced man, for whom probation will take a different form—the normal form of dismissal or 'requested resignation' if he does not prove acceptable to the firm and its staff, or movement out to another post if the job fails to live up to the welfare officer's expectations.

Local recommendation

Probation is quite essential for newcomers to welfare. It is the final sieve in any internal selection process. The first, very coarse sieve is the advertisement itself, designed and distributed in such a way as to catch the attention of every man and woman in the organisation who might be interested in the work. Interest may be recent, or it could have been stimulated almost at the moment of joining, when the new member of staff attended a course in which the welfare officer described his job. The application form provides the next stage in the sifting process; its request for information will deter those who realise that they just do not measure up. The application form should *not* be returned direct to the personnel department, but through the line of supervision and local management, on the assumption that these people are well enough informed about the welfare officer function (and they must be so informed if the function is to be carried out successfully) to assess the potential of the applicants and to refuse to recommend those who in other work have shown that they are not of the right calibre. In an imperfect world, we must of course accept the possibility that good material might be stopped at this stage. The line supervisor or manager may be cynical about welfare or may look sourly at would-be recruits because at some time in the past his own application for a welfare officer post was rejected. This may seem a fairly remote possibility—but it has been known. Generally speaking, people who were not considered suitable welfare officer material in the past are somewhat unlikely to make good supervisors or managers in the present, unless they have suddenly developed qualities which would now put them in the running. And if they have so developed, we are equally unlikely to be faced with the 'sour grapes' situation.

Preliminary interviewing

If the organisation has a 'regional' or 'group' tier between local management and 'national' direction (when it is most likely that a 'regional' or 'group' welfare supervisor will be employed), that tier should be the next stage in the selection process. Its knowledge of the predilections of local management will enable it to weed out many applicants whose case for consideration by the central Personnel Department is thin. Weeding may be done only on paper—by looking at the applications and local assessments of potential—but it is far better to replicate at the regional or group level the interviewing process which the central personnel department will use. 'Replicate' may not be quite the right word here, for shorter personal interviews, without the group selection factor, may be sufficient. But whatever the method, there is still a case for a three-man selection panel (line manager, neutral chairman and welfare supervisor), each member of which will contribute his own specialist knowledge to ensure that the central department will not have to be bothered with any 'sow's ears'.

Induction and training as part of the selection process

After central selection, induction is the next sieve. Here, the man is being looked at in the context of the job, and the local welfare supervisor (or whoever else is made responsible for induction) must be quite firm with the central selectors if he is convinced that they have made a mistake. He has to live with the results of their work, and he must have the courage, for the man's own sake as well as for the thousands of present and future staff with whom he would otherwise deal, to say when they are wrong. Probation begins on the first day the man comes into post, and it must continue throughout the basic training until both sides are satisfied that the person matches the job and the job matches the person. The central training course provides another opportunity to appraise the new welfare officer. In this connection it should be pointed out that the man in charge of central training arrangements is very often the specialist member of the final selection board. He thus appraises a second time—but the second appraisement is not on his own behalf; it is on behalf of the man to whom the new welfare officer reports. But it would be surprising if the trainer's view did not coincide with that of the local supervisor, and together they can plan further experience and on-the-job training for those about whom there may be a measure of doubt. If doubts continue for long, the only workable rule is 'if in doubt, get him out'.

'Getting him out' will rarely if ever involve sending a man back to his old job against his wishes. Every stage of the selection, training and probation sequence should stress that welfare work is not everybody's cup of tea. It should be made crystal clear that probation is a two-way business and that there will be no recriminations if the newcomer decides in the light of experience that he has made a wrong choice. Indeed, the converse should be emphasised; the man who has the courage to abandon pride and to accept that he is better fitted for other work is worthy of respect and admiration. If the welfare supervisor has not the skill of persuasion to get a misfit to go back voluntarily, then something has gone wrong with the selection of the welfare supervisor, as well as the selection of the misfit.

Changes of location

The possibility that probation may not be successful is one of many reasons for the large organisation to avoid appointing a new welfare officer to that unit of the organisation in which he worked in some other capacity. Looked at very superficially, there seems a case to appoint a man who is already known by the staff and by managers and who already knows them; it would seem to streamline the induction process. But in practice this never works out well, for the very obvious reason that the man *is* already known in some other role. If he has been a supervisor, a trade union representative, the secretary of a sports or social club, or just an ordinary employee, he will be regarded by others as having that role, and it cannot be changed at the drop of a hat. It will be many years before he can slough it off and be seen as 'the welfare officer'—and even then he will be 'the welfare officer who used to be so-and-so'. This makes difficulties for the man as well as for staff. Just as they already have their mental picture of him and where he fits in, he too will be habit-bound by all the relationships he made in the past and so less able to make quite new ones. It is much better for him to have a fresh start among people who have not known him in some other role. He will make a better job of it if he does not have to contend with ghosts from the past and with people in the present who may be tempted to do some special pleading from their knowledge of old relationships. There will be special pleading enough, without inviting more of it.

Summary   The emphasis is on in-service training for welfare officers employed in larger organisations. This points to the need for national consideration of the man in the smaller firm. Four basic principles of training are suggested: (a) responsibility for it must be allocated and accepted; (b) it must be based as far as possible on objectively identified needs; (c) optimum training conditions must be provided; (d) the effectiveness of training must be assessed.

Particular stress is laid on the training responsibility of the welfare officer's immediate superior. Training is shown to be a continuous process from induction onwards, and should be based on the derivation of principles from practice. The condensed experience of a centralised course should therefore wait until sufficient *job experience* has been accumulated.

The Need for Training

The suggestions for training in the next three chapters will be based on the assumption of internal selection of staff without formal qualifications, though firms which already employ on other work people with a relevant degree, diploma or certificate who want to become welfare officers start off with a handsome bonus of knowledge and skill. But the suggestions are not intended only for larger firms; they are also set out in the hope that national patterns of training for the 'small firm' welfare officer may develop.

Despite efforts by such bodies as the Institute of Welfare Officers, welfare officers in industry and commerce are not a well-defined breed. When they are—and it is part of the purpose of this book to contribute to a better definition—some of the independent organisations with an interest in industrial welfare may decide to offer training

to match the function. University departments of industrial administration, and technical colleges with experience of providing management and personnel courses, may also show some interest in filling the
gap, perhaps in conjunction with departments which contribute to the
training of social workers. There is considerable common ground
to be covered in knowledge of the social services and in interviewing
skill, particularly counselling. Those who seek to train counsellors,
whether their trainees work in the industrial, educational, marriage-
guidance or other context, should not themselves be amateurs. The
professionals in whose hands the training task should be would no
doubt find closer liaison for the discussion of principles and practice
very rewarding. Current developments in the 'counselling' field are
dealt with in more detail in the Postscript. And although counselling,
as the core of the personal welfare function, is probably the most
important part of a welfare officer's work, it by no means represents
the only training need.

The Principles of Training

As indicated in 'Welfare in Training Courses', the Industrial Training Act has given support to those who favour a shift in emphasis
away from the old concept of 'sitting by Nelly' and towards training
off-the-job. This is only to be expected if one appreciates the lack of
knowledge and lack of instructing skill of the average Nelly. On the
other hand, much training can *only* be given on the job if it is to be
realistic. There is a danger that those in charge of training schemes
may spend a great deal of time and trouble in ensuring the realism of
off-the-job training when they could achieve the same purpose more
economically by making sure that Nelly not only knows the work but
is trained in the skill of passing her expertise on to others.

There would have been little need for an Industrial Training Act
had British industry and commerce been more training-minded, and
had a distinctive British doctrine of training existed. The relevant
literature is still small, but there can be little doubt that the Act will
be a powerful stimulus to its growth. Most training people would
probably agree that four principles are fundamental:

(a) Responsibility for training must be allocated and accepted.

(b) Training must be based as far as possible on objectively identified needs.

(c) Optimum conditions and facilities for learning must be provided.

(d) The formulation of training policy is a continuous process, so that the effectiveness of programmes must be assessed in terms of their success or failure.

How can these principles be applied to the training of welfare officers? The pages on 'Analysing the Job' have attempted to give at least a partial answer to the problem of objectively identifying training needs, while the assessment of the effectiveness of training is basically a task for welfare supervisors in their day-to-day control of the work of their teams. We can therefore best begin by looking at responsibility for training and the provision of optimum conditions and facilities; these will determine broadly what programmes are laid on and the methods which should be employed. Proper selection, based on the paramount need to find people with the right personal qualities, has been shown to be so important that we seem immediately to be faced with a paradox. If the right person has been selected, the best training for a welfare officer may be that which a well-informed and highly experienced welfare supervisor, himself trained in the art of instructing, can give him on-the-job for the whole period of his career, since the feed-back of success or failure in the various spheres of activity can be immediate if the two work very closely together. On the other hand, the welfare officer job is one calling above all for social skills; it is difficult to see how social skills can be acquired and developed more readily than in a social group setting. Welfare officers are therefore best trained in groups, where they can discuss cases, exchange ideas, benefit from the criticisms of their peers and have the gaps in their knowledge filled, supplementing the group experience by personal study and personal contacts with other social workers. In fact the group activity backs up personal coaching just as it does in training for many other jobs. The paradox is thus more apparent than real, stemming from lack of appreciation of the first principle of training—the identification of training responsibility.

Responsibility for Training

No time will be wasted on developing an argument; we shall say quite axiomatically that the supervisor is *responsible* for the training of his staff; he provides much of it by himself directly; and he sees to it that his personal efforts are augmented by the *concentrated* spells of experience which formal group training can provide more effectively than individual instruction. Training is a *continuing* function of the supervisor. He sends his staff to courses and encourages them in private study as part of that function; he does not hand over to the training officer, technical college, university or other independent organisation except as his agents for *part* of the process.

If this is accepted, it follows that even the smallest organisation with only one welfare officer has only itself to blame if it has an 'untrained' man. The welfare officer must be responsible to somebody at a higher level, and this 'somebody' must accept the converse of that responsibility—the responsibility to train. If he cannot do it himself, because he has not the expertise, then he must send his welfare officer away for periods with an organisation which *can* provide it, and meanwhile gain enough knowledge himself at least to be able to find out if his charge is measuring up to the proper demands of the job.

Induction as the Start of Training

Training starts on the first day of appointment, through the process of induction. If selection is wholly internal it can start even earlier, the welfare-officer-to-be discussing his training needs with his supervisor and then beginning his background reading in advance of taking up duty. Induction itself can conveniently be arranged in two phases— induction to the department, office or factory in which the welfare officer will be based, and induction to the welfare officer job itself. The man's first need is to know where he fits in, how his job relates to the jobs of others, local geography and facilities and the general organisational pattern. He needs this information just as newcomers to other work of the unit need it, and there is no reason why he should not attend any 'background' or 'local organisation' courses laid on for them, either in whole or in part, according to the information he starts off with. Similar arrangements should be made if he transfers or is promoted to a post in another part of the organisation, expert though he may be in the welfare officer job as such.

Induction to the welfare officer job can best be linked with initial field training, the objective of which should be to give a broad picture of welfare work (based on the list of duties), with detailed information on specific local arrangements and on sources of information available to the welfare officer. The welfare officer's immediate supervisor must take full responsibility for this. Only he can supply information about managerial and trade union expectations; he should himself introduce the new man to staff—particularly line managers, line supervisors, union representatives, other personnel staff and the volunteers who run the group welfare activities. Only he can say how he wants the job to be run in the office-methods sense, what sort of cases should be referred to him and which are left to the discretion of the welfare officer. In other words, the supervisor must be the interpreter of the welfare policy of the organisation, and he must see to it personally that his interpretation is well-understood and accepted. It does not matter if the new welfare officer is already very adequately trained in the technical welfare sense; he must still be taught the general policy by the man to whom he reports.

The objective could be stated more specifically by saying that the supervisor should aim to bring the new man up to the highest level of efficiency in the shortest possible time, while accepting that later central training will raise it considerably and that the 100-per-cent ideal will never be reached in the man's career. There will *always* be something new to learn, no matter how long a welfare officer stays in the work. To achieve this objective, induction and early field training should be planned with care. The supervisor should draw up a time-table for the first two or three weeks and write detailed notes as his own 'brief' for the programme. These notes should cover the following aspects:

(a) *Introductions*—to managers and supervisors, fellow members of the welfare team, union representatives, outside welfare organisations as required.

(b) *Welfare Policy*—brief history of the welfare officer service in the organisation and its purpose; organisation, consultation and co-ordination.

(c) *Physical Welfare*—working conditions; safety; hostels and lodgings; hygiene; canteens; drying rooms, etc.

(d) *Group Welfare*—First Aid; sports and social clubs; benevolent organisations; retired staff; work with training courses.

(e) *Personal Welfare*—introduction to basic principles of casework; limitations and pitfalls of the personal approach; relationships with people; interviewing; confidentiality; diagnosis and action; liaison with other personnel duties; sick absence; discipline.

(f) *Office Methods*—welfare officer coverage during leave and other absence; welfare records, returns and reports; sources of welfare information.

Training as a Continuous Process

Once training is regarded as a continuous process—a mixture of guided job experience and attendance at formal courses and less formal conferences—it is easier to see how this induction shades into effective work under close supervision and thence into central initial training. At first, the new welfare officer will be mainly concerned with meeting people and finding his feet. He will spend some time in reading, familiarising himself with the detail of office methods, and discussing with his supervisor on the basis of the latter's 'brief'. All this activity should be highly specific, well-thought out, and goal-directed. He should never be left with a pile of books and other documents and told to 'get on with it' for days at a stretch. Nor should he be scheduled simply to 'have a chat with the medical officer' or with the secretary of the local Council of Social Service. He and his supervisor should work out in advance the precise purpose of these visits and should meet afterwards to discuss what has been learned. Is it to find out how the medical officer fits into the organisation, how the medical officer expects liaison with local doctors to be carried out, what welfare cases cause him most difficulty, what are the rules about retirement or dismissal on medical grounds, or what medical services are available to staff? It might be all of these in one visit, or it might be necessary to take several bites at the cherry. This is of no importance. What *is* important is that the aim should be clear, that the newcomer should put his new information on paper (training in report writing cannot start too soon) and that he and his supervisor should later check how far the aim has been achieved.

Wherever possible, the newcomer should sit in with a more experienced colleague, or with his supervisor, to see how personal cases should be handled. Clearly, these have to be selected with considerable care. Some welfare officers regard the personal case situation as so completely personal that in no circumstances may a third-party welfare officer sit in; but this view is somewhat unrealistic. We shall return to it later in connection with the inspection techniques which the welfare supervisor must use. All that is necessary at this point is a useful working rule. The *new* personal case (i.e. the first visit to the welfare officer of the individual in need) should be without the presence of a third party; but *continuing* cases do not demand the same treatment. Once the individual in need has made contact it is far easier for the welfare officer to have someone else present at the interview, particularly if he is introduced as the new man who will take over the duty in due course. In fact, the individual with a problem will often accept that three heads are better than two, and will be gratified rather than alarmed that he has the attention of two experts rather than one.

In this way, continuing cases may be taken over by the new man without a break in the welfare officer contact, and these are the first he should deal with on his own. As he gains experience he should be entrusted solo with new cases which seem prima facie fairly simple ones. The word 'seem' is important here, since the overtly simple are often the cases which need the most skill and effort once the facts are known. But some chances must be taken: the newcomer must start somewhere. As long as he can discuss the case immediately afterwards with his supervisor or more experienced colleague, little harm can result. Close supervision thus gradually tapers off over the first few months, until the welfare officer is virtually standing on his own feet and working within the policy which dictates which cases he should refer up and which are within his own discretion. He must all the time be made aware that he is not only free but also *expected* to ask advice and guidance when his own knowledge or skill is insufficient to meet the situation.

The Need for Central Group Training

Is the welfare officer not now trained? What else does he need? These are fair questions, but the answer is that he is really at the beginning of his detailed training and not at the end of it. He may by now have reached a 50-per-cent or even 60-per-cent level of effectiveness, but he still has a long way to go. At this stage he is working within the confines of present knowledge and skill, and these dictate his approach and attitude. He does not yet know what he would be capable of if by magic he could suddenly see the whole picture—the 100-per-cent ideal. And neither does his supervisor. His supervisor would not know even if he were physically present for the whole of the working day. The time comes when experience gained very slowly on the job must be condensed by means of the first formal training course.

Levels of Effectiveness

It will be useful at this point to spend a little time on what is meant by levels of effectiveness—performance, or adequacy in the job. If we plotted a graph of 'level of effectiveness' against the 'attitude/knowledge/skill' pattern required, we should probably find that it was broadly exponential in character. That is to say: a fairly limited amount of knowledge, a comparatively low degree of skill, and commonsense attitudes would be enough to produce a reasonable level of effectiveness. Many of the problems confronting a welfare officer will in fact demand only limited knowledge and skill and commonsense attitudes. He does not in practice spend most of his time helping with really tough problems, which represent a comparatively small proportion of casework. The basic-grade welfare officer—even the welfare supervisor—can never hope to acquire the 100-per-cent levels of knowledge, skill and attitude which alone would ensure 100-per-cent effectiveness. He may think at some stage of his career that he has got there, but sooner or later he will be disillusioned by the odd case which calls for that bit of extra information, refinement of skill, or insight which he finds to be lacking. He should take some comfort from the thought that even the experts who train professional social workers do not know it all. Lack of detailed knowledge does not matter if it is compensated by knowledge of how and where to find the detail; but attitudes to knowledge and skill in using it are rather different—one aims for perfection, but one knows that one will never quite achieve it. It is here that humility comes in.

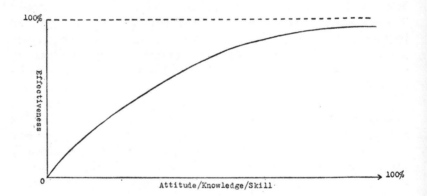

This is of course a generalised 'best-fitting' curve. One could plot a similar curve of 'effectiveness' against 'time' to describe the situation in broad terms from the welfare officer's induction to his retirement. But good selection should ensure that he does not have to start from the zero point, and one hopes that he will continue to improve right up to his final day. One also has to accept that many welfare officers will stick at varying points, unable to progress further because of limitations of intelligence, temperament or other factors. And all 'best-fitting' curves of this sort smooth away a great many plateaux and sudden rises. Every source of information identified, every book read, every insight from local coaching or from mulling over an unusual problem may lead to a sudden upward surge of 'effectiveness', perhaps followed by longer or shorter plateaux when there seems to be nothing new under the sun.

The idea of the 'curve of effectiveness' is not unlike that of the S-curve in the manual skill or operator-training field, but the time-span is different. In general terms, good operator training seeks to achieve 100-per-cent effectiveness 'at one go', the trainees reaching a target standard (e.g. Qualified Worker Standard) based on average shop-floor performance before going on to full production. However, jobs such as the welfare officer's, demanding social skills and the acquisition of more and more knowledge about people and about the ever-changing social scene, are capable of almost infinite improvement of which only a part can be expected during 'basic training'. The effect of these weeks of 'concentrated experience' is probably to provide a sudden and very steep rise in what would otherwise be a fairly long and gentle slope of effectiveness acquired 'on-the-job'. This may indicate the need for a fundamental difference of approach to training for the 'social skill' type of job generally as compared with 'manual skill' training generally.

It is important to point out that the idea of a generalised curve is not based on any scientific analysis; it is offered only for the purpose of illustration. In this type of work, aspects of knowledge, skill and attitude are so interwoven that their separation might defy even the most sophisticated research methodology. In a very real sense the attitude of the welfare officer is part of his skill, and his knowledge of the limits of his skill is one of the tools he will use to help disentangle a personal problem. There is scope for research in this field, to illuminate the nature of what may be called 'social jobs'.

Condensed Experience

The next apparently 'fair question' is why are we assuming that the new welfare officer cannot be given his condensed experience at the outset? Why should not centralised formal training immediately follow induction, to ensure that he knows what he is doing before he is put into the situation where he may risk making a mess of someone else's life? This exposes a controversy at the heart of training philosophy. There is one school of thought which demands that we should tell a man what to do and then ask him to go ahead and do it—

stating the principles and saying that practice must follow them, a view still ingrained in our whole educational system. But there is another school which declares that principles should be educed from practice, for it is only in this way that principles can be realistic and can have meaning for the practitioner. In other words, people should get the feel of the job before trying to organise and grasp the theory which governs it.

This is not the place to philosophise about training. Instead we shall take sides right away, plumping firmly for derivation of theory from practice. There is a great deal in academic learning theory to support this, but it is perhaps better to justify it on a commonsense basis. (In doing so, we must accept that history has often shown what was at one time accepted as 'commonsense' to be sheer bunkum; it was at one time 'commonsense' that the world was flat and, more recently, that hanging was a deterrent to murder—but accumulations of fact have shown up the errors. However, both learning theory and commonsense tell us that we indeed get most of our principles from practice, and the accumulation of new fact in this area is most unlikely to prove differently.) We must *perceive* before we can conceptualise; we must *have* experience before we can organise it. We learn our own language, and we are even getting round to learning other languages, not by first being told the grammar and the syntax and then filling in the vocabulary, but by learning the vocabulary and then gradually conceptualising this knowledge into grammar, syntax, etc. Some people never even conceptualise consciously at all; concepts just grow out of perceptions without our being aware of the process. We may *know* grammar and syntax in the sense of using both correctly, but the conceptual framework of language set out in the textbooks may be completely foreign to us.

What holds good for life in general should equally hold good for training welfare officers. They must have experience of people and their problems in the work context before they are ready to organise this experience, establish the principles which may be found in it and then use the conceptual framework to increase efficiency. When the framework is there they can see their personal gaps in attitude, knowledge and skill and find means to fill them, but they must have enough of attitude, knowledge and skill to build the framework at all. They start with some building material from their general experience of life and their inborn characteristics, they add more during induction—when they are given a rough outline of the framework—but most of it comes from what they have gained in the first few months on the job. Most essentially, they have gained realism and meaning. They *know* what it is like to try to listen with complete concentration, what it is like to try to help put order into incoherent worry, and how necessary it is to possess a sound store of factual knowledge.

Timing for Centralised Training

The new welfare officer will have sufficient grounding to benefit from a central training course after about three months' job experience, but he should not have to wait for it too long. There is an optimal point of time in his experience, which will clearly vary from individual to individual, when he will have acquired enough building material to erect his framework of attitude, knowledge and skill with the help of his colleagues and supervisor, but when he has not yet developed new prejudices and preconceptions which may have to be unlearned. If he goes without his central course for too long there will be a risk that hardening will have set in and he may thus be less trainable.

If central training were done outside the firm by an organisation which offered, say, three or four courses each year, it would be possible to judge quite finely when the new welfare officer was at the optimum point for his condensed experience, and to make arrangements for him to have it without delay. In-service central training is quite another matter, for the biggest organisations would not employ enough welfare officers to run more than one central course each year, and even this would probably have to be augmented, in terms of numbers, by 'outsiders' or by more experienced welfare officers attending for 'refresher' purposes.

Before discussing the advantage of linking the experienced and the inexperienced, we should first spend a little time on the advantages and disadvantages of in-service and external training. These touch on the principle of providing optimum conditions for learning. In-service training has the great merit that the course may be firmly geared to the special needs of welfare officers in the organisation. There is less wasted time in discussing topics which may not be applicable to all. There is also opportunity to see that central policy comes over clearly—perhaps in contrast with some of the predilections of local welfare supervisors, put over during induction, which will inevitably grow up even when communication between the central authority and the local supervisor is as perfect as it could be. And who is to say that such predilections or minor departures from national policy are in fact wrong? The organisation's central policy can best be shaped by the varying views of the local supervisors who provide evidence about its success or failure in practice; the central personnel point which promulgates it and acts as watchdog should only in the last resort lay down the law if that law is not fully acceptable to the majority of welfare supervisors. The practical details of welfare policy should normally result from democratic majority decision (in which the basic grade will also share through local conferences and discussion at central courses) and should not be imposed from above unless the central technical control point has information or direction from higher management which must override the majority view.

The only real disadvantage of in-service central courses is that welfare officers may be denied the benefit of the wider view which comes from comparing the policy and practice of their own organisation with others. And if these contacts are not made at the basic level, it is more difficult for the policy makers and information givers to ensure that they themselves do not become parochial and fail to learn from the experience of comparable organisations; the policy makers then have an even greater need to develop such contacts at their own level.

On balance, in-service basic training is to be preferred if the organisation is big enough to support it, for then it may be tailor-made to known need. It is always possible to expose welfare officers at a later stage of their development to the cut and thrust of discussion with those who follow a different policy. This will be an important part of their continuing training after the basic stage, when they know their own policy well enough to be able to make useful comparisons. Some of this discussion will arise at meetings of local Councils of Social Service, branches or centres of the Institute of Welfare Officers or similar bodies; but these should be augmented by more formal inter-organisation conferences on an area basis.

13 Design of Centralised Courses

Summary   Since principles are to be educed from practice, centralised courses should be based on the case-discussion method. The
cases must be real, never fictitious. Choice of method governs both
the numbers taking part and the length of the course, but there are
other design considerations to be taken into account. Courses may or
may not be residential; initial training of newcomers can be linked
with refresher training for the more experienced. A specimen three-
week course is examined to bring out the need for objectives to be
both clear and limited, and to show how certain subject areas are best
dealt with.

The Choice of Method

A central course must be built up on the basis of the discussion of
real problem cases dealt with personally by those attending it. To
build it otherwise would be to deny our premise that principles should
be educed from practice and experience. Discussion and case study
will thus be the principal teaching methods, although others will have
their place. The choice of main method will determine the numbers
to be invited to any one course, and its length. These and other factors
affecting course design will be dealt with shortly; meanwhile there are
two important general points to be made, the first concerning the
skill of the tutor in charge of the course and the second concerning
the reality of the cases discussed.

Discussion-leading looks easy when done well, but it demands
considerable skill; even professional training officers should not
imagine that they can pick it up as they go along. The tutor must
certainly be well trained in the general techniques of instruction, but
he should also attend a course specifically directed towards discussion-

leading. No-one is a 'natural', and even the most experienced can continue to learn.

Course tutors with limited experience are sometimes tempted to write their own cases, as a way of ensuring that the special points or principles to be learned can be drawn out during discussion by the trainees. Quite bluntly, well-meaning as this approach may be, it is downright dishonest and an invitation to disaster. It is dishonest because seeding a case with the very principles discussion is intended to elicit amounts to no more than sleight of hand, mocking reality; and it is an invitation to disaster because trainees will not accept it as relevant if they know it is fictitious, and the trainer will be forced to invent more and more spurious detail under their questioning if they are not told it is fictitious. Dishonesty and disaster go hand in hand; trainees will recognise both and their confidence in their trainer will be lost irrevocably.

It is quite a different matter to use spurious names of people and places in cases, remove reference to any other identifying characteristics, and avoid using situations which even disguised in this fashion would yet be recognisable if written case studies or notes on them got into the wrong hands. It is similarly a quite different matter to ask each trainee to send in more than one case in advance so that selection of them can ensure coverage of the widest possible range of principles. This latter is another factor affecting course design.

The Number of Participants

There is no experimental evidence bearing on the number of participants of a training course for which discussion is the main teaching method. However, experience has been built up over many years, particularly from the days of the Army Bureau of Current Affairs, whose publication *Discussion Method* (1950) provides an introduction to the subject which has not been bettered since. It is generally recognised that the best range is eight to 16. If there are fewer than eight there are rarely enough distinguishable points of view available to get good discussion going at all; and if there are more than 16, even the best discussion-leader will be hard put to ensure that they all play a full part. One of his main tasks, as a matter of technique, is to encourage the reticent and to prevent the more vocal from hogging the proceedings. If this task is made difficult by the sheer weight of numbers he will be less able to devote time to summarising at intervals, remembering who has contributed what and introducing new themes when old ones are exhausted. In practice, 10–12 has been found just right for welfare officers, as it has been for other groups, e.g. supervisors in training.

Length of Courses

It is clearly necessary to discuss at least one case per trainee, but it may be unwise to have more than two from each person. Participants will remember and distinguish between 'Bill's first case' and 'Joan's second case', but memory may not encompass a third round. Apart from this, more than two per person may lead to duplication and the feeling 'I have heard this one before'—an invitation to staleness and loss of interest. Infinitely varied as personal cases are in terms of detail, many will be strikingly similar in outline. If they were not we could not attempt to classify them, nor could we educe general principles from them.

And although personal cases form the core of the training course, they do not constitute the whole of it. They give leads to the aspects of attitude, knowledge and skill which must be dealt with; they do not deal with them completely. It has been found in practice that personal case discussion can usefully take up a quarter of the training day, and in a four-session day this means one case. This gives us a module of two or three weeks for a course for 10–12 people (allowing half-day travelling time at either end) on a one-case-per-person basis. This is probably enough. Courses should be so intensive that a three-week spell should be followed by consolidation on the job. Training should not be carried to the point where exhaustion leads to loss of interest; it is better that trainees should leave with interest at peak, than that their channels of communication should be so overloaded that they reject information and ideas out of self-defence. If the two-cases-per-person approach is selected, it may be better to run the course in two halves on a 'sandwich' basis, separated by a few weeks' interval. There are considerable advantages in this, particularly if the 'sandwich' spell is utilised for a definite training purpose. An example of this is the inclusion of a short 'personal counselling' session with the course tutor for each trainee (welfare officers of all people would not be averse to this!) towards the end of the first course, during which strengths and weaknesses can be discussed and a short 'tick-sheet' of points drawn up to be considered in the intervening weeks by self-criticism and local coaching and guidance. It may be that some factual knowledge can be picked up by private study or personal contact; that tendencies to impulsiveness have been jointly observed and can be corrected; or that report writing needs special attention. This approach builds an element of validation into the course which would otherwise be difficult to introduce—and lack of validation is a criticism which can be levelled at most training courses.

Joint Initial and Refresher Courses

Even an organisation employing 100 welfare officers will not normally have more than half a dozen or so newcomers to train each year, unless service in welfare is regarded as temporary—a limited spell away from line supervision. Two ways of augmenting the group to a viable size have already been mentioned, and both are almost equally effective. If only six newcomers are available, one can seek four outsiders from another organisation, or four experienced men from one's own organisation can be brought in for refresher training. In the first case one has the advantage of a more malleable group whose experience is roughly comparable, when the course is more clearly one for the new welfare officer. In the second, good use is made of the wider range of experience which exists. On the obverse of these coins, 'outsiders' may be more difficult to draw into discussion because they *know* they are outsiders, and the experienced 'refresher' man with a firm point of view may seek to impose it on the novices. However, problems of this kind merely reinforce the need to have the course in the hands of a well-trained and experienced discussion leader.

Other Design Considerations

There are many other design factors to be taken into account. There will be arguments for and against residential courses or a 'nine to five' office hours approach. Much can be said in favour of a residential atmosphere, particularly when attitudes and social skills loom as large as they do for welfare officers, for a great deal can be learned informally around the coffee cups or pints to supplement what is gained from the class discussions. But a course designer must consider the needs of his visiting speakers as well as his students. Many of the folk he will want to involve in the training job cannot or will not spare the time to make long trips from their headquarters to the training centre. Residential courses also present the temptation to over-fill the timetable, to cram in too much for the student to absorb. On the other hand, a well-packed timetable keeps interest at a high pitch; and many students, particularly married men with families, may well prefer two weeks of concentrated residential effort to three weeks of office hours. Only the designer can weigh up the balance of advantage and disadvantage and make the decision in the best interests of everybody concerned.

A decision will also have to be made on the role which local welfare supervisors will play. Ideally, they too should be well-trained trainers, and capable of acting as discussion leaders for some of the case problems brought by the students. As a minimum, they can take the chair for some of the visiting speakers and 'expert witnesses', and so relieve the pressure on the 'course tutor' in charge. The tutor will then have the additional responsibility of briefing local welfare supervisors in the general philosophy of the course and their particular role in it. Quite often, welfare supervisors will themselves act as visiting speakers; many of them will have expertise in some aspects of welfare work which could not be matched by outsiders. There is in any event a great deal to be said for new welfare officers having early contact with welfare supervisors other than their own. Above all, active participation of welfare supervisors builds the democratic approach and reduces the temptation facing the tutor to deliver *ex cathedra* statements of policy which should really be submitted to proper consultation first.

A Specimen Course

Having listed the main design considerations, we may cut short what is really a long training story outside the scope of this book and move on to look at a specimen non-residential three-week course in which some welfare supervisors participate as 'assistant tutors'. This does not deny other design possibilities, but it will be more fruitful to discuss an example of what was found successful in practice over several years than to consider hypothetical alternatives at length.

Two important aspects of communication must first be stressed. Whatever the course design or general pattern of training, the central tutor must lay his cards on the table at the outset. He must tell his students what he has in mind, how he proposes to set about it, and what people he will be calling on to help him. He thus starts the central training course before the students actually gather together as a group; thinking begins in advance. He achieves this by sending out *detailed* joining instructions—a covering letter with a synopsis of the course, a timetable, and two lists of 'Who's Who' (list of students, and list of speakers and chairmen).

It should go almost without saying that, irrespective of whether they are taking part in the course—and some may be too distant to make this an economic proposition—copies of this material should also be sent to all local welfare supervisors. In doing this, the tutor recognises quite explicitly that he is doing the training *on their behalf*, as their agent. He is doing no more than continuing the training process which the local supervisor started at the induction stage, and which the local supervisor will take up again when the welfare officer returns to his charge. Similarly, when the course is finished and all the handouts are printed, a complete set of the material must go to the local supervisor so that he can follow up in his own way—by personal coaching, or perhaps by raising points for discussion at his own conferences with his team. Finally, the course tutor should ensure some validation by seeking 'feedback' from the local supervisors, either by exchange of visits or at the regular conferences of supervisors with the central body. All these channels of communication must be kept open and clear by regular use. If they silt up, mutual trust is lost; and hostility, or suspicion of too much central control, takes its place.

Specimen 'joining instructions', in the form of a tutor's letter enclosing synopsis and timetable now follow. We shall then discuss some of the points of interest about them.

Specimen 'joining instructions'

Dear

Welfare Officer's Course, ... *196...*

I am glad you will be able to come to this course, and look forward to seeing you again. If past experience is any guide, you are in for a busy but very enjoyable time. I enclose a copy of the synopsis and timetable, a list of the people concerned with running the course, and another list of those attending it. You will see that the course will be held at .... [include full directions, maps, etc.].

This training programme is a very practical one, designed so that all of us who take part can share our experience, whether we are members of the course or speakers. It is built around discussions of cases brought by individual members of the group, and as far as possible each case is allocated to a period just before or just after one of our speakers deals with a topic the case concerns. I should therefore be glad if you would give some thought to this and either bring with you—or preferably send me in advance—a suitable case to put before the group. It should include the usual basic information (age, sex, source, etc.) apart from a brief synopsis of the problem. Names and any other identifying characteristics can be left out or altered in the interests of confidentiality if you wish; but in all other respects it should be a real case which you have actually handled yourself.

We shall provide notebooks and all the reference material likely to be needed.

I expect by now you have made arrangements for any accommodation you may need in ...., but if you do need any help of this kind, please let .... know at this address (telephone: ...).

Yours sincerely,

WELFARE OFFICER'S COURSE, 196..
SYNOPSIS

A CASE DISCUSSIONS

Each case brought by individual members of the group will be discussed in detail, with a view to:

(a) establishing and reinforcing general principles of approach and technique;

(b) underlining the need for special skills;

(c) identifying areas and sources of information and providing links with sessions given by specialist speakers.

These pointers will be summarised in the course of each discussion. The summaries, together with the factual details of each case, will be duplicated as handouts.

B THE WELFARE JOB

1 *Organisation*—The formation of policy; consultation with unions, etc.; patterns of organisation and control in different areas; organisational relationships with management and outside bodies.

2 *Duties*—Guiding principles in the policy statement; codification of practice through information notes and other means; the welfare officer's role in group and physical welfare.

3 *Office Methods*—Recording, indexing and summarising casework; use of diary for follow-up; travelling; accommodation; telephone coverage; typing; background and other reading; duty files; card index of 'contacts' and reference material.

4 *Sources of Information*—The individual and his family; managers and supervisors; outside social workers; local Councils of Social Service; Institute of Welfare Officers; conferences and visits; official material—rules, circulars and other directives; C.A.N.S.; N.C.S.S. circulars; F.W.A. *Guide to the Social Services* and similar publications; Central Welfare Library; the W.O.'s own library; external training courses.

5 *Levels of Responsibility*—Discussion of a case to illustrate supervisory and advisory roles of senior welfare staff.

C PEOPLE AT WORK

1 *Individual Differences*—Influence of age, sex, physique and mental characteristics; heredity and environment; intelligence and aptitudes; how people learn and mature.

2 *Attitudes and Prejudice*—Beliefs, opinions and attitudes; preconceived ideas; seeing and believing; roots of prejudice; how and why rumours spread; how and why we ignore factual evidence; mental defence systems.

3 *The Individual and the Group*—The 'in-group' and the 'out-group'; pressures to conform; group norms and expectations; natural and 'institutional' leaders; group morale; interplay of individual and group morale.

4 *The Welfare Officer's Relationships*—People in need, and their families; colleagues and senior welfare supervision; the Medical Service, managers and line supervisors; union representatives; group welfare voluntary workers; outside social workers; central Personnel.

D SPECIAL SKILLS

1 *Principles of Casework*—Why welfare officers are provided; helping the man to solve his own problem; difference in function between welfare officers and outside social workers; danger of by-passing normal channels; getting rid of 'welfare ghosts'; confidentiality; diagnosing, advising and helping; preserving perspective.

2 *The Art of Interviewing*—Types and purposes of interview; principles and techniques; establishing confidence; leading-in and breaking-off; listening and encouraging; seeking and giving information; the art of questioning; assessing what is unsaid; moral judgments; intimidation; projection of own attitudes and values.

3 *Report Writing*—Types of report; style and layout; standard expected; practical work and self-criticism.

Welfare Officer's Course

Week 1

	9.30	11.00	11.15	12.45	2.00	3.30	3.45	5.15
Monday	Travelling				(2.30 p.m.) Introduction		The Welfare Job 1 Organisation	
Tuesday	Preparations for Case Discussions		Case Discussion No. 1		People at Work 1 Individual Differences		The Welfare Job 2 Duties	
Wednesday	Case Discussion No. 2		The Social Services (1)		Welfare and Discipline		Principles of Case Work (1)	
Thursday	Rehabilitation		Case Discussion No. 3		The Unmarried Mother and her Child		The Mental Disorder Case	
Friday	Physical Welfare		Case Discussion No. 4		People at Work 2 Attitudes and Prejudice		Open Forum	

(Note: Names of speakers and chairman will be given in brackets under the title of each session)

Welfare Officer's Course

Week 2

	9.30	11.00	11.15	12.45	2.00	3.30	3.45	5.15
Monday	Case Discussion No. 5		The National Council of Social Service		The Art of Interviewing (1)		Sick Absence	
Tuesday	The Mental Welfare Officer		Case Discussion No. 6		The Social Services (2)		Principles of Case Work (2)	
Wednesday	Case Discussion No. 7		The Medical Service		People at Work 3 The Individual and the Group		The Welfare Job 3 Office Methods	
Thursday	*Visits* (... Magistrates Court) (... County Court)				(2.15 p.m.) Discussion of Visits		The Probation Service	
Friday	Case Discussion No. 8		The Social Services (3)		The Art of Interviewing (2)		Open Forum	

Welfare Officer's Course

Week 3

	9.30	11.00	11.15	12.45	2.00	3.30	3.45	5.15
Monday	Group Choice Session		Case Discussion No. 9		The Manager's Point of View			
Tuesday	First Aid		The Welfare Job 4 Sources of Information		Case Discussion No. 10		Young People Today	
Wednesday	Report Writing				The Welfare Job 5 Levels of Responsibility			
Thursday	Report Writing—Practical Work		Discussion of Reports		The Art of Interviewing (3)			
Friday	People at Work 4 The Welfare Officer's Relationships		Summary and Open Forum		Travelling			

E SPECIAL AREAS OF KNOWLEDGE

The social services, the National Council of Social Service, physical welfare, First Aid, sick absence, the Medical Service, mental disorder, the Mental Welfare Officer, unmarried mothers, rehabilitation, the work of the courts, the Probation Service, discipline, young people today, the manager's point of view.

Discussion of 'joining instructions'

INTRODUCTORY LETTER

This brings out several important points. First, the course is practical; anxieties of the non-academic are allayed. Yet the emphasis on shared experience encourages a 'set' to participate to the full. With the forewarning that a personal case actually handled by the welfare officer will be discussed, this produces what has been found in practice to be just the right level of 'expectancy tension' to ensure that interest is high at the outset. No time is wasted in building it up. The joint-enterprise nature of the training is further pointed out by showing that visiting speakers are going to depend to some extent on the material provided by the trainees; and, conversely, that their contributions will illuminate what the trainees provide. It is made clear that the course is well-grounded in reality. Finally, the trainees are given a rough idea (by reference to the synopsis) of what sort of note-taking they are going to be required to do; they know that there will be handouts and that they will not have to scribble furiously all day. These may appear trivial points, but good training rests as much on careful attention to detail as on the philosophy which informs it.

SYNOPSIS

This incorporates a clear statement of the aims of the course, and these aims are shown to be limited. The overall aim is clearly to give the trainees the opportunity of becoming better welfare officers than they were before, but a broad statement of this kind would be quite superfluous. It must be broken down in such a way that the participants know where and how far they are expected to go, and by this means they have a better yardstick to measure the degree of success. The declared aim of 'establishing and reinforcing general principles of approach and technique' expresses the hope that the main attitudinal part of the job should be covered by the end of the three weeks. But 'underlining the need for special skills' and 'identifying areas and sources of information' explicitly accept that although the course will thoroughly cover the *groundwork* of skill and knowledge, these areas have to be further explored and developed both on the job and by means of refresher training.

For example, 'Sources of Information' are dealt with in the round. Provided that the new welfare officers appreciate what these are, so that they can use them effectively on the job, there is no need to go into the mass of detail which, if it is ever finally acquired, would represent the 100-per-cent level of knowledge required for 100-per-cent effectiveness. This important session links closely with the one on 'Office Methods', when the problems of keeping up to date are discussed. The session also establishes the place of external training courses in continuing the learning process.

Similarly, the sessions on 'People at Work' are designed only to give an introduction to psychology and to whet the appetite for more. One cannot presume to do in four sessions what the professional psychologist has to cover in not less than four years—but one can show that the professional psychologist's area of knowledge is a relevant one. If one only succeeds in explaining the differences between psychologists, psychiatrists, psychotherapists, psychoanalysts and kindred people, and in dispelling some of the myths of our time, one has achieved a great deal. It is of course essential that these sessions are taken by an expert—for preference a professional psychologist recognised by the British Psychological Society. In passing, one should also add that the title of the series has been chosen with some care. 'Human Relations' is abhorred; 'Work Relations' is a little better, but what the welfare officer is really concerned with is 'People at Work'. His own relationships to these people are treated separately, and on a commonsense rather than a technical psychological basis.

Just as 'People at Work' provides an introduction, so one should not try to go too far into the 'Art of Interviewing' during initial central training. The use of the word 'art' is perhaps a little pejorative. There can be little doubt that scientific investigation has thrown considerable light on what used to be regarded as a highly individual business. Some of these findings can be brought to attention but, bearing in mind their introductory nature, the three sessions are better handled practically than theoretically. It has been found useful to devote the first two to discussion of tape-recorded interviews *and to discussion of the kind of discussion they evoked*, using the third to bring out general principles for blackboard or overhead-projector summary and later printed handout. Once again, this series is designed to be an appetite-whetter. Interviewing will be dealt with more thoroughly during a later follow-up course specially designed for the purpose, in which techniques such as closed-circuit television should be used.

Similar considerations apply to 'Report Writing'. One cannot teach it in a day; it can be learned only over a long period by coaching and self-criticism. But the central course must set the standard required by the organisation, for without it coaching and self-criticism cannot be goal-directed. The most effective way has been found to relate report writing to the session on 'Levels of Responsibility'. An introductory session based on a combination of the booklet published by B.A.C.I.E. (1961) and Gowers' *Plain Words* is followed by discussion of an actual and very complicated personal case which involved first the basic-grade welfare officer, then his first-line supervisor, his chief welfare officer and finally the top level of personnel control. During discussion, the levels of difficulty are established, and the trainees are then asked to write a report of the case as if they were chief welfare officers submitting it to their personnel controllers. This exercise is first discussed by passing the reports around the table for neighbourly criticism and the course tutor then offers to take them away to be returned later with his own criticisms and a model report. These supply the basis of later coaching and guidance from the local welfare supervisor.

It will be seen that Section E of the synopsis covers the bulk of the special areas of knowledge required by the welfare officer. They are all areas which should be dealt with by visiting speakers brought in as 'expert witnesses' for questioning rather than lecturers. A short introductory talk (20–30 minutes) is followed by discussion under the chairmanship of the course tutor (or welfare supervisor deputising for him), and this will be specifically related to points brought out in earlier group discussion of a personal case which bears on the specific area of discussion.

TIMETABLE

A few comments on the example given may exemplify the approach and put more life into the bare titles of sessions. First, the construction of the timetable will depend to some extent on the availability of visiting speakers, but forward planning rather than last-minute phone calls will usually ensure that they can fit in with the needs of the training group. And following the doctrine of educing principles from practice, speakers should as far as possible come in *after* the relevant personal case has been discussed.

As discussion leader, the course tutor has to be a man of many parts. The individual presenting the case must have his head in choosing the manner of presentation. Most will choose straightforward talking, but more adventurous spirits will see the value of role play or tape-recordings of 'acted' interviews. The tutor will then have to arrange for the briefing of one or two outsiders to act out the parts. It is distinctly preferable to have outsiders for *rehearsed* role play, but the tutor will encourage *spontaneous* role play during the ensuing discussion, particularly when trainees take up rigid attitudes. This can often lead into the more refined and very valuable technique of 'role reversal'. His most important function is to sum up at intervals, and he may achieve this best by a running blackboard or overhead-projector summary for later duplication as a handout to accompany the write-up of the case itself. In the process of summarising he must also be prepared to spend a few minutes now and then on direct teaching of points of fact, although he will never take time off to impose his *opinions* in the role of self-appointed lecturer.

Films should be fully integrated with the teaching session, and not dealt with separately as a 'film programme'. For example—although examples date rapidly—a Ministry of Labour representative may well be the 'expert witness' for the Rehabilitation session, in the course of which the film 'New Lease of Life', on the work of the Ministry's Industrial Rehabilitation Units, might be shown. Similarly, one or two films on First Aid and Safety should be integrated with the session on these subjects (often best treated as a combined session so that the possible results of unsafe practices are brought home forcibly). There is only limited value in showing specialised films when there is no specialist available to answer questions about points of detail.

The day on the work of the courts and of the Probation Service is planned as a whole. A useful approach is to divide the group into two 'syndicates' (on the basis of existing knowledge of Magistrates' and County Courts) and have them report back in the afternoon so that the differences may be brought out in the presence of the probation expert. He will then provide any necessary factual correctives and lead into his own session from the discussion of the work of the courts.

The session on the Manager's Point of View is best treated as a symposium of, say, three managers carefully selected as representing sub-organisations or groups of different size or function. If the tutor knows his managers well, he will also try to select them with regard to their differing approaches to welfare, briefing them in advance to be completely frank and to look forward to a controversial and possibly argumentative session. His briefing will also include the seemingly trivial point that names will be drawn out of a hat for order of speaking; he must firmly resist any basis of seniority which might only result in the junior managers following the lead of the first speaker, dotting his 'i's' and crossing his 't's'. If in doubt, he can bring them in one by one. The session is quite valueless without controversy, and it first has to be accepted that trainee welfare officers are as much entitled to question and perhaps criticise management as managers are to question and perhaps criticise the activities of welfare officers.

It is essential to keep the tempo of a training course going to the last minute; it should never be allowed to run down to the feet-shuffling and watch-glancing level which tells the trainer he has failed. It is also dangerous to finish on an exhortatory plane—sonorous and pompous speeches are definitely 'out'. The final few hours should be reserved for the full treatment of the core of the job. Interviewing is the crucial skill of the welfare officer, and his relationships are at the heart of that skill. They will govern his acceptance or rejection by those he seeks to serve and those he is there to support. He must get them right and keep them right—and this is perhaps the most appropriate note on which to finish.

14 Continued and Refresher Training

Summary   Training should be continuous from selection to retirement, and the organisation should recognise this by running internal courses of a specialised follow-up nature, and refresher courses. Local welfare conferences are another important tool of internal training. Apart from this, the firm should encourage external training and education, including membership of local external welfare groups, short external courses, and longer external programmes which may or may not lead to a formal qualification in the social sciences at diploma or degree level. The educational system must be fully explored to match the need of the individual welfare officer to what is available. This knowledge will also often be of practical value in personal welfare work within the organisation.

The two previous chapters have already made the case for regarding training as a continuous process which extends from selection through induction, initial field training, central group training and onwards to final retirement. Even retirement from full-time paid welfare officer work may not be the end of the story. One trains oneself for retirement, and formal 'retirement' may be only the beginning of a long era of part-time or voluntary work which demands new knowledge, different skills and a change of attitude. The National Council of Social Service has for some time given close attention to the proper selection and training of 'retired' people for the voluntary social work field, about which even the ex-professional has something to learn when he leaves the statutory services, industry or commerce.

We must now examine more closely what forms of training should be available after the first stage of central group training. In doing so, the welfare supervisor's responsibility must again be stressed, since training is as much a method of organisational control as are more commonly recognised systems of records, returns and reports—and the less commonly recognised ones of staff appraisal, manpower budgeting and career planning. Indeed, paper control systems are effective only in so far as people are well-trained in their operation. However, the local supervisor does not bear the whole responsibility. He is one leg of a tripod of which the others are the welfare officer himself and the central welfare or personnel organisation which reports to the highest echelons of management and shares with management in the formulation of general policy. All three legs take something of weight and between them achieve balance.

The central role is to ensure that continuous training is accepted as part of general policy, and, when this is willed as the end, also to will the means. This involves the provision of other forms of internal training to follow up the basic central course and the granting of time off and financial support for approved external methods. The supervisor's role also falls into two parts: the provision of local internal training, both in groups and by individual coaching and guidance, and encouragement and advice to the individual on external facilities which are appropriate to him. Finally the welfare officer himself has a dual responsibility: to participate to the maximum in local in-service training and thus assist in its improvement, and to augment this by accepting the need for private study and then by doing what he can about it according to his own choice.

Thus continued training as a tripartite responsibility will have both internal and external elements, and this might provide the most suitable classification for looking at ways and means.

Internal Training

Specialised follow-up courses

The first and most obvious form of continued training are specialised follow-up courses after the basic central course, the objectives of which have been shown to be limited. Broadly, the basic course sets out to give a bird's-eye-view of the welfare officer job as a whole, plus specific initial training in its more important aspects. One cannot, for example, bring interviewing skill to a high level in a few hours, nor report writing or any other essential area of skill or knowledge. One must provide special courses later, reinforcing and being reinforced by local coaching and guidance and self-criticism. These are not to be

confused with the 'refresher' training which has already been mentioned and to which we shall shortly return in more detail.

It is suggested that special courses should be of short duration,
providing further highly intensive 'condensed experience', and that
they should be spaced over the first two years. This is especially convenient when a two-year probationary period is a key element in the
selection, training and appointment policy. One-week courses are
probably ideal (strictly, four-day courses with half-day travelling
time allowed at each end), so that difficulties of coverage during
absence are minimised. Essential 'candidate' subjects have been mentioned, but one can also envisage short intensive courses on specific
social services; on the problems of sick absence and its relation
with welfare and discipline; young people; counselling for
retirement; group welfare; and office methods, including records and
returns.

'Skill courses' must clearly be based firmly on practical work, for
there is no better route to the acquisition of skill than carefully
supervised practice. But practical work—in the more general sense of
very active participation—is also necessary for the 'knowledge' areas.
A series of lectures by an expert, followed by questions and discussion,
is doubtless more effective than simply absorbing the material from
books; but even more valuable is the relation of the new knowledge to
real problems brought by course members. In other words, the
special courses are best designed around case discussions in the same
way that the initial course is designed, but discussions should be
taken to greater depth and detail. This does not imply that there is no
need for the visiting 'expert witness'; in fact the need for him is
greater than in initial courses.

Refresher training

The purposes of refresher courses is quite different. They are not
designed to take special areas to depth, but to provide those who have
been on the job for some years with the opportunity of getting a more
up-to-date 'bird's eye-view' of the organisation's philosophy, policy
and practice. Refreshment of this kind is necessary *at least* every five
years if people are not to grow stale or develop a local and parochial
outlook. The suggestion has been made that refresher training is best
linked with the initial training of newcomers, and it is worthwhile
repeating the advantages of this policy in the present context. First,
there is the practical advantage of having enough group members to

make initial training possible at all; even the largest organisations will rarely have enough newcomers to welfare work to give them separate treatment. Second, the contribution of the experienced adds immeasurably to the realism of the course; newcomers may not readily believe that such-and-such a type of problem could arise at all unless their colleagues can point to a similar occurrence in their own period of service. Third, the experienced man is brought sharply up against the learning difficulties of the 'new boys'; he thus re-lives some of the problems he himself encountered and can with humility take his prejudices out of the cupboard and view them with a clearer eye. Finally, and certainly not least, cooperation and camaraderie can be developed among people from different areas, under different local supervision, who otherwise may rarely meet each other.

Local welfare conferences

Local conferences under the chairmanship of the welfare supervisor (if one is employed) should have many purposes and many elements; but, whether specific training elements are overt or not, they all fuse into an overriding objective. This can only be to improve the quality of the welfare officer service given to the staff of the organisation as a whole. And this, in the long run, is a training task. What are these many elements? There are the elements of direct control: discussion of policy developments, adjustment of individual loads (both short-term to cover absences and long-term to cope with major trends in the incidence of work), settlement of queries on case classification and on recording systems. There are elements of information: announcements and discussion of new legislation, books, pamphlets, press reports and comments, personnel changes in local statutory and voluntary services. There are elements of more direct training: showing a film, listening to an expert visiting speaker, discussion of recent difficult or unusual cases. It is all training in the broader sense, and the welfare supervisor learns as much as members of his team. He particularly learns from the 'feed-back' the team supplies—information which he in turn may pass on to the central welfare organisation either direct or through supervisors' conferences. He gets to know of the complaints and grievances of his staff; as human beings, welfare officers are bound to have some! He learns how the organisation's welfare policy is working out in the field and how it should be modified. He is also able to identify further training needs; he can better appreciate what further information is required by the team as a whole, and which individuals display gaps which he must help to fill by his own local training effort.

This ideal can be realised only in large organisations, but something similar can be achieved in the smaller organisations without welfare supervisors by participation in local conferences of managers and/or supervisors. Welfare supervisors, where they exist, should naturally take part in management conferences, since they are part of the managing team.

External Training

Once again, we may discuss this best in terms of central policy, the role of the local supervisor and the responsibility of the individual. These are better taken in reverse order, starting from the principle that individuals, supervisors and the central organisation must all accept that people learn in different ways. Some welfare officers may be academically inclined; some may learn more from informal contact with outside professionals than by reading texts on social welfare. Some, although academically inclined, may have too many domestic commitments to be able to attend regular evening classes; or such classes may not exist in their areas. Others could face a short series of lectures lasting a term, or even an academic year, but may have no taste for long-term diploma, certificate or degree courses with examinations at the end of them. All must be catered for, but they must not be forced into a common mould. The supervisor must know his man well enough, and know the available facilities well enough, to advise and help him in the choice of the pattern most appropriate to him. The central organisation must admit the range of possibilities, offering financial support and a measure of time off, where necessary, for individuals to develop themselves according to their needs.

Local external welfare groups

Starting at the informal level, it should be apparent that welfare officers should be encouraged to join and take an active part in any local Council of Social Service, social workers' discussion group or other organisation which brings together people with welfare interests. (Subscriptions are usually nominal and could reasonably be met from the welfare officer's incidental expenses account. If the central organisation encourages, the central organisation should meet the cost; the individual should not be expected to pay even a nominal subscription from his own salary.) It is not only the training element which is important; successful day-to-day cooperation is more likely if the outside social worker is known personally and well, than if he remains a signature on a letter or a voice on the telephone. What is sauce for the internal welfare officer goose in the context of re-fresher courses is equally sauce for the external social worker gander in the context of external local groups. There will naturally be times when urgent personal casework must take precedence over attendance at these meetings, but they should be very rare. Purpose-ful meetings with other social workers must be put high on the priority list and not neglected because one is generally 'busy'. Wel-fare officers should always be busy—but they should also get their priorities straight and not let the long term suffer because of short-term pressures.

Short external courses

These may be residential or non-residential. The six-monthly *Calendar of Residential Short Courses* published by the National Institute of Adult Education (35 Queen Anne Street, London W.1) often lists courses from which a welfare officer may benefit. The local supervisor should be provided with a regular copy so that he may keep in touch with what is available. He will sometimes find, for example, that an adult education centre within reasonable travelling distance is offering a long-weekend conference on the problem of particular groups of immigrants, which would provide very useful background for one particular member of the team serving an office, factory or building employing a considerable number of such staff. The welfare officer's appreciation of cultural differences in habits of personal hygiene, or of eating—both of which have been known to cause strikes—may make all the difference to his own approach to indi-viduals in need or to questions of group morale which may come his way. And he can pass on his enlightenment to supervisors and others whose ignorance of these differences results in trouble rather than bliss. The *Calendar* always lists the dates of one course which deserves special mention. This is the one-week course on 'Human Aspects of Management' run by the Roffey Park Institute—a 'must' for all welfare officers in their early years of service.

Apart from the 'official' education system, relevant courses are also offered by such independent organisations as the Industrial Society. Most of these are directed to line management and supervision and to the higher 'personnel' echelons rather than to the basic-grade welfare officer; and most of those which come within the definition of welfare used in this book (as distinct from training, industrial relations and other personnel functions directed to welfare ends in the broader sense) deal with the physical rather than the group or individual welfare field. But many of them are relevant to the needs of welfare *supervisors*, particularly courses on interviewing techniques which deal with selection interviewing as well as personal counselling. The welfare supervisor has a role to play in the selection of welfare officers, and he cannot perform it satisfactorily without adequate training in selection interviewing.

Reports on external courses are often regarded as a chore, but how else is the central organisation to learn which courses are useful and which are not? The welfare officer samples courses as an agent of the whole organisation, and not simply for his own benefit and that of the group of staff he serves. Furthermore, a report ensures that at least some of the benefit may be shared in the reading, and other welfare officers with similar interests and needs may be stimulated to go to the fountainhead themselves.

Longer external courses

These could be classified in several different ways—according to level, location or duration, including whether they are part-time or full-time. Level is important because it is not merely the basic-grade welfare officer who needs to continue his training; welfare supervisors and members of the central personnel or welfare organisation have the same responsibilities and obligations in this respect, although their needs should certainly differ. The other factors are very much interlinked. Only those welfare staff with unusual self-discipline and determination will tackle part-time courses of the type which lead to diploma or degree. Only the unmarried, or those without normal family commitments, will be willing to undertake full-time courses which take them away from home for several weeks or months. And only the very enlightened of industrial organisations will be prepared to release welfare staff for long full-time courses. It is really not only a matter of enlightenment; there are many practical difficulties of welfare coverage during absence to be considered. Should the gap be filled by stretching the other members of the team to limits which may be excessive; or is the answer temporary promotion or temporary appointment? If the organisation wishes to follow a progressive policy of release for further training and education, its welfare officer complement and organisation must be adapted accordingly.

It may be useful to list types of courses, irrespective of level, in an ascending order of 'release' difficulty. In all cases it will be taken for granted that financial assistance will be provided, together with a measure of time off when all or part of the training is done in private time.

Correspondence courses

These are at present a poor substitute for the *group* training and education methods which most aspects of the welfare subject demand. However, there is no reason why the substitute should continue poor, and there is in fact every hope of modernisation. A University of the Post and/or University of the Air is slowly developing from experimental tutorial schemes in various parts of the country (see Peterson, 1964). There are already systems in which home study by correspondence with expert tutors is augmented by regular discussion meetings 'on the job'. All these are pointers which show great promise for the future, and there is no reason to suppose that some of the needs of welfare officers cannot be catered for on these lines.

Lecture series

Many university extra-mural departments and other colleges of further education, often jointly with the Workers' Educational Association, run regular series of a dozen or so lecture/discussion sessions on topics which are part of the essential background of the welfare officer in industry or commerce. The National Assistance Board was particularly active in stimulating courses on the Social Services for its own staff. One of the duties of the welfare supervisor should be to keep in touch with local facilities of this kind and bring them to the attention of members of his team.

Diploma and certificate courses

A good example is the London University Extra-Mural Department's Diploma in Sociology. The course covers four years—Social History, Social Structure, Social Psychology ('Psychological Aspects of Society') and Social Philosophy (or Social Policy and Administration as an option for the final year). In addition to sessional examinations students have to meet certain attendance requirements and to submit a number of essays. Although the attendance is only one evening a week, the real time commitment is nearer three, since one must allow a minimum of three hours for reading and more for written work. Follow-up extension courses, and summer schools at Wye College, are also available. Similar courses are provided in other parts of the country, and such is the rate of growth of adult education that others will doubtless be offered before this book is in print. Some local sleuthing by the welfare supervisor may be necessary, or he can direct his enquiries to the National Institute of Adult Education.

The main focal point of professional training for social work *per se* is of course the National Institute for Social Work Training, which is developing the 'generic' and other courses recommended by the Younghusband Report. Most of this effort is directed to full-time training which at present may be inappropriate to the needs of the basic-grade welfare office in industry or commerce. However, the needs of welfare supervisors and of senior staff of the central welfare organisation may not be dissimilar from those of the social worker in the statutory services who has supervisory or controlling responsibilities. The central organisation should therefore develop close contact with the Institute and establish what is common ground between them.

Degree courses

Part-time degrees are going out of fashion in certain educational quarters, the view being taken that every young man or woman with the capacity should have the opportunity to develop it by going straight from school to college or university. The vision is no doubt splendid, but there are late developers at 18 just as there are late developers at 11-plus. There are also folk who just do not know what they want to do at 18, although some of the general first-year courses provided by the newer universities are designed to help meet this problem as well as to be correctives to over-early specialisation. There are also many people who through domestic circumstances cannot go direct to full-time studies; and there are those whose first experience of full-time university level education whets their appetite for more— but in a quite different direction. For example, training and experience in teaching has stimulated many to go on to degree courses in their specialist subject, or in psychology, sociology or other disciplines related to teaching as such. Some people come to the social sciences comparatively late in life, when their experience of engineering or whatever else it might have been has shown them that their real interest is in human factors. Welfare experience itself can often be the link between vocational training at a lower level and professional training at graduate level. These people can rarely give up their careers to take another full-time course; they must perforce ease out of one career and into another by the part-time route.

The best-known institution providing part-time *internal* degree courses is probably Birkbeck College, University of London, where the biggest single group of students consists of teachers who are following their pet subject to degree level or moving out into disciplines related to teaching. The London School of Economics also offers part-time courses, mainly in the specialised social science sphere. Here and elsewhere, London degrees may be obtained on an external basis. (The degree-conferring powers of many of our new universities in fact derive from their earlier provision of courses for London external degrees.) Some colleges run full-time courses only, some part-time as well; and certain correspondence colleges specialise in courses for external London degrees.

In summary, the educational system of this country provides many ladders and bridges for the welfare officer to use if he has the interest, the determination—and the time. There is somewhere a level appropriate to every individual, and it is up to him, his supervisor and the central organisation to find it. It cannot be found unless the ladders and bridges are first precisely and accurately identified. There is at present a major gap in the system—part-time day release courses for adults which welfare officers (among others) could attend if complements are adjusted to a shorter working week—but it is beyond the scope of this book to do more than point to its existence.

Finally, one may point out that time spent in finding one's way around the territory of education and further training is time well spent in more than one sense. It may provide a useful store of information to be drawn on when counselling the individual in need; problems of loneliness and shyness may often be cured by finding an educational interest which brings one into contact with others of like mind. Normally, the firm's Education and Training Officer would be expected to take over from the welfare officer any counselling which had led into prospects of further education, but informal agreement on where the line is to be drawn between the two spheres of advisory interest should not be difficult to achieve.

Part four

ORGANISATION AND
CONTROL

15   Welfare Information

Summary   Information is a subject which links training with organisational control. In order to ensure a dynamic welfare policy, specific 'information channels' must be identified and properly used. In this chapter we are mainly concerned with channels *to* the welfare officer; the next chapter considers information *from* him. We look at channels as 'types' of information and distinguish four: broad policy information; specialist information combined with policy guidance; permanent specialist reference material; and current 'background' and 'controversy' material. The last of these provides a measure of short-term 'feedback' on the effectiveness of welfare policy, since welfare officers themselves contribute much of the material.

Some 'Information Theory'

Information for the welfare officer can be regarded either as an aspect of his training or as an aspect of the organisation and control of his function. The recent section on Local conferences as part of internal training showed that keeping him informed had elements of both training and control. The subject of information is thus a linking one, but it is so important in its own right that it needs separate treatment. It is convenient to consider it immediately after chapters on training and immediately before those which deal with the more easily recognised organisation and control problems.

Without going too far into the special languages of cybernetics or organisation theory, one may point to the need for various information *channels* which link to form a dynamic system. 'Feedback' is the essential feature of a dynamic system which differentiates it from a static one. A static policy will result unless 'feedback' is deliberately built into the system and consciously maintained.

An organisation's welfare policy should develop dynamically in three main stages, the second and third of which provide short-term and long-term feedback for the first. The stages are: formulation of policy, its implementation, and the assessment of the effectiveness of the policy.

1. Policy should be *formulated* on the basis of objectively determined needs, but in the context of certain limiting factors. Some of these factors will be legislative in character (e.g. Factories Acts; Shops, Offices and Railway Premises Act, etc.). Others will be social in the broader sense (e.g. the existence of voluntary social organisations), and other limiting factors are provided by the shape and size of the organisation itself. The objective assessment of needs may of course show scope for differences in judgment about how they can be met; but although one cannot dispense entirely with subjective factors of this kind, the final policy should be drawn up as far as possible in terms which are measurable. If one does not start with measurable terms, one cannot later measure the effectiveness of the policy. It should go without saying, but it has to be said over and over again, that management can be successful only to the extent that its objectives are clear and specific—and thus measurable.

2. When policy has been agreed, it has to be *implemented*. Once again, implementation will be within the context of limiting factors, some of which may be new (since policy was formulated), or may not have been foreseen at the formulation stage. These new or unforeseen factors immediately provide a corrective (i.e. feedback) which may lead to short-term reformulation on points of detail. The need for any major changes would be an indication of lack of realism in the original analysis of needs, or poor judgment concerning the subjective factors taken into account with objective needs.

3. The third stage is the longer-term *assessment of the effectiveness of policy*—its validation and evaluation. At this stage one measures what is measurable, and one collects subjective opinions to augment and illuminate the cold facts. But the collection of opinions must be done expertly, the right questions must be asked and the answers quantified wherever possible. It is only when long-term validation and evaluation are firmly built into the system—and carried out even though everybody concerned may be convinced that the policy is 'right for all time'—that short-term decision making is really recognised as a poor substitute for long-range planning and foresight. One must avoid the situation where short-term decision making has led to

so many breakdowns that a drastic review has to be made in a hurry, when insufficient time is available to do it properly. Hurried reviews rarely provide a sound foundation for policy; they simply lead to the perpetuation of 'muddling through', the biggest enemy of efficiency.

There is nothing particularly novel about this three-stage approach; the novelty lies mainly in the rareness it is used in practice. However, 'management by objective' is beginning to gain ground, and the concept of feedback is essential in 'business games'. These owe much to military exercises, and it is not difficult to discern 'strategy' and 'tactics' in the distinction made between long-term and short-term decision making.

This brief look at 'information theory' points not only to the need for information channels as such; it also indicates that they should be devised strategically with conscious care, each a part of the whole and having a thought-out objective, and not set up tactically on a 'good thing' basis. What welfare information channels are required beyond those identified in the chapters on training? We may best answer this by trying to differentiate the *types* of information the welfare officer must have to do his job effectively. Some of it will be given to him during training, but training handouts may date. They must be supplemented and revised from time to time, they must illuminate and follow through the training process so that training really is a continuous process. It is suggested that he needs four distinct types of information which should flow in four distinct channels; overloading and confusion would result if only one channel were used. They are: broad formal policy; detailed application of policy to specialist problems; purely specialist material for permanent reference; and current 'background' and 'controversy' material. Welfare officers will themselves contribute much of the last-named type of information and thus provide some short-term feedback on the effectiveness of policy. To complete the picture, the next chapter will be concerned with another channel—objective information *from* the welfare officer in the shape of his records and returns, which provide most of the evidence required for long-term validation and evaluation.

Before considering each of our present four types of information in detail it is worthwhile pointing to a fact which may seem surprising. Only one of them—specialised reference information—seems to concern the welfare officer alone. The rest to a greater or lesser extent are also for managers, supervisors and others. Even specialised reference material should be available to these other interests if they want it.

The more managers, supervisors and others know about the welfare function the better it can be carried out—as long as they do not then claim to 'know it all'.

Policy Information

Welfare policy, which includes the duties of welfare officers but is more concerned with measurable objectives, should not only be well thought out but also written down, manifestly approved by the highest level in the organisation, and made available to any interested party. A general understanding based on word-of-mouth transmission is quite insufficient; such so-called 'understandings' are notoriously prone to distortion and misinterpretation. Newcomers to the firm get slightly different versions, which will change as they are passed on to others, and within a comparatively short time local 'old Spanish customs' will grow up because there exists no authoritative statement to act as a basis of reference whereby to challenge and correct them. Distortions and misinterpretations will arise in much the same way as they arise in the spread of a rumour. Certain aspects of policy will be selected by the 'transmitter' (not necessarily with conscious malice) in so far as they conform with his own prejudices. This process of selection will over-simplify and sharpen some features, and level down the total amount of information to the point where it is easy to remember and to transmit to others. The oral transmission of information presents real problems. (Readers who want to take this fascinating subject further may like to look into some of the experimental work on rumours, e.g. Krech and Crutchfield, 1948.) The availability of a written document on welfare policy will not of itself *prevent* rumour-type distortions from arising from time to time, but it will certainly reduce their number and enable them to be scotched very rapidly.

The policy statement is of course written against the background of the limiting factors provided by the organisation's policies in related areas. Thus there will be policies and rules on sick absence, discipline, joint consultation and kindred subjects. These must be regarded as 'reference' material to which the welfare officer must have easy and rapid access. He must have staff handbooks and copies of relevant rules on his bookshelf and not have to go to another office to consult them. His time is valuable; the cost of providing these reference sources is negligible in comparison. Keeping rule books up-to-date is a problem which must be considered in the same context of realistic rather than cheese-paring cost consciousness; it is a task for lower-level clerical people. The general topic of clerical assistance to the welfare officer will be discussed when we turn to office methods.

The welfare policy statement will not have to be kept up-to-date in the sense of issuing rule amendments. Its nature is quite different. It should be designed broadly, to set the scene for a considerable period of time. It should be rewritten only when the regular validation and evaluation review points to the need for restatement, or when a major change in the social scene demands it. Tinkering with policy from time to time leads to instability, and neither staff nor the welfare officers who serve them know where they are.

Specialist Information and Policy Guidance

However, a broad policy statement needs amplification in respect of detail. It is, for example, easy to state as policy that the welfare officer should work in collaboration with the organisation's medical staff, the local G.P.s and the Mental Welfare Officer on problems of mental ill-health; it is quite another matter to spell out how this should be done and to provide sufficient information about the Mental Health Act, and about delicate questions of responsibility and referral, to enable it to be done smoothly. This is of course a major topic to be dealt with during basic training, but basic training must be backed up by permanent reference material.

The policy statement will also need periodic amplification in respect of *changes* in the limiting factors inside or outside the organisation which are not drastic enough to force a major review. We can take as an example the introduction of a new medical/social service, such as cervical tests which may help in the early identification of cancer. The general policy will probably be on the lines of 'bringing medical services to the attention of staff', and this need not be changed. But new services not only *cater* for new needs; in a sense they also *create* them by making explicit what was hitherto vague and ill-defined. They thus point to new areas of welfare information, and to the need for guidance on its practical application. In the present example, recognition amongst staff that the welfare officer is knowledgeable about facilities for cervical tests will almost certainly lead many women to consult about problems which in their minds are associated with the menopause. The welfare officer must know something about this to recognise problems and have clearly in his mind where his task finishes and where the tasks of other specialists begin. The required information is therefore twofold—technical material and policy guidance.

Experience suggests that this sort of technical information should be put out through a single channel, which, if accurately labelled, is readily identified and not confused with others set up for different purposes. Anything savouring of a rule book is quite inappropriate; on the other hand, it is not the sort of thing which should be published in a newsletter or other vehicle designed to cater for the informal 'background' and 'controversy' channel. A series of 'welfare information papers' has been found to be a most effective method. They should be published by the central welfare authority and sent direct to all welfare staff and to the senior managers of the staff served by each welfare officer. And joint consultation should be so well developed that copies 'for information' should be supplied to the trade union members of the organisation's joint welfare committee. It is for senior managers to decide to what extent the papers should also circulate to junior managers and line supervisors. The central welfare department should supply copies on request for this purpose but should not seem to dictate what *technical* welfare information should go to line managers and supervisors who are under the control of others. To do so would deny the basic premise that the welfare function is an advisory one. Thus technical information stands in sharp contrast with the information to staff dealt with in Chapter 2. Once policy has been decided, no manager can refuse the use of notice boards or change the content of training courses, but he should have a voice in how much technical information his staff need or can digest.

Welfare information papers need not invariably be written in their entirety by the central welfare department. They may well take the form of pamphlets, extracts from or copies of articles from journals and other publications not normally seen by 'field' staff, usually with an exegesis or other form of covering statement which relates the material to current policy. Where 'outside' material is used, the best form is the paper itself, written by the central department, with the pamphlet, copy or extract as an appendix, since this makes it quite clear who has contributed what. The policy guidance or interpretation should not be so interspersed with specialist fact or opinion culled from elsewhere that the reader cannot distinguish the two contributions. Credit or criticism must go to whomsoever it is due; acknowledgments must be made to the external source (particularly when authority to reprint has to be sought because of copyrights), and the facts and opinions from this source must be presented precisely as in the original. They should not be condensed in the interests of brevity without the approval of the author, nor should they be slanted in any way. Any summary, slanting or interpretation should be manifestly a separate contribution.

The usefulness of information papers, which bring to attention material not normally seen, will be readily apparent. A welfare officer will not have the time—nor should complements be so generous that he can be given it—to read through a mass of journals on the off-chance that something will be relevant to his work. This is a task which the central organisation is far better equipped to tackle, one man or group acting for the whole organisation. Only when the material is seen to be important enough to go to all welfare staff and their senior managers, should the 'information paper' vehicle be used. There is of course a great deal of background material in the regular journals of less importance or of ephemeral interest which will have no repercussions on policy. This kind of material may be labelled 'circulating' to distinguish it from permanent specialist 'reference' material. Circulating material can itself be broken down into sub-categories.

First, there is material which is known from experience to be of general interest to basic-grade welfare staff. This should be supplied direct to the local welfare supervisor. He can either attach a general circulation slip, letting his team choose for themselves what if anything they will read; or he can act as 'first reader', marking off the items to which he wants to draw attention. Examples are the weekly *New Society*, the monthly journal of the Industrial Society, *Social Service Quarterly* (National Council of Social Service) and the quarterly bulletin of the National Old People's Welfare Council (also published by N.C.S.S.). The second sub-category consists of highly specialised welfare material which the central welfare or personnel organisation feels that local welfare supervisors should have the opportunity of seeing, on an open circulation or on first-reader basis. It is a matter for local discretion whether this should go further, to basic-grade welfare staff. Examples are *Case Conference* (Association of Social Workers and Case Conference Ltd), *Social Work* (Family Welfare Association), *Rehabilitation* (British Council for Rehabilitation of the Disabled), *Mental Health* (National Association for Mental Health), and similar periodicals.

The third category consists of those many learned journals, and other publications of organisations concerned with aspects of people at work, which senior people involved professionally with the person- nel function can be expected to see. These periodicals are received by the central organisation but are not circulated to local welfare super- visors as a matter of course—only when a particular issue contains something relevant to the job. The list in this third category could be almost endless; in practice it will depend on the time available in the central organisation to deal with it. Large organisations with good library facilities can solve this problem easily enough, but the central welfare organisation has to ensure that the library is fully aware of its range of interests. Examples are the journal of the Institute of Person- nel Management, *BACIE Journal, Journal of Management Studies, Occupational Psychology, Personnel Magazine, The Manager, Vocational Aspect*, and *British Journal of Industrial Relations*. Although the cardi- nal principle is to be as generous as possible with information, it is clearly unwise to expect the busy welfare officer to skim through journals of this sort on the off-chance that he might find something of value; somebody must select on his behalf. But we must enter one caveat—that if any individual welfare officer expresses a particular wish to see a journal regularly (it may be relevant to a part-time academic course he is taking) then steps must be taken to ensure that his name goes on the circulation list. The majority of welfare officers will be only too glad to have 'first readers' who will save them time, but those who think differently must also be catered for.

Permanent Specialist Reference Material

In this section we shall be concerned only with *published* reference material. Discussion of other reference sources required by the wel- fare officer (e.g. card indexes relating to outside social services and their personnel) are best discussed in the context of office methods. With a few but very important exceptions, this reference material should be kept in the local office. (When two or more welfare officers operate from the same building and share clerical assistance, only one copy each of the recommended publications need be supplied.) The exceptions are those documents, pamphlets and small books which can easily be slipped into pocket or briefcase when out of the office, enabling the welfare officer to visit as the fountainhead of *fact*, not relying on memory of details of the enormous range of social welfare knowledge. These 'portable' sources will be dealt with first, dividing them into external and internal publications.

The most important external publication is the Family Welfare Association's *Guide to the Social Services*, revised annually. This has already been mentioned as providing a large proportion of the day-to-day social service information required for the welfare job. The second is the National Assistance Board's *Help for Those in Need* or such version as may be issued by the Ministry of Social Security. A small stock of these leaflets should be held in the office so that copies may be left with any individual in need who can benefit from the reading and perhaps left to make direct contact with the Ministry's staff. Although it contains little which is not published in the F.W.A. *Guide*, the Institute of Welfare Officers' *Welfare Officer's Guide* also deserves mention.

If they have been written with a keen eye to day-to-day needs, internally published welfare information papers often come into the category of reference material which can be carried around. They are of course written for the welfare officer's own information and should not be left with individuals in need of help. However, appendices to a paper may be designed expressly as handouts. For example, a paper on Wills, Probate and Letters of Administration (an area where there is a clear need to gather together information from many source documents) may have as appendices a short guide on making a will, and the National Citizens' Advice Bureaux' leaflet *Practical Problems following the Death of a Relative* (published by the National Council of Social Service).

As far as 'non-portable' reference material is concerned, the N.C.S.S. publication *Citizens' Advice Notes* (C.A.N.S.) is quite indispensable. It performs on a bigger and more detailed scale the same function for the welfare officer in his office as the F.W.A. *Guide to the Social Services* performs when he is out of it. C.A.N.S. is a loose-leaf publication offered on a down payment and subsequent subscription basis, amended and up-dated sheets being sent out quarterly to subscribers. It covers in summary form most of the social legislation and related information the welfare officer should have at his fingertips—literally at his fingertips, since there is no reason at all why he should try to keep it all in his memory, a most imperfect instrument for storing detailed information. Naturally, time-lags between public announcements of social changes and their appearance in C.A.N.S. are inevitable, but to help close the gap the N.C.A.B. publish a monthly circular, a copy of each issue of which should go direct to every welfare *office* (not necessarily every welfare *officer*).

The N.C.A.B. circular also announces new or revised leaflets issued by the Ministry of Social Security, another most important reference source. There is no reason for the central welfare or personnel organisation to act as intermediary between the M.S.S. and the individual welfare officer in the distribution of leaflets, although it can perform the useful service of issuing an annual list of current leaflets as a check that local supplies are complete. It is much better for the welfare officer to get his leaflets direct from his nearest M.S.S. office. In this way he will maintain personal contact with people who are a considerable help to him in his day-to-day work. To digress for a moment, one may point out that social legislation put out by M.S.S. and other government departments is often drafted in complicated legal phraseology, and even the experienced welfare officer is sometimes at a loss fully to understand it. While this state of affairs exists the welfare officer must clearly go direct to government servants who should be in a position to do the interpreting. However, it is possible that such leaflets may in future be put out differently. There will perhaps be a trend away from continuous prose and towards presentation in analytical and semi-programmed form—logical trees in the shape of visual graphs and ordered lists of conditions and exceptions. Research work is being done at University College, London, to this end (see Dr Sheila Jones' article on 'Why can't leaflets be logical?', *New Society*, 10 November 1964).

All these reference sources are essential; they are in what one may call the front line of personal welfare service. As a second line, the welfare office needs a small library of the sort of publications which lie in the area between factual reference and background textbook. Many of these are revised annually, and the category also includes annual reports and brochures of the major welfare organisations—the Industrial Society, National Council of Social Service and bodies linked with it, National Marriage Guidance Council, National Council for the Unmarried Mother and her Child, National Association for Mental Health, etc. One must also include relevant government reports such as 'Albemarle' and 'Younghusband', and a considerable number of leaflets and pamphlets dealing with specific and general topics. Examples (which will seem dated by the time this book is in print) are *Using Hire Purchase Wisely* (Finance Houses Asscn. Ltd), Audrey Harvey's *Casualties of the Welfare State* (Fabian Society), Nesta Roberts' *Everybody's Business* (N.A.M.H.), and certain of the Ministry of Labour's Safety, Health and Welfare book-

222   ORGANISATION AND CONTROL

lets (H.M.S.O.). Most of the published output of the National Council of Social Service is relevant, and up-to-date lists may be obtained from the Council at 26 Bedford Square, London W.C.1. None of them costs more than shillings, and the expenditure of a few pounds will see the welfare office well supplied. Selection may imply invidious comparison, but *Advising the Citizen, Interviewing in the Social Services, Loneliness, Voluntary Social Services* and *Public Social Services* merit special mention. The *Annual Charities Register and Digest* published by the Family Welfare Association is in a similar category.

These are all quoted only as examples. One cannot exhaust the list, for it is continually growing. It is one of the main duties of the central organisation to keep track of everything which may be of local value, partly by maintaining direct contact with the many organisations in the field, partly by ensuring that the organisation's librarian is fully acquainted of welfare needs, but most of all by closely reading the reputable dailies and weeklies. One cannot hope that the information will flow in uninvited; one must be in constant search of it.

There is yet a third line of support, where reference shades into background education. There are two opposing views about the location of libraries of this kind. One school says that such texts are so rarely consulted by field welfare staff busy keeping up with day-to-day pressures that general libraries in local welfare offices cannot be economically justified. The other says that texts certainly will not be consulted if they are held centrally and welfare staff have to ask specially for them. The balance of argument is more likely to be with the second school of thought, for the economics are in reality trifling. One may for example buy the whole Pelican 'Psychology' series (edited by C. A. Mace) for two or three pounds. A few more will buy a good selection of some of the standard texts on social welfare and social administration—Wootton (1959), Timms (1964), Rodgers and Dixon (1960), Farndale (1965), to name but four examples. The more general social background should be represented, e.g. Mackenzie (1966), Welford (1962). Welfare officers should also have the opportunity of relating their work to personnel management. One should therefore include all the publications of the Institute of Personnel Management, some of the general personnel management texts (e.g. Northcott, 1960), and some dealing with special skills which are common to several branches of the subject. In particular, one needs books on interviewing (e.g. Sidney and Brown,

1964, which is itself a useful source book of other work on interviewing) and counselling (e.g. Harms and Schrieber, 1964; Halmos, 1965).

Central welfare organisations or local welfare supervisors should have no difficulty in compiling a suitable list for a good working library at minimum cost; but if advice on the available range is needed such bodies as the National Book League (7 Albemarle Street, London W.1) would be glad to give it. One cannot take everything on board; one must select. But if selection is to err, it should err in the direction of generosity rather than parsimony.

Current 'Background' and 'Controversy' Material

Our fourth information channel, or fourth type of welfare information—it does not matter very much which way we look at it—is a fairly obvious one, but only when it has been identified and consciously built into the system. The obvious is too often taken for granted; one supposes that everybody in the organisation with some concern for welfare knows that he can offer facts or opinions which may contribute to policy making, and will in practice do so. In theory the facility may exist, but in practice it may never be used. If one asks why, one often finds that the wrong channel is offered. Ideas are supposed to come through the '*proper* channels', and what the organisation means by the proper channels are the formal lines of supervision and management. Yet almost by definition the formal channel is not one which can cope with informality; the nature of the material dictates the need for an *informal* channel to provide a forum for controversy to flourish.

The shape and size of the forum will depend to a very large extent on the shape and size of the organisation providing it. In the small and geographically compact company it may only be oral, the direct face-to-face contact and discussion between welfare officers, their 'personnel' colleagues, and the managers, supervisors and union representatives of the staff they serve. Organisations of this sort perhaps have an even greater need to commit their welfare policy to paper than larger ones, for unless it is 'externalised' in this way one strong-minded but possibly insufficiently informed individual could change it almost daily. Policy would then be determined not by an objective assessment of need but by the state of a liver, ephemeral successes or failures on the job, or frustrations at home.

While still retaining the oral channel, organisations big enough to run a house magazine represent the next size gradation. The magazine could well include a 'welfare newsletter' or similar section for open and public discussion of a service which is available to all staff. A little further up the scale there is scope for an independent broadsheet, quickly and economically duplicated; while the biggest organisations can produce a regular 'Welfare Review' or similar publication which may even rival in its size and coverage the more general house magazine put out by a smaller company. Large or small, printed or duplicated, regular or irregular, the purpose of the publication should be stated and adhered to. It should not, for example, be used to save the trouble of putting out information papers, nor for circulating technical information which welfare staff should have more authoritatively from C.A.N.S. or the N.C.A.B. monthly circular. It can of course be a most useful vehicle for reporting conferences and meetings which welfare staff have attended, for points made at external gatherings of this kind are often controversial in themselves or may arouse controversy between welfare staff and others within the organisation. Other useful material can be in the form of articles on day-to-day problems, reports of illuminating incidents (generalised in such a way as to preserve anonymity of the people involved), and, almost without saying, Letters to the Editor.

16   Records and Returns

Summary   Records and returns may often be regarded as a chore, but they are essential not only for the assessment of the effectiveness of welfare policy but for many other reasons as well. It is better to regard them as 'aids' rather than 'controls'. At local level they are aids to the welfare officer himself and through him to the person needing help, to his substitute when he is away, and to his supervisor. At central level they are still as much aids as controls; they are aids to formulating general welfare and welfare training policy and to matching complements to needs. Work must be classified if trends are to be watched, and levels of work—for example, time-consuming 'cases' and briefer 'enquiries'—must be differentiated. Criteria to judge 'what is a case?' are suggested, and the use of diaries, daybooks and monthly summary sheets is examined. The problem of retention or destruction of records is also considered.

The Need for Records

'Good manners, ability and willingness to listen, and efficient methods of record keeping are the principal elements required.' So says Wootton, 1959, in discussing 'generic' social casework courses. Perhaps this is too low a common denominator, for one might say that at least the first two of these three elements should be common in the selection and training of anybody who works with people rather than things. But what is true for social case-workers is equally true for welfare officers in industry and commerce. In an article on the good receptionist (*New Society*, 29 April 1965) Denis Rice makes similar points, although emphasising the good manners and listening elements. The receptionist, even in a social casework agency, may be so concerned with facts for the record that manners go by the board. To quote Rice, 'At the reception counter I was met with an immediate barrage of questions; Name? Address? Age? With maximum efficiency and minimum humanity the vital facts were secured; then "Sit down over there!"' Tempting as it is to go straight into the whole question of when, where and how to take notes, we are now concerned with records and returns as such, not with the skill required to gather the raw material for them from the individual in need.

It may be that some are born good record-keepers, some achieve good records under the inexorable pressure of experience, common-sense and self-discipline, and others have records thrust upon them by the employing organisation. Certainly attitudes to records vary, and even the best welfare officers (and social workers) may sometimes regard them as an irksome chore instead of the aid they are designed to be. Perhaps the differences are temperamental; perhaps clerical duties sort ill with the sensitivity required for hours of patient listening; or perhaps an anti-record attitude is a clue to the impatience which leads into the dangers of short-cutting and God-playing identified earlier. But records and returns there must be. Any organisation which claims to do without them is also claiming that it doesn't know what its welfare officers do, how they are doing it or indeed whether they are doing it at all—and doesn't care sufficiently to find out. In such organisations we will find amateurism and weak sentimentality based on vague objectives, instead of the more astringent insight and understanding which characterises the real professional whose purpose is clearly thought out.

In the last chapter we were concerned with information *for* the welfare officer, as a linking topic between his training and the control of his activities. Although the emphasis is now on information *from* him, one must not lose sight of the fact that records and returns provide him with information about the people he deals with and about the state of his work generally, quite as much as they provide 'control' information for those higher in the chain of welfare command. They are indeed instruments by means of which he exercises control over his *own* activities; and self-control is much to be preferred to control from above. Because of this, records and returns are best regarded as aids—to the welfare officer himself, and through him to the individual needing help, as well as aids to his colleagues and those senior to him.

Thus there are many good reasons for having an efficient system of records and returns. The most important are as follows:

1. An aid to careful thinking and to the adoption of common standards, classifications, and criteria.

2. An aid for the welfare officer and, through him, the individual being helped. The inefficiency of the human memory system has already received comment, and it is quite essential that facts should go on the record. Once there they do not have to be sought again.

3. An aid for the colleague who may take over the task of helping an individual transferred to a different part of the organisation or who may 'stand in' during sick or holiday absence.

4. An aid to the welfare supervisor and the central welfare organisation, who must watch area and national trends because of their influence on general and training policy, in particular their periodic validation and evaluation.

5. An aid to those who have the task of matching complements to the demand for welfare officer service. This is frequently the local welfare supervisor, in his role of sharing work within his team, but also the central personnel representative who may have power to lapse or create posts.

What is a Case?

If 'cases' have to be classified and recorded, what is a case? How, for example, is a case to be differentiated from a casual enquiry? This is the first question to be asked and answered if the welfare officer and those who control his activities want to know how he is spending his time. Both should be concerned to know that as much as possible of the time available is being used on work which really does need a specialist. The distinction between cases and casual enquiries is thus an essential one. It would be absurd to give every request for information, answerable in minutes, the same weight as a real case needing perhaps hours. For some welfare officers who serve staff spread out over a wide geographical area, or whose office is a little out of centre of the population, casual enquiries are reduced simply by physical absence, and work connected with them is not onerous. But for others, who may be located in and serve only or mainly staff in a large building (and who are therefore physically present most of the time), casual enquiries may take up a considerable part of the working day. This is not to say that all such enquiries are proper to be dealt with by welfare officers; but if they in fact deal with them, or even only receive them and then channel them elsewhere, the time necessary to do so must be taken into account when work is allocated or when loads are

examined for complementing purposes. Indeed, an unduly high proportion of casual enquiries might reveal the need for supervisor
training rather than for an additional welfare officer. One should not
use specialists on work which non-specialists are capable of doing.

Analysis of work will usually reveal that most *real* enquiries or
requests for factual information normally take no more than 20
minutes to deal with. *Time taken* is therefore one workable criterion
to distinguish them from cases, and 30 minutes provides an ample
safety margin. Those 'enquiries' which take longer are usually symptomatic of the individual's wanting to come to the point of his visit
after 'trying the welfare officer out' (for sympathy, efficiency, knowledge, etc.) or to pluck up courage to tell the whole story. On the
other hand, many real *cases* may initially take less than 20 minutes—
but they are judged to be likely to recur or to need a follow-up check;
or will involve the welfare officer in subsequent work, such as information from or consultation with another member of the organisation or
an outside agency.

These considerations imply three criteria of a 'case', now defined
as 'any problem, irrespective of source, which: (a) takes at least 30
minutes to deal with; or, irrespective of initial time, (b) is likely to
recur or require follow-up check; or, irrespective of initial time, (c)
will involve information from or consultation with a third party.'

These are to an extent arbitrary criteria, but have been found easy
to apply in practice. In practice, it is rarely necessary to record the
details of enquiries. It may be useful on occasions to keep a stroke
record of the number for the monthly return, but a fine analysis will
only be required when the weight of enquiries is such that inadequate
line supervision or some other similar cause is suspected. It will
become clear when we deal with the machinery of records how such a
fine analysis could be made.

New and Continuing Cases

Just as cases must be differentiated from enquiries, any system of
records and returns must also distinguish new cases dealt with during
the period under review from continuing cases 'brought forward'
from the previous period. This is a central element in self-discipline,
since the explicit recognition of the pressure of new cases is an
incentive to conclude the old ones. If cases continue too long, and
become 'welfare ghosts', the welfare officer must ask himself whether
his disengagement technique is becoming blunt or whether they con-

tinue because of his own interest in them rather than the interests of
the individuals in need. The definition of a continuing case is thus a
very simple one—'any problem recorded in the previous return which
is not concluded and has led to welfare officer activity in the current
period'.

Classification of Casework

The time of a welfare officer will be apportioned between:
(a) personal welfare 'casework' and casual enquiries;
(b) physical and group welfare 'casework' and casual enquiries;
(c) travelling on duty;
(d) miscellaneous activities such as conferences, meetings, training
courses and sick and holiday absence.

It is essential to have a heading for travelling on duty, since the location of groups of staff served will be an important factor in complementing, whereas 'miscellaneous activities' should be broadly the
same irrespective of location.

The classification of physical and group welfare presents no difficulties and the headings which one would expect to find on a monthly
return of work have already been used as headings in Chapters 6 and
7. Similarly, classification of personal casework was foreshadowed in
Chapter 4. This classification must be a little more arbitrary; it is at
least much more difficult. It is not always possible to judge at the outset whether an individual problem is mainly financial, mainly accommodation, or mainly ill health. It could well be a blend of these; and
even after helping with the problem to a final solution, the welfare
officer might be hard put to decide on the classification. But this is by
no means a crucial consideration. The purpose of case records at local
level is to provide a history and an aide-memoire *to help a person*, and
to help him irrespective of how his problem is to be classified. At area
or national level the purpose of records is to enable trends to be
followed—and occasional misclassifications will tend to cancel each
other out. If the welfare supervisor sees that one of his team seems to
be getting an undue proportion of one class of problem, he will
want to know why. There may be a valid reason, which in itself
would throw up interesting lines of further enquiry, or he may find
that persistent misclassification is the answer. If it is, the supervisor has identified the need for training in the form of personal
coaching.

There is no reason at all why the criteria offered for the definition of a case should not be applied equally to personal, physical and group welfare if one really needed sound measures of the proportion of time spent on each. There should be little head-scratching over how to record time actually spent on First Aid, Benevolent Funds or Hostels. However, a great deal of physical and group welfare 'contact' work can be done most economically and conveniently in the course of visits connected with personal casework. Similarly, a long discussion with a manager may range over several aspects of physical, group and/or personal case work. 'Contact' work is simply oil in the social machine, and meetings with managers, unless related to highly specific personal or other problems, are best classified under 'meetings and conferences'.

Local Records

Now that the preliminary 'criteria' work is cleared away, thought can be given to the actual machinery of 'recording and returning'. Since we are looking at records and returns as aids rather than controls it is better to start at the person-to-person end—what is needed by the welfare officer in the face-to-face situation. Starting from the other end of the scale could just possibly lead to the collection by the central organisation of facts and figures for their own sake. Thus we start from written notes of one sort or another. Perhaps the first thing to recognise is that it is an assumption of omniscience or infallible memory, as well as more than a little patronising to a person in trouble, to assume that the only reminder one needs of his problem is a few scribbled words in a diary or on an odd scrap of paper. Diaries and odd scraps are quite 'out' for note-taking, save in emergencies.

We are not concerned with personal diaries. They are quite another matter, and the welfare officer can put in them whatsoever he likes—except the details of the personal cases he deals with. It is the office or desk diary, so frequently abused as a notebook, which is often the enemy of a good record system. Desk diaries should be used for what they are designed—appointments, visits, forward reminders of follow-up and other action. And they should be non-confidential, kept where anyone—supervisor, colleague or clerical assistant—with a right to know where the welfare officer is likely to be found can consult them freely. Diaries are valueless to these people if kept under lock and key, or carried around on visits doing a job which the pocket diary should be doing. Thus the open nature of the office diary rules it out as a working note-book; and scraps of paper are easily lost, with subse-

quent risk of loss of confidentiality. What is clearly needed is a pur-
pose-designed working notebook.

The Daybook

Lovers of language will not fail to appreciate that a diary has a limited
and specific use, because we have brought words almost identical in
basic meaning to describe similar but different uses. 'Journal' has
long since ceased to have the 'daily' connotation, but 'daybook' still
has, and could not possibly lose it. Daybooks are common in the
C.A.B.s and some other social casework agencies, police forces, etc.
The hallmark of the daybook is that it has prepared headings for the
special needs of the organisation concerned. If these are chosen with
care they are invaluable time-savers when information has to be
extracted for the monthly return. Further, prepared headings clear
the path for the use of codes or symbols, which reduce the amount of
physical writing in the daybook. Those who seek to 'save time' by
using diaries or odd sheets of paper would no doubt be surprised if
they did a word count and found out how much time was in fact being
wasted by using the wrong instrument for the job.

There is no need for even the largest organisation to go to the
trouble of having daybooks specially printed and bound. Printing can
reduce to a minimum the proportion of space taken up by headings,
but 'petit-roman' typed headings on duplicated sheets for a standard
loose-leaf binder are all that is required. Quarto size is probably the
most convenient, balancing the advantages of portability and maximum proportion of writing space, and using the sheets lengthwise to
clear the binding rings when writing. Completed sheets are then taken
out and filed elsewhere when the summaries for the monthly return
are made out. This is of course 'completed' in the real sense of finished
with, not in the sense of 'filled in'; one must keep a close check on
one's continuing cases and bring the diary into use for follow-up reminders. This is done with no loss of confidentiality—no name in the
diary, just the daybook serial number entered on the day the follow-
up is to be made. An example of a daybook sheet is given below,
followed by some notes on the use of codes as time and space saving
devices. Column rulings should be quite bold, but horizontal rulings
very faint indeed—if required at all.

Col. 1 gives the serial number of the case, each being recorded con-
secutively, from the beginning of the calendar (or financial) year if

TABLE TWO

No. 1	Date 2	Name 3	Location 4	Source 5	Grade 6	N/C 7	Category 8	Notes 9

for annual reports, or in $1/1$ ... $n/1$, $1/12$ ... $n/12$ form if monthly
totals are required.

Col. 4 gives the location, often codable for office, factory, group,
section, shop, etc., of the individual in need of help.

Col. 5 gives the source of the case—the route by which the individual
has come to the welfare officer—and can be coded, e.g.

P   personal direct approach.

M   referred by manager or supervisor.

T   referred by trade union.

O   referred by outside agency or other means.

This information is useful from many points of view. The welfare
officer and others in the chain of command will wish to know how far
managers, unions and outside agencies are making use of the service.
It also discloses differences in attitude between managers. If the pro-
portions are too high or too low, if there is anything unusual about the
figures, these are items of 'control information' which serve as pointers
to action.

Col. 6 can also be coded—general categories such as J for juvenile, R
for retired and D for dependants (widows, etc.) as well as the grades
in which staff are employed.

Col. 7 is for the identification of N = *New* or C = *Continuing* cases.

Col. 8 provides for the final classification of the case, also coded by the
number of the category of personal, physical or group welfare problem
which represents the main element. These numbers will correspond
with those of the monthly summary (see Col. 1 of Table 3, pp. 236–7).

Col. 9 This column for 'Notes' may appear cramped, but notes on
the problem may of course be extended to other columns as long as
spaces are left to make the previous and subsequent entries in them
stand out clearly.

Index or Facing Sheets

The next step in the recording machinery is a sheet of thin card for
detailed notes on 'continuing' cases and/or as a facing sheet for filing
reports and correspondence on particular cases. When such a card is
started, the code F (file) should be entered alongside the serial number
in Column 1 of the daybook, as an indication to the duty welfare
officer or whoever may be standing in for him that further details have
gone into the filing system. He will then use the file for recording new
material, thus avoiding scattered notes in various parts of the daybook. However, a very brief daybook entry is required each time a

continuing case is dealt with—otherwise it might not show up in the monthly return. All that is necessary is a new serial number and the name of the individual, with the original serial number in Column 9 (Notes). There is no particular reason for any daybook serial numbers to appear on the card, unless cross-checks are required, since the daybook provides two other more useful means of entrée to the filing system. If the welfare officer serves staff in one location only, the file can be in alphabetical order of surnames; but if he serves staff in several small sites it may be more convenient to file surnames alphabetically *within* location groups, also alphabetical. He can then take all relevant case notes with him when he visits each location.

The Monthly Summary Return

Why monthly? Those who consider records and summaries a chore will argue that quarterly is quite enough, but this is a doubtful proposition. In the first place, quarterly returns obscure seasonal trends, particularly in sick absence. It is well worthwhile knowing, for example, where the peaks and troughs of personal casework fall, so that training courses and conferences may take place in the least busy times—a purely practical consideration. And when the evaluation review of welfare policy takes place, the correlations between use of the welfare officer service (broken down into direct, via management and via trade union use) and other variables such as sick absence and casual absenteeism may provide highly significant information. Secondly, one does not reduce a chore by putting it off for a couple of months; one merely finds that the task takes three times as long as it would have done. An experienced welfare officer can make out his monthly return from his daybook in under an hour, and it is a very busy man who cannot find this much time. It is far less easy to find two or three hours—approaching half a day's work.

The summary form sketched out as Table 3 is in four parts. Part A, Personal Welfare, is based on the daybook sheet already discussed and provides for numerical totals of the main categories of personal casework according to source and a cross-check in terms of grades of staff employed. Very fine subdivisions would be required if anyone expressed interest in a question like 'How many clerks approached the welfare officer through trade union representatives about new bereavement problems during February?' Such questions are so unlikely that the multidimensional analysis form required to answer them would be a large steam hammer for a very rare nut. But it is clearly important to know what type of personal casework is coming from which grades of staff. This is a hardy annual of control information, a question asked as frequently as another—how far managers and supervisors are making use of the service for their staff. The form must be designed on the basis of what questions are likely to be asked, but even more important than this, what value the answer would have. That is, is it a *productive* question the answer to which can lead to remedial action, or is it simply the sort of question people like to ask until somebody points out that the answer, though correct, would take them no further? Thus, the incidence of *new* cases of sickness coming through union channels can tell us something about the quality of the executive control of sick absence—or the lack of it. The number of *continuing* financial cases in a firm with security problems would also be of some interest. The N (= new) and C (= continuing) subdivision of the four sources can therefore be worthwhile, although the grand totals of these two, irrespective of source, may be sufficient.

Part B provides a place to summarise group and physical welfare activities, but in far less detail. 'Grades' are clearly irrelevant but, 'source' may not be. The 'source' breakdown in Part A can therefore be used in Part B if the need exists; but in practice it is usually found that a brief note of the major commitments during the month, and an assessment of time taken by them, are sufficient. Any special analyses which may be required from time to time can be taken straight from the daybook in whatever form best answers the questions which have been posed.

Part C needs little comment. It provides for the welfare officer's more subjective analysis of the trends of the month, his highlighting of particular events, his drawing attention to problems better dealt with by his supervisor (e.g. excessive load of enquiries which should be going to others), his comparisons with last month or with the same month of the previous year. In short, he can spread himself as far as he wishes, and show how far he is on top of his work—or vice versa.

Part D, for Miscellaneous Information, can be useful in many ways. It can provide a central point for various items of general control information which might be scattered elsewhere (e.g. annual and sick leave taken, car mileage travelled on duty) as well as more specific information concerning aspects of casework (e.g. the number of visits to private homes, to hospitals, and to the firm's other locations, the number of references to outside bodies) which might be under review from time to time.

TABLE THREE

Welfare Officer Activities

A Personal Welfare

CATEGORY	SOURCE													
	Direct		Manage-ment		Trade Union		Other		TOTAL					
	N	C	N	C	N	C	N	C	N	C				
1 Domestic														
2 Financial														
3 Sickness														
4 Bereave-ment														
5 Living Accom.														
6 Employ-ment														
7 Retire-ment/ Resig.														
8 Misc.														
TOTAL														

B Group and Physical Welfare

9 First Aid	
10 Sports and Social Clubs	
11 Benevolent Orgns.	
12 Retired Staff	
13 General Physical Conditions	
14 Safety	
15 Housing, Hostels, Lodgings	
16 Welfare in Training Courses	

C Trend Reports and General Remarks (*please continue overleaf*)

asework Summary and Analysis for period_____

ffice_____

GRADES OF STAFF

										Juvenile	Retired	Dependant	D Miscellaneous Information	
													New Cases	
													Continuing Cases	
													Visits— Homes	
													Hospitals	
													Ref. to Outside Bodies	
													Holidays	
													Sick Absence	
													Car Miles	
													Meetings/ Conferences	
													Training	

Signature:

.... 196....

Retention or Destruction of Records

Unlike daybook sheets and index cards, monthly summary sheets are quite impersonal, anonymous and statistical. They do not need the seal of confidentiality (unless the welfare officer has spread himself too far in his trend report). They are part of the general personnel records and statistics system and should be preserved (carbon copy to welfare supervisor, photocopies if others are required for local managers or central welfare organisation). Their final destiny is the organisation's archives.

But daybook sheets and index cards should be destroyed when they have served their purpose. It would be quite intolerable for anything in the nature of 'personal dossiers' to be built up for reference by anyone inside or outside the welfare line of command. Tempting as it might be to keep on file one's 'difficult' cases for the background information they supply if the individual comes with a fresh problem, one must resist it. People can change a lot in the course of two or three years and the welfare officer should not look at a new problem in the blinkers provided by the old one. Save in rare instances when very long-term follow-up is clearly necessary, one could question the need to keep any daybook sheet or index card longer than one year after the case was completed.

Note on analysis of enquiries

Many welfare officers will prefer to enter *all* enquiries in the daybook along with cases—because one often cannot tell at the outset whether one or other of the three criteria of a 'case' will be met. Once satisfied that one really has dealt with an enquiry and not a case, the prefix E is inserted in Column 8 (Category) of the daybook to distinguish the entry from case entries. Thus E 6 will denote a personal welfare *enquiry* about employment, E 9 a group welfare enquiry about First Aid. If a fine analysis of enquiries is required, *two* summary sheets are made out at the end of the month—one for cases and one for enquiries—taking care that each sheet is correctly labelled. Local or central statistics could be vitiated if the wrong set of figures were incorporated!

Summary   Careful attention to the practical detail of working methods will reap good dividends. The welfare officer will need an efficient system of *information files,* including card indexes of internal group welfare and external organisations with which he deals, and he must keep them up to date. He must ensure the provision of adequate *telephone answering* arrangements at work, but he should not advertise his home number. *Correspondence and typing* need special care: headed paper should be provided, but even then a 'signature description' is necessary; he needs to be able to type himself if he cannot have the services of a part-time confidential typist. Some other *clerical assistance* is also required, and this might provide useful 'on-the-job' training for a welfare officer 'cadet' or assistant. The needs of the job he is doing will dictate what *accommodation* is necessary. The welfare officer must learn to *take notes* during an interview with unobtrusive skill, or get his facts on paper immediately afterwards when circumstances preclude note-taking in the face-to-face situation. He must plan his *travelling and appointments* with foresight; for his time, and that of the individuals he serves, is valuable.

As analysis of the job led through selection to training, and training led through information to records and returns, so we go naturally on to work methods. Records and returns are in fact so much part and parcel of methods that we can complete in the new context a point started in the old—the destruction of records when they have served their purpose. Methodical and regular weeding is much to be preferred to irregular purges on the rare occasions when 'business' is slack. The 'paired month' system has a lot to commend it, since it can be operated when the monthly summary sheet is made out. On this basis, records for the same month of the previous year are examined and thinned, leaving only those few cases which are still incomplete or which await long-term follow up. These are then transferred to a special file and action reminders noted in the office diary.

Local Information Files

The same rotation principle can be applied to the upkeep of local information files, of which the welfare officer may need more than one. He will certainly need a card index of all the internal group welfare organisations, giving names, addresses and telephone numbers of chairmen, secretaries and other officers of sports and social clubs and benevolent organisations. He will need a similar index of staff of statutory, local authority and voluntary services in the locality—and nationally where required (see *Social Welfare Directories and How to Prepare them*, N.C.S.S., 1966). Indexing should of course be alphabetical by name of organisations, not individuals; names of people-in-posts change frequently, names of organisations only rarely. These index cards should also be noted with any relevant points of policy or practice stated in the annual reports and other publications of the bodies concerned, or learned about them in any other way. There is no need for lengthy extracts. 'See page 9, annual report 19..' is a sufficient reminder that there is a point to be checked before writing the letter or making the telephone call. As with records and returns, the welfare officer should develop the habit of glancing over his shoulder at the needs of the man who may take his place, either temporarily or permanently, and jot down any point which will save time, oil the social wheels or otherwise advance the interests of the individual in need. What is second nature to the experienced occupant of the post may not be so apparent to his stand-in or successor.

The second type of local file contains more general information. It may be quite separate, but for preference the 'organisation indexes' are part of the whole: for example, part of an overall decimal classification or similar system in common use by all the welfare staff in the organisation. Possible major headings come readily to mind—Physical, Group, Personal, Liaison with Outside Organisations, Welfare Training, Information Papers and Newsletters, Conferences and Meetings, etc. Minor sub-headings are then developed as necessary (e.g. the lists of personal, group and physical welfare categories on the monthly summary form). The great advantage of the decimal type of classification system is that it can be expanded indefinitely once the major headings are settled, and cross-referencing is a simple matter. But advantages also carry disadvantages: the major headings have to be very carefully chosen to stand the test of time, and there is no built-in limit to the mass of paper which can accumulate. One has to build it oneself by the rotation system of weeding. One takes out a major or minor file each month and thins it as rapidly and ruthlessly as possible, avoiding the terrible temptation—akin to finding old newspapers in a box-room or under linoleum—of browsing over the past.

Warnings over the accumulation of paper may leave the unfortunate impression that the welfare officer must spend a good proportion of his time in keeping it in order. He must not, since he is not employed as a clerk or librarian. Every 'office' job carries its own irreducible personal clerical load, but this minimum should decrease as the specialist or technical content rises. A welfare officer will have an 'irreducible personal clerical load', but he needs a measure of clerical-level support to keep it at minimum. However, the need is so rarely for a full-time clerk that the main difficulty is finding ways and means of arranging such support on an economic basis. Since filing and weeding are not the only clerical jobs to be done it is worthwhile keeping the problem in abeyance until two other aspects of office methods have been examined.

Telephones

There are two telephone problems, one 'official' and one personal. If the welfare officer's 'official' telephone number is advertised (as it should be to cut down nugatory personal visits to his office), then it follows that someone must be available to answer it when he is out. This does not mean relying on the good nature of the occupant of the next room who may sometimes hear the bell when both windows are open. Ideally it means the special designation of somebody whose duty it is to take messages, consult the diary and generally make it clear to the caller that he is being attended to. A simple extension system with secrecy on the main telephone is therefore the best solution, and the G.P.O. will always advise on the most appropriate method. Other possibilities are automatic answering and recording devices, switchboard interception or alternative numbers. The first may be thought a little inhuman for the welfare context, and the other two are usually considerably more costly in staff time than the installation of an extension.

Although it is clearly necessary to make the best possible arrangements according to local circumstances for receipt of telephone calls during working hours, there is surely no case whatever for making use of the welfare officer's private telephone at home. On the contrary, there is something wrong with the attitude of the occupational welfare officer who on his own initiative has his private telephone number printed on a visiting card and encourages individuals in need of his services to use it. It is almost better to go to the other extreme and be 'ex-directory', since staff who feel they really must make contact in private time will probably get the number from the book anyway. Those wanting help who 'declare a state of emergency' would be far better off dialling 999, the Samaritans (see Varah, 1965) or other '24-hour' general community services. If there is no real emergency the problem can wait until the morning anyway. There is also something wrong with the attitudes of the managers of a commercial or industrial organisation who ask the welfare officer to make himself available out of normal hours in this way—availability quite different from the clear need of the welfare officer to do a limited amount of work on *current* cases when contact is possible only in the evenings. No welfare officer in industry or commerce should be expected to be 'on tap' all round the clock, and it is no part of the responsibility of industry or commerce to provide such a service in competition with general community emergency services. Readers so far unconverted to an unsentimental approach to staff welfare may raise an eyebrow at this apparently hard doctrine, but the lines have to be drawn—and this is one of them. We are talking about people who have an essentially different role from those in the statutory services. The fact that Mental Welfare Officers often have their private telephone advertised is neither here nor there. In such cases the M.W.O. *works* from his home base, his work load is organised quite differently and he has different conditions of service.

Correspondence and Typing

As with telephones, little can be said about correspondence and typing which is not already enjoined by common sense. The points are obvious, but it is the obvious which we frequently overlook. For example, an organisation willing to employ a welfare officer should not cavil at supplying him with special headed writing paper or an overprinted version of the firm's standard paper. It is essential that the recipient should have no room for doubt about the identity of the writer. Special headed paper, though necessary, is thus insufficient; it is just as important to type in a signature description:

Yours sincerely,

J. Jones,
Welfare Officer, Bloggs and Son Ltd.

In case it should be felt that this is overdoing it, one may point out: first, that we do not always read the printed headings of writing paper until we want to reply, but we all have an immediate interest in the signature; and second, that other internal organisations (e.g. sports and social clubs, benevolent funds) may use the standard paper or an overprinted version of it. It is not unknown for John Jones the welfare officer to get correspondence destined for Jim Jones the trade union welfare secretary, or vice versa, and this can lead to loss of confidentiality as well as to confusion.

Except for very brief notes of an ephemeral nature, all correspondence to individuals in need, as well as to organisations, should be typed with a carbon copy; there is something absurdly antiquated and unbusinesslike about long manuscript letters on 'official' paper. There has been controversy even over this very simple point. Some 'manuscripters' hold that typescript is inevitably cold and impersonal and thus militates against the development of a personal relationship. They say they would not 'insult' a personal friend with a typed letter and argue that individuals in need of help should be dealt with on a similar friendly basis. But this logic seems faulty on two counts. First, one wonders how many personal friends would in fact be 'insulted' by typescript and how many would on the contrary be pleased to be relieved of the trouble of reading one's execrable handwriting. Second, a personal relationship with a friend is a different matter from a friendly relationship with a person.

If self-typing is not possible, the welfare officer must have the services of a confidential typist, chosen for discretion rather than for seniority or technical skill. In these days, when we seem to treat typists as goldfish and put them in 'pools', this may be much easier said than done. The welfare officer is often forced into the position of having to hawk his work around the secretaries of various managers.

Clerical Assistance
The need for help with filing and file-weeding, telephone answering and typing may indicate that the ideal solution is a part-time secre-

tary. Where several welfare officers operate from the same building (by no means uncommon in large organisations) there is almost certainly a case for one full-time post to serve them on a shared basis. In other circumstances the load may be made up by sharing assistance with others having similar needs: there are almost certainly junior managers who cannot justify a full-time assistant. However, 'secretaries' are in short supply, and it should be pointed out that the only really *skilled* assistance required is with typing. Telephone answering does not save the welfare officer's time; it saves other people's. Filing assistance does save time, but any good clerk can do it at a cost of a couple of hours a week. But is any time saved when the welfare officer dictates or prepares a manuscript draft for the typist? Once the negative answer is recognised, alternative approaches present themselves.

One feels that the best one—although long-term for the community generally—is for typing to come to be regarded as a useful practical skill of the same kind as the ability to drive a car. In the shorter term, welfare officers, who have a special problem arising from the confidential nature of their work, might blaze the trail and acquire typing skill. The job has to be done properly if it is to be done at all; two-finger 'hunting and pecking' can never lead to speed and accuracy. But with self-discipline it is by no means difficult to learn touch-typing on a do-it-yourself basis from special texts. Even better, it is probably very much in the firm's interests to arrange for intensive part-time courses for welfare officers and others with similar needs. It should not take many hours to produce a good and sufficient level of speed and accuracy, since the full range of work of the professional typist (tabulation, audio tape, etc.) need not be taught. If the welfare officer is really too old to learn a fine manual skill, one could look to the future and make typing part of the training of assistants employed in a sort of welfare-officer-cadet capacity. One may thus encourage younger people whose age may militate against their being selected as welfare officers in a firm which reckons to 'grow its own' rather than recruit from outside. Such cadets could not only take on the full range of clerical assistance but could also be entrusted with routine enquiries and correspondence (e.g. preparation of 'contact' letters to sick absentees) which do not call for the skill of the experienced welfare officer.

We tend too much to assume that typing skill is rather low-level—exclusive to young girls who come up the secondary modern stream—but the spread of comprehensive education may slowly change this pattern of thinking. Typing may in future be regarded as part of one's comprehensive education in another sense. This may be a long way ahead, but it may not be so long before it is recognised as an essential part of the training of all social workers. If training time is at a premium one could argue with some force that typing is more practically useful than some of the areas of academic knowledge now regarded as essential.

Accommodation

The size, style and furnishing of offices, particularly in the larger organisations, is often so bound up with status that accommodation for the welfare officer can be a very delicate matter. In the chapter on Analysing the Job, it was suggested that the salary of the basic-grade welfare officer should be comparable with that of any other basic-grade personnel officer dealing with safety, training, wages, negotiation, or other subdivisions. It would be unusual, especially with the growing trend towards 'open-plan' offices, for any of these people to have separate rooms. One must not indulge in special pleading for the welfare officer as a person. He has no greater claim to privacy than anyone else at his level in the organisation, but this is looking at the problem from the wrong point of view. The type of accommodation provided should be based on the needs of individuals seeking his help. His own are incidental except in so far as they relate to the needs of the staff he serves. From this point of view a private interviewing room is essential, and there are clear advantages in giving the welfare officer a room to himself. If this is not possible, access to an interviewing room at recognised periods of the day is the minimum. It should not be difficult, for example, to allocate the mornings to the welfare officer and the afternoons to someone else, part of whose work also requires privacy. If this is the case, the times should be strictly adhered to so that they may be advertised on notice boards, and privacy should be made even more certain by a red/green light or similar warning system which keeps casual callers away when the room is in use. Such a warning system is desirable even when the welfare officer has a room to himself.

Looking at the accommodation problem from the 'customer' point of view enables one to identify several other requirements. First, callers should not be expected to walk through large open-plan offices and thus expose themselves to the curious as people needing help. A small room slightly away from the centre of population is far better, and has the additional advantage of reducing the number of casual visitors—who would be more inclined to telephone for an appointment if they had to walk a hundred yards or so. Second, the room should not be overlooked; if it is, blinds provide the answer. Third, particularly when the office is on the periphery, there should be mats for wet shoes, pegs and hangers for outdoor clothes—and an umbrella stand. Simple things, and it is the simple things which make the difference. Fourth, to generalise from this, the room should be comfortable and welcoming but yet give an impression of business and efficiency. One should err neither in the direction of chintzy chumminess nor in the direction of soulless rows of filing cabinets. The fifth point is one which has already been mentioned in another context—the chair in which the visitor will sit. 'Putting the visitor at ease' does *not* mean putting him in a deep armchair from which he has to *look up* to the welfare officer. The other context mentioned the 'one-down' position of the individual needing help; one does not want to emphasise this physically. Similarly, one should not force the visitor to look at the welfare officer silhouetted against the light; expressions on the latter's face are as important to the visitor as are the visitor's to the welfare officer. One is aiming at a practical man-to-man situation, and neither party should be at a disadvantage.

Taking Notes

If anyone is at a disadvantage in the practical man-to-man situation it may well be the welfare officer. It is more difficult to listen than to talk, it is even more difficult to remember what one has heard without distorting it (see Sidney and Brown, 1961), and it is more difficult still to get the bones of the story on paper. Most difficult of all is to take notes in the other's presence so naturally, so openly and yet so skilfully that he is hardly conscious that you are doing it. This is a hardy annual of all training in interviewing, whether for selection, vocational guidance or any other purpose where the exchange of facts is essential. There are of course differences of opinion about it, some claiming that if attention is to be undivided notetaking is impossible. But one thing seems quite certain. It is not the notetaking—or lack of notetaking—itself which causes trouble, but the manner of doing it or not doing it. It may seem surprising that *not* taking notes can cause trouble, but 'Aren't you going to write anything down?' is by no means an uncommon reaction to what one thought was undivided attention but what has been interpreted as lack of interest or plain boredom. If the daybook is ready, open on the desk, this is a reaction which could be turned to advantage—'Yes, I must; I was so engrossed' or 'I like to hear the whole story first'. On the other hand, if one had to fish the daybook out of the drawer, the *real* answer to such a question can only be 'Yes, if you insist', and will be so registered, irrespective of the words actually used.

If one wanted to go into the 'Ten Golden Rules' business (tempting, but golden rules about dealing with people, who are infinitely variable, are a trap for the unwary), the first is probably Be Ready to Take Notes—even if you don't intend to; you cannot otherwise be unobtrusive about it when you do intend to. Rule number two may well be Never be Apologetic about it. Questions like 'You don't mind if I take some notes, do you?' are most unfair. They expect No for an answer and therefore usually get it, whatever the feelings of the individual may be. And what precisely does one say to the bold spirit who replies 'Yes, I do mind'? A brisk 'Right, we'll manage without' is a little difficult after an apologetic opening gambit, and bold spirit asks himself (or you) why you couldn't manage without notes in the first place. Anyone can guess rule number three as a logical extension —Take Consent for Granted ('I'll jot down a few points') unless one's first impression of the interviewee is that he is angry, hostile or suspicious. If challenged, by a look or a pause if not by words, one must be quite honest about it. 'I'm here to try to help you if I can and have to get the facts straight', or similar implicit recognition of the fallibility of memory should be quite sufficient. If it is not, the chances are that one is dealing with a character whose suspicion borders on the paranoid or is burdened with either well-merited or neurotic guilt. In any event, resistance to notetaking is a warning light, must be seen as such and the issue must not be forced.

The welfare officer himself must be the final judge of the situation he has to deal with, not seeking golden rules but finding guidelines for his own behaviour. Some of these are in the early discussion of confidentiality (Chapter 3), in the mention of the receptionist (at the beginning of Chapter 16), and elsewhere. If attitude is right and good manners are paramount one cannot go far wrong. For example, one cannot then rap out 'Name, Age, Address', etc., as a start for an interview. One gets information of this sort as one goes along, or at the end, when the need for further action has become apparent. It is of course important to remember that one cannot get *everything* down on paper during the interview; to try is to reduce too much one's attention to what is being said and *how* it is being said. One very firm rule is to complete notes immediately after the individual has left, before any distortion of memory creeps in. Similarly, there will be occasions, when interviewing outside the office, when it is hardly possible to take notes at all. The welfare officer sometimes has to take the individual aside from his work, to a quiet spot—perhaps even an outside café—to ensure privacy. In such circumstances the production of the daybook would be an intrusion, and all notes have to be made afterwards, but they have to be made *immediately* afterwards.

Travelling and Appointments

Even those welfare officers who serve only the staff of one large unit will spend a considerable time out of their offices, but in these circumstances travelling is an incidental problem. Those serving several scattered units must give a good deal of attention to *planning* travelling. No longer incidental, it is a core problem demanding specific techniques for making the best use of time. Some of these are: zoning areas better reached by public transport than by car; arranging circular car journeys instead of a series of out-and-return trips; spacing or concentrating appointments according to location; ensuring that small units are not neglected from the group welfare point of view when there are no personal cases on hand to 'justify' visits to them; arranging to be at different locations on regular days of the week. It is not an easy matter; regular days at different places, for example, will raise awkward accommodation problems. We shall see when we come to discuss complements that a careful balance has to be struck between using one welfare officer, much of whose time is 'dead' travelling, and two people with less need to travel who may both then be underloaded. The economics of paying the fares of a member of staff to visit the welfare officer (once the need to do so is firmly established) compared with car travel by the welfare officer to visit him, must also be taken into account. This is not simply a question of comparative travel costs; it is a question of comparative wage or salary costs as well. The main thing is to avoid the *a priori* assumption that it is always the welfare officer who makes the journey.

One can do little more than indicate the problems of making the best use of time. Their solution by specific techniques depends upon so many local factors that it would be fruitless to suggest any principles beyond the application of a simple work-study approach—the analytical and questioning approach which takes nothing for granted. This may be exemplified by looking at the appointments problem, particularly as relevant research evidence is available. The use of hindsight, *after* research findings are published, makes us realise how odd it is that many doctors, hospitals and other social agencies have taken it for granted, year after year after year, that one should announce hours of availability and then work on a first come, first served, basis. There is little excuse for hospitals and other agencies which employ non-professional supporting staff and which thus have the facilities to offer firm appointments.

In 1958 the Ministry of Health suggested that, when patients had appointments in out-patient departments of hospitals, 75 per cent should not have to wait more than half an hour; and only three per cent should have to wait over an hour. Yet in 1963/64 a Nuffield study team visiting 60 hospitals found that 49 of them were *below* the Ministry's standard and only 11 succeeded in reaching it. The *average* waiting time was 25 minutes; 11 per cent of patients waited over one hour, 34 per cent over half an hour. The two main causes of delay were late arrival of doctors, and underestimation of the time required by each patient (Nuffield Provincial Hospitals Trust, 1965).

Industry and commerce should not tolerate a situation where staff are queuing up to see the welfare officer, in a waiting room or any-where else. It is too costly a situation, it is a situation which breeds rumours about why so-and-so has gone to see him, and, most impor-tant, it is a situation destructive of human dignity. Welfare officers could learn much from the apparent failure of many hospitals, and design simple appointment systems that work. This means that although specified hours of availability might be advertised on notice boards they should not be so limited that waits are almost inevitable; and it means that 'dropping in' without an appointment or prior telephone call should be discouraged.

One final point while we are on the medical analogy. No occupa-tional welfare officer should think it natural to use the term 'surgery times' when referring to his advertised hours of availability. If others start using it he should make discouraging noises. If he uses it himself he should be sent off for refresher training. He needs it badly if he has begun to regard himself as a medical *manqué*.

18 Complementing and Controlling

Summary   One must decide how many welfare officers are required in a firm of given size. Some clues may be found in an analogy with medical G.P.s, but the basic criteria are level of staff and the location of both staff and welfare officers. The small firm may manage with a general-purpose personnel officer, provided he has been trained in occupational welfare work and has no executive responsibilities; but joint schemes between firms, which can employ experts whole-time on welfare, are a better proposition. In the larger firm, complements cannot be determined until one welfare officer has established the need by providing the evidence of his records and returns. The accuracy of complementing will depend on the sophistication of the 'yardsticks' which are evolved. Welfare supervision and control may be wholly specialist in the large organisation or wholly non-specialist in the smaller one. 'Welfare appreciation' courses are required for non-specialist supervisors and controllers. Full-time active and participatory specialist supervision is needed when two or three welfare officers are employed; a second 'tier' of technical supervision is needed for a team of about six to eight welfare officers; and three technical levels are required in the really large-scale organisations. The basic techniques of welfare supervision and control are subjective assessments, direct observation and analysis of records and returns. All three are necessary, but the hard facts represented by the third are essential.

How Many Welfare Officers?

Although the use of the phrase 'surgery times' has been rejected, opinions on the optimum size of a G.P.'s list are as good a starting point as any to try to answer a very important question: how many employees can a welfare officer serve? Or, in another form: how many welfare officers should a firm of given size have? The G.P.'s position is not too dissimilar from the welfare officer's to rule out the analogy, and providing we do not push it too far we may get some clues from it. The similarity rests in the fact that the G.P.'s list contains a great many people who may never see him; his real work load is very much smaller, comprising only those on the list who claim his services. So with the welfare officer. A large proportion of employees will never seek him out; some will need him two or three times in the course of their service with the company; others, like the chronics and hypo-chondriacs in the doctor's waiting room, will be back time and time again, just as difficult to help if they need help and just as difficult to shake off if they do not.

When the B.M.A.'s 'Charter for the Family Doctor Service' was published, a *Guardian* first-leader (9 March 1965) started off with the obiter dictum that in an imperfect world 2,000 patients were about the right number for one G.P. to look after (more care would have dic-tated *potential* patients!). It went on to suggest that the 1,000 or so which was customary in 'good' private practice gave too much scope for conspicuous consumption on the part of the patient, and elaborate and expensive public-relations procedures on the part of the doctor. The leader continued in the vein that for a true health service, which must include education and prevention, as distinct from a system of comprehensive medical care, 1,500 would be a better figure, but for the foreseeable future 2,000 would do.

This strikes several occupational welfare bells—particularly the opposite but linked dangers of conspicuous consumption and the lack of time for educational and preventive work. It is rather tempting to claim the analogy as exact and leave it at that. However, to do so would beg several questions apart from comparability between welfare officer and G.P. work, which could be assessed only after a careful survey. The most important question is of course whether the *Guardian* or the B.M.A. are right in plumping for global figures. This is not a question for us to consider, but one is inclined to feel that the number of 'active patients'—the direct work load—in an ageing and worn-out mining area might be different from the active list in a well-heeled suburban or 'stock-broker' belt. Whether or not the global assessment for doctors was accurate we must certainly take this and similar points into account in considering welfare officer staffing ratios. There are probably two main factors or groups of inter-related factors, some of which have already been mentioned in different contexts. One is level of employees and the other is their location.

Level of Employees

'Employees' is used here, as it is used elsewhere in this book, in the sense of everybody employed by the organisation. When we speak of 'level of employees' as affecting complementing, we are mainly concerned with the educational-social-economic level of the bulk of the personal users of the welfare officer service, but we must also take into account the degree of knowledge of the service possessed by managers and supervisors.

Personal users

The lower the educational and social level of the bulk of the personal users, the larger the 'active list' will be. This is the converse of the point made earlier, that the higher levels in an organisation will produce fewer personal cases. It is not only that people of higher social and educational level are normally more capable of dealing with most of their own problems and better know their way around the social services. It is also because social and educational level is usually closely correlated with pay level. The less well-paid will be those who produce more debt problems, who will be more affected by shift working, and who have less security of tenure.

Managers and supervisors

Managers and supervisors are still potential users of the welfare officer service in a personal capacity, but it is the degree of their interest in and knowledge of the welfare function which has a more direct bearing on complementing. The higher the level of knowledge and interest, the fewer enquiries should reach the welfare officer which managers and supervisors are capable of dealing with themselves. On the other hand, sympathy for the staff they control and encouragement to them to use the available services may result in more *real* cases coming the welfare officer's way.

Location of Employees

The sub-factors which have to be considered under this heading are location of the welfare officer himself, the location of the personal users of the service and the *type* of location. The last of these relates mainly to the marked differences which will be found when complementing for 'big city' or for more rural areas.

Location of welfare officer

In the last chapter it was pointed out that if the welfare officer were housed a little way from the general centre of employee population, perhaps making people think twice about going out in the rain or climbing the stairs, he would be less bothered by trivia. But there is an optimum point; if too far from centre he might not be consulted as often as he should be. It is not easy to assess the optimum point even when a choice of accommodation is possible. More often there is no choice at all, but it is none the less a significant factor in complementing and must be borne in mind for any future reorganisation of premises. If new buildings are planned, the architect should certainly be made aware of the needs of the welfare officer service.

Location of personal users

This is not quite the other side of the same penny. Location of users refers to whether they are on a compact site or whether the firm is composed of small local units which may be scattered over a fairly wide geographical area. This factor clearly links with level of management interest. In small units, where the manager knows all his people, and frequently their families as well, the expectation of welfare officer service should be considerably lower than in larger units. Large units mean longer chains of command and these often lead to less time for and interest in personal problems. The factor links also with travelling commitments, an increase of which tends to counterbalance 'time savings' to be made from low expectation of service. Fine judgment based on a cost analysis is required to decide the point at which an additional post is required to reduce dead travelling time; but as a rough guide one-third dead time should be a warning signal, one-half dead time requires a cost analysis.

Although personal problems should occupy most of the welfare officer's time, one must not overlook the influence of location and size of unit on group welfare problems. The most critical factor is the way in which group welfare is organised. If voluntary group activities are on a purely local basis, each unit having its own clubs and societies, the welfare officer will need a good time allocation to keep in touch with them. On the other hand, 'national' organisation of group welfare which reduces the scope for local differences of approach will mean that the welfare officer's contacts will be more centralised. It will be the 'national' voluntary officers themselves who have the prime responsibility of looking after the interests of the local branches. The amount of welfare officer time to be allowed for group welfare work depends on company welfare policy. Only company policy can determine how this affects complementing, but a personal opinion may not be out of order. It has been suggested that a welfare officer's perspective may be wrong if he deals exclusively with the seamier side of life; he needs a strong injection of normality of work to maintain a good balance. As another 'rough guide' it is therefore suggested that about a quarter of his time should be devoted to group welfare—which is to a large extent comparable with the 'education and prevention' work mentioned in the analogy with the medical G.P.

Type of location

Although it is not easy to support the argument with figures, it is virtually certain that employees in more rural areas throw up fewer personal problems than employees in urban areas, particularly the 'big cities'. This is partly a matter of level. Jobs may be in short supply in rural districts and selection is possible; better-quality staff are thus available. Living costs are usually lower and debt problems less frequent; housing is more plentiful, or at least it is less expensive when it is available, and fewer problems arise from this source. At the other extreme, in the big cities, firms can often scarcely recruit, let alone select; they have to employ lower-quality people. More debts arise from the higher cost of living, and they arise too from more pressure to 'keep up with the Joneses' and from the activities of door-to-door salesmen. Housing is a very serious problem indeed, and is likely to remain one for many years.

These are the principal factors, but others should not be overlooked. The attitudes of managers, supervisors and trade unionists are very powerful influences. There are some parts of the country where the natives are renowned for rugged independence and other parts where they are not. Some towns and villages are so community-conscious, so 'caring' for their neighbours that few problems arise which they will not seek to solve themselves. Some are served by Citizens' Advice Bureaux which open in the evenings, some have no C.A.B. at all. It is therefore quite futile to lay down any hard and fast figures for complementing. The need will vary so much from place to place that figures could be more of a hindrance than a help. All that one may reasonably do is to suggest broad guide-lines, with special reference to upper and lower limits.

Clearly there is an upper limit of staff numbers beyond which one welfare officer is quite insufficient. The *Guardian* leader quoted above mentioned 'tragically under-doctored areas ... where one practitioner serves 5,000 patients'. In spite of the difficulty of arguing from one situation to another which may not in fact be comparable, one is inclined to suggest that this should be regarded as a firm upper limit for occupational welfare officer service also—even when our criterion factors of level and location indicate the most favourable circumstances possible. Many hard-pressed welfare officers would put it a great deal lower than this. On the other hand there is just as clearly a lower limit below which even the most *unfavourable* level and location factors cannot justify a full-time welfare officer. One names a figure with some trepidation, and it may be best to do so somewhat obliquely by pointing out that the famous 'Hawthorne Investigations' employed one 'counsellor' for about every 300 staff to do a more intensive and specialised job.

The smaller firm might manage reasonably well with a general-purpose personnel officer with specialist occupational welfare officer training—provided he has no hire and fire responsibilities—or the job may be linked with another personnel specialism of a non-executive nature such as safety. But a different solution has been foreshadowed earlier, and it is time to discuss it more fully.

Joint Welfare Officers

Firms are naturally reluctant to share any services with other companies they consider as rivals, especially where technical or commercial 'trade secrets' are thought to be involved. There are three points to be made about this. First, there is sometimes a tendency towards an ostrich in the sand attitude which labels some things as secret which are not in fact secret at all—the 'open secret' type of thinking. Second, advancing technology means that firms in the same sector of industry or commerce are increasingly forced to pool their research and development facilities and thus share what used to be labelled as secret. Third, parochialism is often carried too far; a suspicious and uninformative attitude extends to firms in different sectors in which so-called secrets are of no real interest at all.

Occupational welfare is surely one field—training is another—where cooperation could be of inestimable value. It can be argued very cogently that the part-time services of a full-time expert are far more useful than the full-time services of a man who has to cover so many functions, each of them on a part-time basis, that he cannot be expert in any one of them. Not only is part-time coverage inimical to the development of expertise; what most frequently happens is that the part-timer never even gets basic training in any of the specialisms. We thus get the uneasy situation where an untrained man tries to do some 'welfare' as a sideline, or the situation where no welfare work is done at all beyond compliance with legislation.

There seem to be three possible ways of achieving shared expert service. First, private consultants may set up shop. Many are reputable and offer highly skilled advice and assistance based on a wide experience, but some may be self-styled experts only. Firms should make careful enquiries before using them, and satisfy themselves about qualifications and experience. Second, one of the bigger companies in the area, perhaps having a case for a half-time man, could offer services to smaller firms on a repayment basis. The basis of repayment is a matter for local agreement, but number of actual cases dealt with, time spent, or a fixed proportion of salary and overheads calculated according to the number of staff on the various payrolls, all suggest themselves as possibilities.

The third and perhaps best approach to shared occupational welfare officer service is for Rotary Clubs, Chambers of Commerce or similar local bodies to employ welfare officers themselves in return for special subscriptions determined by mutual agreement and based on one or other of the three possibilities mentioned above. However, it would be essential for this to be done imaginatively and without cheeseparing, taking all our complementing criteria into consideration. Otherwise it might be found that the sum total of staff covered by one man was far in excess of what would be tolerated in a single firm. However, a modest start with one joint occupational welfare officer who can begin to measure the work load is preferable to an over-ambitious scheme, started in an excess of enthusiasm, leading to 'conspicuous consumption' and in turn to 'woolly welfare'. It must also be borne in mind that a new complementing factor will arise in joint schemes. It will arise from the fact that the joint occupational welfare officer would have to relate his activities to different managements, different welfare policies and different conditions of service of employees. The total number of staff covered in a joint scheme should therefore be smaller than in a single organisation made up of several geographical units which nevertheless has a common senior management, an over-all welfare policy and common conditions of service. The joint welfare officer needs an additional allowance of time to accommodate the differences.

To anticipate an inevitable question, there is a real difference be-tween a joint occupational welfare officer scheme sponsored by a Chamber of Commerce or similar body, and the support of that body for the setting up of a Citizens' Advice Bureau in the district if one does not exist. Even if staff are allowed time off to visit such a c.a.b., the function of the c.a.b. is quite different. It will deal with a good range of personal problems, but can never deal with those personal problems which are firmly in the man-in-his-job context, and natur-ally it cannot be involved in group welfare or any aspect of physical welfare.

Inspecting Complements

It is far easier to assess how many welfare officers are required in an organisation when at least one is already employed, than when the organisation is starting a welfare officer service from scratch. This is not as silly as it sounds. Until an expert is there, doing at least part of the job, nobody has any real idea of how many more are needed. The situation is rather akin to offering Stone-Age man a wheel; he has no conception of using it until he has done so. Stone-Age man may use logs or round stones partially to achieve his purpose; managers, supervisors, trade union branch secretaries and other people un-selected for and untrained in welfare officer work are acting as logs or stones. They can do a certain amount of rolling but they are not really designed for the job. Complementing can only start when they know what a wheel could do and are convinced that a wheel is more effec-tive, but they cannot be fully convinced until they have actually tried one.

One carefully selected and trained welfare officer will be adequate in the smaller firm, and no question of increasing the complement will arise. Larger ones in which managers suspect that a singleton will not be enough will none the less be well advised to start with one rather than several. If his records and returns are adequately kept, the complement can then be expanded to the optimum point on the basis of proven need, avoiding both conspicuous consumption and overloading. The individual responsible for complementing must make himself thoroughly familiar with all aspects of the work and listen carefully to views expressed by managers and others as well as the welfare officer himself and the latter's immediate chief. For preference he should also be the individual responsible for complements in other spheres. Staff inspecting as part of the manpower-planning function is a skilled job in its own right when done properly and not on the basis of hunches and prejudices. The tools of the trade are mastered by training in general 'O & M' and related systems analysis work, and it is to O & M that we turn for an example of careful inspection in the social work field in default of any published studies of occupational welfare officer complements inspection.

Cooper, 1964, reports aspects of an O & M review of staffing arrangements carried out by the L.C.C. (now G.L.C.) in the light of experience of the scope and development of services for the mentally ill and subnormal required by the Mental Health Act, 1959. The article relates how 'yardsticks' for complementing were fashioned on the basis of subjective and objective measures of work needed and actually done in these two separate spheres. (Similarly, separate yardsticks are required for personal, group and physical welfare work in the occupational field.)

Subjective appraisal of need by the social workers themselves was checked by the O & M team in two ways: direct inspection of work done by accompanying the social workers on their rounds of visits, and analysis of their worksheets. This procedure led to the establishment of three criteria: each visit (including associated office work) will take about two hours; mentally ill persons need on average 20 visits a year; and the mentally subnormal on average four or five visits per year. The next step was to work out the annual visiting potential of one mental health social worker. Each officer should be available, on average, for visiting for the equivalent of 42 weeks a year (allowing time for leave, training, lectures and discussions and similar activities as revealed by the work sheets). The yardsticks were then derived by the formula:

$$\text{Weeks available} \times \frac{\text{Weekly hours}}{2}$$

= Potential no. of visits per year ÷ No. of visits per year per case
= yardsticks

The results were 1:40 for the mentally ill and 1:160 for the mentally subnormal. To ascertain the staffing complement required, the yard-sticks were applied to the active cases currently carried by each social worker, due account being taken of any extraneous duties and other local circumstances.

It is clear that very similar *techniques* can be developed for measuring occupational welfare officer staffing needs, but naturally it does not follow that the actual yardstick ratios will be found to be the same. Nevertheless, there is probably some similarity between work for the mentally ill and personal welfare on the one hand, and work for the subnormal and group welfare on the other. The mentally ill person needs short-term and frequent attention—he has a *current* problem which it is hoped can be solved by treatment; but the mentally subnormal is a longer-term problem to which there is rarely a complete solution. Group welfare is not dissimilar. It is a long-term problem, always with us, but as long as a voluntary social, sports or benevolent organisation is going along satisfactorily (as the subnormal person probably is in a satisfactory environment), little is required but the occasional but regular 'checking' contact. This over-simplified analogy may have limited appeal to the mental welfare officer, but it does illustrate the fact that different yardsticks are required to measure need for personal and group welfare work. The value of Cooper's article is that she has shown how yardsticks can be derived from a well-considered blend of subjective opinion, direct observation of the work as it is carried out in practice, and analysis of the records of work done. All three are necessary, and no source of information is adequate on its own.

Welfare Supervision and Control

The techniques required for inspection of complements are very closely related to those which the welfare supervisor must employ in his day-to-day work if he is to run an efficient team. There can be no question of 'management by exception' in the welfare field, the supervisor coming into the picture *only* when something has gone wrong. However, we first have to clarify what is meant by supervision and control, since the supervisory role will vary considerably according to the size of the welfare officer force and the pattern of organisation within the company. These two are the main considerations which will determine whether first-line welfare supervision will be primarily technical or primarily administrative. Clearly there will be differences between firms which have only one welfare officer and thus cannot justify a full-time technical supervisor who should know the job better than the welfare officer himself, and the very large organisation which has several teams of welfare officers justifying at least two and sometimes three levels of technical supervision. And there are many gradations between these two extremes.

The cardinal principles are that there must be someone in the organisation to whom the welfare officer is responsible; and that the 'someone' must know enough about occupational welfare to make a sound judgment of how effectively the duties are being carried out. To acquire this knowledge means effort, and effort is wondrously concentrated by proper training. 'Welfare appreciation' courses are as much needed for people without direct experience as welfare officers, to whom a welfare officer is accountable, as similar appreciation courses are required for people who have to control any other specialist activity. The days of the amateur, who claims to see it all in a flash by virtue of superior intelligence, are passing as technical developments change the scene with increasing rapidity. Unless the non-technical supervisor makes the effort he cannot win the respect and confidence of the man who has to work for him. When respect and confidence are lacking, resentment and personal tensions rush in to fill the vacuum. No personnel function—least of all the welfare function—can flourish in this atmosphere. This principle has already been stated in the chapters on training, but no apologies are offered for restating it in the organisational context. It is of such fundamental importance that repetition must be quite merciless until the lesson is accepted.

When two or three welfare officers are employed there is a sound case for full-time technical supervision of an active and participatory nature. That is to say, one welfare officer will be regarded as senior and in charge, directly responsible for the work of the others. This line of command must be clear and definite, with no 'primus inter pares' nonsense as an uncomfortable compromise. Either he is accountable or he is not, and if he is accountable he must be seen to be fully accountable. He will participate in the sense of taking a considerable direct case-load himself and also in the sense of being able to give advice and guidance when it is required and to take over more difficult cases when the need arises. He must be responsible for watching loads, easing the burden by transferring work to others less hard-pressed—or doing the job himself. Although a direct personal load is necessary with this pattern of organisation the supervisor must have a generous time allowance for supervision as such—and this means the development of another yardstick for complementing purposes, particularly related to travelling and office time.

Geography will be of as much importance as numbers at the next level of organisation, where the second tier of technical supervision is required. The general principles of 'span of control' tell us that one man can look after the supervision of about six others, the exact number varying according to the similarity of their work, their knowledge and experience, and other factors affecting ease or difficulty in communicating with them. It is very unlikely that a firm will employ more than six welfare officers in a geographically compact area, and even in a compact area it is doubtful whether the nature of the work permits six to be exceeded without creating a higher level of technical supervision. We thus have the 'chief plus one senior' pattern of organisation. Here the chief will still have a direct load, but one essentially restricted to the immediate locality of his office so that his direct-load travelling time is kept to the minimum. According to geography, the senior will either act as deputy in direct line of command of other members of the team, or the chief and the senior will split the staff according to location and thus control two sub-teams. Obviously, the next pattern up the scale of complexity is a 'chief plus two seniors' with diminishing direct personal loads, and then upwards by similar steps until the third level of technical supervision becomes necessary—a stage reached only by the organisational giants.

The *use* of the basic techniques of welfare supervision and control thus depends on the level at which they are employed and the organisational context of that level. The techniques themselves are the same, the major variable is the degree of expertise of welfare which illuminates their use. As in complementing, they fall into three main classes:

1 *Subjective assessments*

This will cover not only the supervisor's or controller's own subjective assessments arrived at by keeping his ear to the ground but also the use of the *welfare officer's* subjective assessments of welfare need. Inherent in the latter is the *continuous* assessment of the man himself, not simply 'annual appraisement'.

2 *Direct observation*

There are no difficulties here as far as group welfare is concerned. The supervisor or controller must make it his business to accompany his welfare officer (or the chief or senior, depending on the level of control under consideration) on group welfare business from time to time. It is far more difficult with personal casework. The senior or chief welfare officer has a comparatively easy entrée to some interviews when he is known to the interviewee, especially when he has been asked to come in on the 'two heads better than one' basis. But it may be very difficult for the non-technical supervisor or controller, if he is known to the interviewee as also having powers of selection, dismissal or discipline. He has to take a great deal on trust, but he should base his trust on as much direct observation as he can manage.

3 *Analysis of records and returns*

The general use of records and returns for control purposes has been fully covered in the chapter dealing with them, but two points deserve special mention. First, the monthly report on trends provides a cross-check on the use of subjective material from the welfare officer or from elsewhere. If a trend is stated, the more objective evidence of the breakdown of casework on the summary sheet should support it. If it does not, questions must be asked. Second, monthly records and returns supply the material for what could be called an 'audit check'. The supervisor or controller can pick out a trend and then ask the welfare officer, at whatever level, to come along and discuss it, bringing the supporting evidence with him. Similarly, daybook sheets can be sent 'up the line' monthly, or carbon copies of entries can even be supplied daily. Inspection can then be based on the overall picture, on a chosen or random selection of cases (e.g. every fifth or tenth case) or on specific types of cases, all with or without discussion, and penetrating into supporting case records to whatever extent is required.

Some people, conditioned perhaps to a more amateurish and less professional approach to occupational welfare, will probably find something quite foreign or even abhorrent in what has been said about supervision and control. If they have not been convinced by the arguments which have led to it, one can only draw the conclusion that the arguments have not been convincing. If this is the case, there is one more argument to use. It is that if occupational welfare is to be an integrated and efficient function in an organisation, it must be controlled efficiently. The basis of efficient control is objectivity, and the only source of objectivity is fact. Subjectivity can never be ruled out; it never should be ruled out where human beings are concerned. But subjective opinion by itself is valueless. The welfare function deserves something far better, and only hard facts can supply it.

Postscript—Past and Future

The identification of the modern occupational welfare officer and his job will raise many questions. I have described him as a 'jack of all social welfare trades, but master of none but his own', and I think this is a fair summary. Does this necessarily mean that he is basically a social worker in industry, owing his inspiration to the developing professionalism of the social workers categorised in the Foreword? Is he perhaps the occupation-based counterpart of the general-purpose social worker whose emergence was stimulated by the Younghusband Report?

I have also pointed to his relationships with his colleagues in the general field of what is now described as 'personnel management'—training, safety, industrial relations officers and the like. Does this mean that his inspiration should come from the development of industrial administration rather than social administration? Should he have a tour of duty as occupational welfare officer en route to a post as personnel manager, or should a spell as an occupational welfare officer be valued as part of the job experience of the man or woman who aspires to supervisory or controlling posts in the social services?

Is there yet a third possibility, that the occupational welfare officer has been identified as a 'professional' in his own right, independent of both social administration and industrial administration, but drawing inspiration from both sources—and elsewhere—and at the same time building his own discipline, raising his own professional standards and improving the training facilities available to newcomers? Although the context is different, similar problems face the modern training officer and others who can at present best be described as 'interdisciplinary specialists'.

Some of these questions have been touched on in the numbered chapters. For example, the limited interchange between the social

services and industry and commerce was mentioned in Chapter 10 in
the discussion of attainments to be sought at the selection stage. It is
perhaps time to try to ask them more specifically, or at least to try to
point to some of the problems which must be faced if useful answers
are to be found.

A Postscript can be only a very modest contribution to the debate
which should be mounted. One can do little more than offer personal
views on what seem to be some of the more important issues, leaving
it to those who are actively engaged in welfare to follow through if
they think fit. The Institute of Welfare Officers, the only professional
body which caters for both occupational and social welfare officers,
may have a very important role to play, in collaboration with other
interested organisations, in providing a forum for such a debate.

The past has shaped the present just as surely as the present will
shape the future. The starting point is therefore a brief survey of the
concept of welfare in industry in the post-war years. This will be
followed by some notes on how functional analysis could be applied
with profit to the many diverse jobs which 'personnel management'
now seeks to encompass, and to other jobs which are related to occupational welfare. Finally there will be a short section on some of the
barriers to mutual understanding which exist between occupational
welfare officers and their social welfare counterparts, with special
reference to 'counselling'.

The Post-War History

There are so many books on personnel management and its related
subjects that the most erudite of personnel officers can scarcely have
read them all. But even books with Welfare in the title give very little
information about welfare officers, what they are supposed to do, how
they should be selected, trained, kept informed and made to account
for their activities. Indeed, in the early days welfare and personnel
management were used virtually synonymously. The contributors to
what was perhaps the first major handbook—*Welfare in Industry*
(Blayney Thomas, 1949)—wrote of Welfare and Personnel Departments, or Personnel and Welfare Departments, of 'welfare officers'
doing selection testing and training, running house magazines and
doing many other things now accepted as specialisms within or outside personnel management. The role of this general-purpose 'welfare
officer' was seen as a 'benevolent spider' (*sic*) whose tentacles reached
into every part of the organisation. The book starts off in fine style, on

the lines that the experiences of war-time emphasised the individual human need; physical amenities were shown to be insufficient; the 'welfare officer' was no longer confined to the organisation of recreational activities and the supervision of physical amenities. It gave us a glimpse into the future—he was expected to be able to help and guide individuals in their personal problems and to 'assist them in attaining a right perspective of themselves in relation to circumstances'—but the effect was rather spoiled in a subsequent chapter which suggested that when asked for advice on personal problems the 'welfare officer' may as a rule refer enquirers to the nearest (Citizens' Advice) Bureau.

A little later, Brook (1952) touches lightly on welfare officers but offers only one firm principle—that 'the nature and substance of all discussions between the welfare officer and the employee are completely confidential'. (I hope that Chapter 3 has shown this rigid doctrine, which would put the welfare officer above the law, to be quite unacceptable.) Brook also says that 'the whole subject of personal problems in industry is one which poses many problems'. He lists six issues in this sphere which he says every concern must face, but no help is offered towards their solution.

Three years on and we get another *Handbook of Industrial Welfare* (Hopkins, 1955). Hopkins lays his cards on the table immediately. In his preface he tells us that 'there are certain subjects which fall within the outer framework of industrial welfare but are also major subjects in their own right, e.g. wages structures, catering and training'. In the first chapter he admits the confusion between welfare and personnel management but goes on to say that his book is concerned with welfare in the broadest possible way, and that he will regard it as providing a background for personnel management if not actually synonymous with it. He wishes to discuss it within the definition provided by the Ministry of Aircraft Production (Production Efficiency Board), as follows: 'Welfare is fundamentally an attitude of mind on the part of management, influencing the method by which management activities are undertaken', a statement which contributed in some measure to the vagueness of the concept.

None the less, Hopkins goes on to differentiate:

1. Legal requirements—'what the manager *must* do if he employs (say) over 200 people'.
2. Economic welfare—'what he *should* do to underwrite the economic efficiency of his labour force'.

3. Social (or humanitarian) welfare—'what he *may* do to *encourage a wider will to work* and superior team spirit within his organisation' (my italics).

Hopkins' first group of mainly economic features clusters around the prime function of employment, and includes recruitment, selection, induction, training, methods of payment, merit awards, profit sharing and employee advancement. The second group of essential or desirable features of a mainly economic character comprise social security, pensions, use of elderly workers, benevolent funds, suggestion schemes and a few incidental items of daily factory life such as tea breaks. He deals rather sketchily with these, but fortunately the general level is well above that of the concluding sentence, which says that the serving of cakes is favoured and profitable, but managements which have endeavoured to include buttered buns in this service have generally withdrawn this commodity after a short trial!

The ground covered by the present book is entered by Hopkins in his fifth chapter. Here he claims that British employers have a happy instinct for general relationships, morale and climate, suggesting that while the Americans may have more impressive personnel organisations, this country probably leads in the rather more subtle field of employee counselling, sport and recreational activities, and sick visiting. However, no evidence of such leadership is given. Employee counselling is dealt with in five pages which skip over lodgings, domestic issues, loans, holidays, queries arising around a man's job, younger people, older people, retirement, spiritual welfare (by visiting padres), and the problem of retention after conviction for an offence. It is difficult to avoid the conclusion that no matter how good the British may be at it, employee counselling is in fact an afterthought or casual spare-time activity. It may be significant of the era (little more than a decade ago) that sports and social clubs merited eight pages of the author's attention against five on counselling. Significant of the era, for this is a useful book in most other respects. It comes right up to its publication date with ergonomics, sociometry, the need for local research, and an excellent bibliography.

When only five years later we read the most recent edition of Northcott (1960), one of the best-known British books on personnel management, it is rather surprising to find that the word 'welfare' has virtually disappeared. We find a great regard paid to the personal element—in aims, principles, policies and procedures, and the psychology of the working group—but somehow the individual John Smith is absent. One gains the impression of the personnel manager on Olympian heights, full of sympathy for 'the workers' (the customary phrase) in the busy toiling ant-heap beneath, the ad-mass from whose condition the general principles of justice, mercy, democracy, consultation and the like may be abstracted. However, he does not perpetuate the confusion of earlier writers by the synonymous use of 'welfare' and 'personnel management'. Personnel management seems to have come of age; no longer the province of the amateur who has a guilty feeling that he ought to know more of the sub-specialisms than he in fact does, it is shown as a highly expert area within which separate experts may flourish. Northcott suggests seven of these areas (based on Moxon, 1949)—Employment; Selection and Training; Employee Services; Wages; Industrial Relations; Health and Safety; and Education. They are not unlike the seven main areas offered by the Ministry of Labour as a broad guide to those matters on which the personnel officer should be readily informed—Recruitment, Placement and Termination of Employment; Payment and Hours; Education, Training and Promotion; Communication and Consultation; Health and Safety; Employee Services; Organisational Structure.

Northcott does not seek to establish personal welfare as an identifiable function. He has a section on 'The Unguided Interview' which points to the 'emotional release afforded to the employee by discussion of a topic spontaneously chosen by him' and goes on to say that again and again some personal situation unconnected with employment will prove to be the real root of the trouble. However, there is nothing about who should do the interviewing, how he should do it and how he may be trained to do it properly, perhaps on the assumption that such interviews will be so rare that the who's and how's are points only of academic interest. Yet a few pages further on one is reminded of the famous American Western Electric ('Hawthorne') investigations (see J. A. C. Brown, 1954, for an introductory account), in the course of which the Company 'decided to extend the use of this *method of promoting satisfaction*' (my italics) by appointing personnel counsellors on a full-time basis, each being assigned about 300 people.

Welfare appears eventually as a subdivision of Employee Services, and Northcott suggests specific duties as follows:

'To devise, where necessary, and *administer* [my italics] sick club, benevolent and savings schemes.

To arrange suitable treatment for, and otherwise help sick employees and ensure assistance from the social services to those eligible.

To arrange for long-service grants, leaving grants, the payment of
pensions where applicable, and loans to employees.

To assist employees in transport, housing, billeting and other
problems, including any arising out of national service.'

The same employee services section is concerned with canteen
provision and management; the organisation and control, with
employee cooperation, of Youth Clubs, Girl Guides, Boys' Clubs, and
various sports clubs, and 'to organise other *recreational* activities (e.g.
St. John's Ambulance Brigade)' (*sic*); and the encouragement of
holiday travel for education and pleasure.

Perhaps because it started out so all-embracing yet so woolly,
'welfare' has now been diminished to a mere subdivision of one of
seven main sections of personnel management. What was once the
whole dog is now but a tail. Yet the list of duties which the Northcott
'tail' suggests, contains in it the seeds of the tripartite analysis of
welfare into its physical, group and personal areas which the present
book adopts.

A recent synoptical view of personnel administration (Lupton,
1964) has a little to say about physical welfare, but personal problems
and help towards their solution do not find a place. There is a cogent
section on 'Human Needs and their Satisfaction' in which what are
called 'ego needs' (i.e. needs to be recognised, to be esteemed and well
regarded, to be cared about) are picked out; but it is all 'needs' in the
abstract, and not the personal needs of Bill Smith and Mary Jones.
This is not to say that this synopsis lacks humanity; indeed, it is
suffused with it. Some may argue that if all personnel management is
suffused with humanity, there will be plenty of people around to help
with personal problems. I have taken a quite different view, based on
a different concept of 'help' and 'counselling'.

To conclude this survey, I should like to mention Fox's (1966)
contribution, entitled 'From Welfare to Organisation', to a series of
articles in *New Society* on the future of personnel management. He
identifies three crucial stages in development:

1. The 'betterment of the individual', based on ethics and pioneered by such people as Seebohm Rowntree.
2. The activities and methods of industrial psychology. (This is
   limited to the contribution made during the 'heat, light and

sound' era of the subject: Fox does not deal satisfactorily with the current contribution of modern *occupational* psychology which grew from the meagre limits imposed by emphasis on the physical environment.)

3. The trend towards 'scientific management' and its growing concern with organisational problems.

Fox suggests that the 'act of faith' on which the 'betterment' pioneers based their philosophy, 'has, with time and progress, been drained of its promise. This means that personnel officers who take their stand as repository of the company's long-term conscience will argue their case with diminishing validity, and will become even more the men-in-the-middle, decreasingly relevant to policy-making.' He concludes with the thought that those who see personnel specialists as a species of 'social worker in industry' are increasingly wide of the mark.

There is of course no reason why personnel officers should be repositories of their companies' long-term consciences. Conscience is part of the organisation as a whole, just as it is part of the human organism as a whole. If conscience is to be regarded as an aspect of leadership rather than something which is part of the total 'ethos' of the organisation, the only man who should act as 'repository' is the chairman or managing director himself. But I do not think it fruitful to identify conscience in this way.

Nor is there any reason why personnel specialists *generally* should be a species of social worker in industry. I have tried to show that personal welfare work, that aspect of the occupational welfare officer's job which comes closest to the social worker's, cannot be carried out effectively if it is combined with executive functions of the sort undertaken by many personnel officers. The same point comes out regarding group welfare. There is a considerable difference between *running* a benevolent scheme and acting as an adviser to volunteers who run such a scheme. While it would be quite wrong for all personnel specialists to be regarded as a species of social worker in industry, this does not invalidate the case for *someone* in the organisation to be given a role which is similar to a social worker's. I am suggesting that this man is the occupational welfare officer. The question to be resolved is whether or not he should be part of the personnel management team.

The Functional Approach
To answer this question we need a very much more precise definition of the scope and limits of personnel management than we have at

present. So much information is flowing in from theory, practice and research that the term has burst at the seams. It is increasingly clear that few personnel managers can cope with all the areas of knowledge and skill which are being accumulated. The result is that they have to to specialise, but at the same time they may be reluctant to admit that others may be better equipped to deal with areas hitherto classed as part of the generality of personnel management. Their own specialisation may thus be a temporary focus of attention on new developments from research or from legislation; they have to deal with them because nobody else in the organisation is willing or able to take the initiative. This inevitably leads to neglect of areas which were once their prime concern.

Fox's article shows this very clearly in terms of the subject of personnel management as a whole, rather than in terms of individual personnel managers, and I think my own review of the history supports his analysis. The first area of concern was broad and ill-defined 'welfare', but the pace of development was such that only in the very large organisations, which began to employ sub-specialists, was it possible to develop the concept of welfare to any degree of precision. The 'singleton' in the smaller firm had to hurry on and get acquainted with industrial psychology. 'Woolly welfare' was left behind. No sooner did he begin to learn this 'new' area, usually at a superficial level, than industrial relations presented a fresh challenge. Thus there was another shift of attention. Only the larger organisations began to employ industrial psychologists *per se* to develop the detailed application of the subject. Employment legislation followed thick and fast, with training rather aptly sandwiched between 'contracts of employment' and 'redundancy payments'.

And now it is 'organisation'. Recent contributions of industrial sociologists and others now point the need for organisations to look at themselves *as organisations* and to re-shape themselves to meet new needs. (For example, organisational structures designed for batch production are probably quite inappropriate for automation and computerisation.) When there is nobody else in the firm to do the necessary re-thinking, it falls to the personnel manager. If it has not happened already, he is in danger of becoming the firm's dustbin or rag-bag and it is only a short step from this to becoming the scapegoat when things go wrong. If he accepts responsibilities which ought now to be allocated to others he will himself encourage the process—and make a rod for his own back.

It seems to me that personnel managers are engaged in a fort-holding operation, awaiting the reinforcements which *manager training* should provide. Putting this in another way, they have been pioneers in the exploration of new territory and they are waiting for line managers to catch up. Line managers are rarely trained as such. Most of them still 'come up the hard way'. They learn new developments (for example, the engineer learns of automation techniques), but in the name of their own specialisms and not in the name of management. The long-term answer to 'What is personnel management?' almost certainly lies in manager training based on a re-allocation of managerial roles, a fresh look at the old type of 'line and staff' management theory.

But the short-term is pressing, and we cannot wait for general management theory and training to rescue personnel management from its predicament. There is an immediate job to be done. Perhaps we should start off with the name itself. Without stepping too far out of my occupational welfare patch, would it be unfair to suggest that the very term 'personnel management' may be forcing us into a strait-jacket, or equipping us with unnecessary blinkers?

Not to put too fine a point on it, the one thing that personnel managers never do, except in relation to their own staffs, is to *manage personnel*. This is what line managers are supposed to do. Personnel managers might claim to manage the *personnel function*, but this is quite another matter. One must in any event ask whether 'personnel function' is a meaningful term; quite frankly, I think it as woolly as 'welfare' ever was. Could we think of a better term? The only way to find one, or to arrive at a definition precise enough to obviate the need for a new title, is first to analyse every sphere of current 'personnel management' interest and activity in functional terms—what is actually *done* and for what *purpose*? The next step is to determine what level of expertise is necessary to do it, and this will tell us what kind of person should be selected and trained. Finally, which of these activities might be grouped together, and what organisational pattern does this grouping require?

I have tried to do part of this task in relation to occupational welfare officers. Similarly, the stimulus of the Industrial Training Act has led to functional analysis of training (see Taylor, 1966). There are other hopeful signs. Research of a survey nature has already begun. Crichton and Collins, 1966, have reported the results of an arithmetical count by employers of their personnel specialists, part of a study of the occupational role of the personnel officer. The authors' comments on the facts they have collected are most interesting. They suggest that little can be said about the welfare specialists except to note how few in number they now are, and that the statistics seem to confirm the demise of the personnel specialist as social worker in industry (cf. Fox, 1966). But they did not know how important welfare work was in the jobs of general personnel officers. A survey based only on job titles is therefore of limited value.

The authors go on to ask whether the general personnel officer is trying to cope with such a wide range of activities that he cannot take much initiative in any of them because he lacks the expertise. They also ask whether we should now train for a speciality within the personnel function. It will be clear that I think the answers to both these questions are affirmative, but proper research is badly needed. Anticipating such research, some suggestions may not be out of order.

First, functional analysis implies that we should try to find *active* ('doing') words for job titles wherever possible. A manager manages; 'training manager' is therefore quite explicit, since 'training' is a doing word. A training manager manages the training function and merits 'manager' in his job title. There is no reason why other 'personnel' functions should not be analysed in the same way. As with training, such a scrutiny might well show us that some current functions are so specialist that they must be separated out from the traditional 'personnel' sphere and stand on their own or be re-grouped.

The notion of re-grouping leads to the second suggestion. It seems very likely that the current activities of personnel selection officers, management development officers and those in charge of appraisal and promotion systems would be identified as the *manpower planning* function, worthy of equal status with training. Naturally the two relate closely; the training manager must know a great deal about the firm's selection and promotion processes, but it does not follow from this that he has to manage them. The relationship is in reality no different from the relationship between training and safety, safety and production, production and sales, sales and finance. The sales manager (*selling* manager ?) has already been identified as a separate breed, and we must identify other specialist areas.

A third functional group might well be based on the 'organisation and methods' concept pioneered by the public services and having twin roots in the traditional management theory and work study areas.

'Organising manager' would be a suitable title for the man who takes responsibility for devising new forms of organisation to cater for changes in methods, and technological developments. The 'doing' words in the field of industrial relations are conciliating, negotiating and consulting. 'Negotiating manager' might prove suitable for this area of work, which would probably take in the analysis of wages and salary structures.

It does not follow that firms with one personnel manager will in future need four or more extra people operating in the sphere which he has traditionally coped with alone. In fact, differentiation of functions resulting from an analysis of actual activities might show that it would be very much more useful to allocate some of them to people who are at present regarded as being exclusively line managers. An activity analysis in a given firm could possibly reveal that certain line managers were already doing some of the things which were shown on the organisation chart as falling within the personnel manager's responsibilities—but they might not be doing them expertly. It would clearly be more economic to invest some training time in such line managers than to employ additional people.

Final decision on allocation of work would depend very much on the size of the firm, the nature of its activities, and the quality and experience of its managers. Work has to be done by people, and it is better to draw up an organisation chart in terms of what the available people can do or could be trained to do, than to fashion it in theoretical terms which are remote from reality. We have also to bear in mind that more and more personnel specialists are likely to go into general management. They are thus ready trained in a certain specialism, and might well carry managerial responsibility for it as part of their general management load. Or, if additional posts are justified, two or more 'personnel functions could be grouped under one manager—e.g. Manpower Planning and Training. Smaller firms could link together in group schemes or employ consultants on a part-time basis when they cannot justify a full-time specialist in each of the separate areas.

In contrast with manpower-planning managers, training managers and others, it is not so easy to find 'doing' words for people like safety officers and welfare officers. This may be a sure sign that their work is purely advisory and should remain so. I hope I have shown this to be true for welfare officers; the section on safety in Chapter 7 indicates that safety officers may be in the same position. The appropriate verb is in fact 'advise'. One can plan, train, organise and negotiate, but there is no possible verb to cover the 'doing' of safety and welfare. This suggests that there is an advisory function left over when the *executive* personnel tasks have been separated out for possible allocation to line-managers or for re-grouping.

The linkage of health, safety and welfare in some large organisations already recognises the difference between the executive and the advisory personnel functions. It would be of considerable interest to know whether this recognition is by accident or design. Do the functions just 'seem to go together', or has the common advisory element been identified? Another common element is that health, safety and welfare seem to be more 'person-centred' than many of the other 'personnel' areas. Naturally, training must relate to the individual's need as well as the company's; one *selects* individuals, and one *negotiates* with people. The term 'personnel' would be quite meaningless if this were not true, but 'personnel' has a *group* rather than an *individual* ring about it. Health, safety and welfare seem—to me at least—to go closer to the 'individual' heart of the matter than do other personnel areas.

If the firm has one, its medical officer could take charge of this group. Nobody expects a doctor (or a legal or financial *adviser* for that matter) to be part of the management team except in terms of status and salary. Where there is no medical officer there is clearly a need for someone of comparable professional level, if only on a part-time consultancy basis. Some large firms are already employing 'advisers in the social sciences' who could not only take responsibility for the health, safety and welfare part of the organisation but who may also be equipped to advise managers working in the executive 'personnel' spheres which have been mentioned. Industrial sociologists, occupational psychologists and, more particularly, people with post-graduate training in social welfare administration, should be competent to 'manage' or act as consultants on the advisory health, safety and welfare functions.

Counselling

The excursion into 'personnel management' will no doubt lead many people to ask why I am content with 'occupational welfare officer' as a job title, when I am suggesting that others ought to look around for 'doing' titles. This has been answered only in part by pointing out the difference between the executive and the advisory elements in present-day personnel management. A critic could suggest that 'employee counsellor' is already in vogue and is to be preferred to 'occupational welfare officer'. This is a perfectly fair point and one which must be examined, particularly as it bears on the relationship between occupational and social welfare.

In the first place, the title does *point* to this relationship, and it is an important one. The areas of knowledge shared by the occupational welfare officer with the outside social worker may be at least as great as those he shares with people inside his own organisation. Second, it contains no implicit contradiction of the 'personnel manager' kind. Some people may dislike 'officer' for its armed services connotation, but it is in such wide use—Housing, Probation, Children's, Youth Employment, Administrative, Training (to name but a few)—that this is not a serious objection. Third, as pointed out in the Foreword, there is no reason why 'welfare' should be abandoned because the term has been allowed to degenerate. It is one without which we would be distinctly poorer. 'Employee counsellor' is open to objection on several grounds. It is a limiting title. It limits the man to 'employees', which usually but quite wrongly excludes managers, who are equally employed by the organisation. It limits his role to personal counselling, which I have tried to show is but one aspect of occupational welfare work; it does not acknowledge his interest in physical or group welfare. Furthermore, the word 'counsellor' is being applied to so many quite different contexts in such a haphazard fashion that we may find ourselves with yet another degraded word on our hands, and wish in the future that we had not adopted it.

Employee counsellor specifies the context in the same way that *occupational* welfare officer specifies it, but the title introduces quite as many risks of confusion with other roles, without any compensatory gain. *Counsel* already has a legal meaning; in the U.S.A. *counsellor* more often than not means lawyer. *Vocational guidance counsellor* and *marriage guidance counsellor* have been in use for many years. *School counsellor* and *college counsellor* have recently joined in. In his book *Student Guidance*, Palmer (1965) deals only with problems in the further education context, and anyone reading it will agree that the job of the college counsellor is some distance from that of the occupational welfare officer. We may expect a fair spate of writing on educational guidance counselling as a result of courses now being run at Reading and Keele Universities and Edgehill College, and many different concepts of counselling may grow up.

Halmos (1965) in *The Faith of the Counsellors* has given counselling a specific meaning, and it is one which industry and commerce may be very reluctant to accept. In fact, I suspect it is one which many social workers and others with counselling responsibilities will be equally reluctant to accept. He uses *counsellor* to describe (as the dust-jacket has it): 'the new secular professional . . . the social case worker, the psychotherapist, the psychiatrist, the probation officer, the marriage guidance counsellor—the person whose job it is to help others through personal care for them'. His conclusions, that counselling is based on a morass of paradox deriving mainly from Freud, and that the faith of the counsellors is as much religious in origin as that of the priests and ministers they have supplanted, seem to me generalizations erected on highly selected evidence.

Halmos selects his evidence in three steps. He starts by appropriating 'counsellor' exclusively for psychiatrists, psychotherapists, psychologists and social case workers. In doing so, he ignores others with a right to be included (e.g. lawyers) and probably includes some who would rather be left out. For example, he estimates that around 1960 there were 150 psychologists engaged in some counselling practice, but it is not clear whether those working in vocational guidance or youth employment are included in this total. Next, he documents his 'portrait of the counselling ideology—*shared by all, from the medically trained psychiatrist to the social case worker* [my italics] by citing admissions, whether inadvertent or not, from the literature of counselling of all kinds'.

This statement covers two stages in the selection of evidence. First, there is the assumption that the 'trade journals' adequately represent the views of the memberships of the organisations which produce them. One has no means of knowing whether this is true. One indeed suspects that the average 'social worker' is a busy eclectic with neither the time nor the doctrinaire inclination to contribute articles. Admittedly, the survey of the selected literature is backed up by some questionnaire studies, but these were restricted to the already selected groups. And some of the conclusions drawn from the responses are odd. On page 160 one finds great play made of the fact that the respondents agreed both with the statement that people should be accepted as responsible agents who *by and large* (my italics) mean what they say; and another statement to the effect that the 'presenting problem' is *not always* (my italics) that in respect of which they need immediate help. It would be a poor social worker who did not agree with both of the statements. They are not mutually exclusive, particularly when loose terms such as 'by and large' and 'not always' are incorporated. Halmos finds a paradox where none exists.

Second, Halmos has himself selected from the *content* of the literature. Opposing views are scarcely mentioned, except when they are used in the paradox-hunting game; but in my own reading of the journals I have certainly not gained the impression of *unanimous* support for, for example, Halmos' description of psycho-analysis as the 'arche-theory of counselling'.

We need some of the Barbara Wootton type of commonsense antidote to all this. There is no need at all for a mystique to be built around a common human activity often based on simple kindness and interest. When we 'counsel', we try to listen to the other's troubles or problems and try to help him sort them out or solve them. We do so in many situations and for many different reasons. We may counsel another at home, work, school or play. We may counsel because we know him or because we don't; because we are paid to or because we are not; because we can offer an audience or something from a bigger store of knowledge or experience; or simply because we are 'there'. Our counselling may sometimes be just listening (the 'get it off his chest' variety); sometimes it is inextricably blended with giving advice or information; sometimes—as with a welfare officer helping with a debt problem—we do a bit of 'teaching' as well.

There is a generality, communality, or basic common ground which could be overlooked if people raised their own brand of counselling to such a pinnacle of importance as to cut themselves off from related professions. Occupational welfare officers and their colleagues in outside social work could be much closer in thought and action if they appreciated this common ground. Their services to the community are complementary: the more they know of the jobs of their opposite numbers the more efficiently they can perform their own.

I am not suggesting that we need take 'counselling' no further than recognising its generality. Good training is necessary before we can claim to counsel professionally, and the precise form of the training must depend on a thorough functional analysis of the job *and its objectives*. 'What is the counsellor trying to achieve?' is a very much more important question than 'What does the counsellor do?'

Counselling has been chosen as an example of the barriers to understanding between occupational welfare officers and social workers mainly because of its relevance to the choice of job titles. But the brief review of Halmos' book also illustrates how difficult it may be for one group to understand, if not actually accept, the ethos, ideology or vocabulary of the other. The occupational welfare officer will be able to communicate better with the social worker if he has some appreciation of the psychodynamic mode of thinking, and if the social worker is familiar with the language of industry and commerce; but the difficulties in achieving this kind of cross-fertilisation should not be under-estimated. There may be good personal contacts at local level, and these should be fostered. Yet it is the ideology of those who are responsible for training which is of crucial importance. We need cross-fertilisation at this level in order to achieve long-term results. If Halmos is right in his conclusion that social workers are trained on the basis of faith rather than evidence, the gulf is likely to grow as industry and commerce proceed swiftly in the opposite direction. The development of scientific management, which relies increasingly on evidence rather than faith cannot be ignored.

To conclude this discussion on a practical note which further illustrates the gulf which has to be bridged, I draw attention to the invariable use of 'client' in social welfare as synonym or shorthand for the person the social worker is trying to help. Forms of shorthand are inevitable in professional circles, but it is difficult to see the justification for using a word with so suspect a history. It apparently stems from 'plebeian under the protection of a noble', thence to 'dependant', thence 'employer of a lawyer or other professional man', and finally 'customer'. There seems to me a certain absurdity when it is used in respect of a person under probation order, or of a child, or indeed in any context where there is no direct passage of money for services rendered. 'Patient' is equally archaic, even if it were not reserved for the exclusive use of the medical profession. One may ask 'What's in a name?', but it will be clear that I think the correct answer to this question is 'a great deal'.

However, I must admit the difficulty of finding a better term. I have used the more cumbersome description 'individual in need' throughout this book partly because a simpler one is so elusive, but also as a constant reminder. In welfare work we need to spell out in our thinking that we are in fact dealing with *individuals*, and that these individuals are in *need* of something—advice, information or support. Perhaps we should shun forms of shorthand which do not provide this reminder. In any event, we are not dealing with 'clients' in the 'customer' sense used by industry and commerce. The occupational welfare officer talking about his 'clients' is likely to generate considerable misunderstanding amongst the managers and others with whom he deals.

Finale

I hope I have shown the occupational welfare officer's job as both limited and essential. I do not want him to be 'a repository of the company's long-term conscience', for this would be an intolerable burden. But I do hope that his existence, with one foot in the social welfare camp and the other in his firm, will be a constant reminder of the need for a *collective* conscience. In recent years there has been a reaction, maybe a healthy one, against Elton Mayo's famous writings on the moral obligations of industry. It probably began with Levitt's article on the 'Dangers of Social Responsibility' published in the *Harvard Business Review* (September–October 1958) which arrived at the conclusion that 'in the end, business has only two responsibilities, to obey the elementary canons of everyday face-to-face civility and to seek material gain'. Levitt's fear was that when companies interested themselves too much in their social responsibilities they were likely to transform 'an all-important and desirable economic functional group into an all-knowing, all-doing, all-wise father on whom thousands become directly dependent for cradle to grave ministration. This is the kind of monolithic influence the corporation will eventually have after it becomes so occupied with its social burden, with employee welfare and the body politic.'

But there are signs that the pendulum may be swinging back from Levitt's extreme—and to my mind unduly pessimistic—position. In analysing the earlier swing from Mayo to Levitt, Allan Flanders (1966) has recently given it a push in the other direction. I should like to end with a quote from him:

> Whether a nation in its law takes a broad or narrow view of what it regards as anti-social activities on the part of industry, we can be sure that the mere observance of its legal obligations is never a sufficient acknowledgment by industry of its social responsibilities; often the things most worth doing no law can demand, still less effectively enforce.

I think this can stand as a text for the provision of a businesslike and unsentimental occupational welfare officer service. No law could ever demand it, but I believe it to be one of the things most worth doing.

References

ALBEMARLE, Lady (Chairman)
The Youth Service in England and Wales, Cmnd 929, H.M.S.O., London, 1960.

Annual Charities Register and Digest
Family Welfare Association and Butterworth, London.

ASHWORTH, H. W.
'Why Bother to Go Back to Work?', *Personnel Magazine*, 1966, 32, no. 308.

BLAYNEY THOMAS, F. J.
Welfare in Industry, Caxton, London, 1949.

BROOK, F. H. C.
Personnel Management and Welfare, Burke, London, 1952.

BROWN, J. A. C.
The Social Psychology of Industry, Penguin Books, 1954.

BROWN, W. and JAQUES, E.
Glacier Project Papers, Heinemann, London, 1965.

BUREAU OF CURRENT AFFAIRS
Discussion Method, Staples Press, London, 1950.

COOPER, Mary V.
'Staffing Standards for Social Workers', *O. & M. Bulletin*, 1964, vol. 19, no. 2, pp. 59–62.

CRICHTON, A. and COLLINS, R. G.
'Personnel Specialists: a Count by Employers', *Brit. J. Industrial Relations*, 1966, vol. 4, no. 2.

ELLIOTT, A. G. P.
Reviewing a Merit Rating Scheme, Institute of Personnel Management (Occasional Papers No. 7), London, 1955.

FARNDALE, J. (ed.)
Trends in Social Welfare, Pergamon, Oxford, 1965.

FLANDERS, Allan — 'The Internal Social Responsibilities of Industry', *Brit. J. Industrial Relations*, 1966, vol. 4, no. 1.

FOGARTY, M. P. — *The Rules of Work*, Geoffrey Chapman, London, 1963.

FOLLETT, M. P. — 'Dynamic Administration' (*Collected Papers*, ed. H. C. Metcalf and L. Urwick), Pitman, London, 1941.

FOX, A. — 'From Welfare to Organisation', *New Society*, 1966, vol. 17, no. 193.

FRANK, E. — *Using Staff Training Techniques*, Industrial (Welfare) Society, London, 1964.

FRYER, D. H. — 'Training, with Special Reference to its Evaluation', *Personnel Psychology*, 1951, 4, pp. 19–37.

GRIEW, S. — *Design of Work for the Disabled*, H.M.S.O., London, 1963.

HALMOS, P. — *The Faith of the Counsellors*, Constable, London, 1965.

HANDYSIDE, J. D. and SPEAK, Mary — 'Job Satisfaction: Myths and Realities,' *Brit. J. Industrial Relations*, 1964, vol. 2, no. 1.

HARMS, E. and SCHRIEBER, P. — *Handbook of Counselling Techniques*, Pergamon, Oxford, 1964.

HERON, A. — *Solving New Problems*, National Council of Social Service, London, 1961.

HOBMAN, D. — *A Guide to Voluntary Service*, H.M.S.O., London, 1964.

HOPKINS, R. R. — *Handbook of Industrial Welfare*, Pitman, London, 1955.

JAQUES, E. — *Measurement of Responsibility*, Tavistock, London, 1956.

JAQUES, E. — *Equitable Payment*, Heinemann, London, 1961.

KRECH, D. and CRUTCHFIELD, R. G. — *Theories and Problems of Social Psychology*, McGraw-Hill, New York, 1948.

LUPTON, T. — *Industrial Behaviour and Personnel*

Management, Institute of Personnel Management, London, 1964.

LUPTON, T. — *Management and the Social Sciences*, Hutchinson, London, 1966.

McGEHEE, W. and THAYER, P. W. — *Training in Business and Industry*, Wiley, New York, 1961.

MACKENZIE, N. (ed.) — *A Guide to the Social Sciences*, Weidenfeld, London, 1966.

MANDELL, M. M. — *The Selection Process*, American Management Association, New York, 1964.

MARTIN, A. O. — 'The Assessment of Instructors', *Occupational Psychology*, 1965, vol. 39, no. 1, pp. 45–55.

MARTIN, A. O. — 'The Assessment of Training', *Personnel Management*, 1957, vol. 39, no. 340, pp. 88–93.

MAURICE, Spencer G. — *The Charities Act, 1960, with annotations*, Sweet & Maxwell, London, 1961.

MINISTRY OF LABOUR — *The Appointed Factory Doctor Service*, H.M.S.O., London, 1966.

MITCHELL, Ewan — *Your Factory and the Law*, Business Publications, London, 1966.

MOXON, G. R. — *Functions of a Personnel Department*, Institute of Personnel Management, London, 1949.

MULLEN, J. H. — *Personality and Productivity in Management*, Columbia University Press, 1966.

MURRELL, K. F. H. — *Ergonomics: Man in his Working Environment*, Chapman & Hall, London, 1965.

NATIONAL COUNCIL OF SOCIAL SERVICE — *Age is Opportunity*, National Council of Social Service, London, 1961.

NATIONAL COUNCIL OF SOCIAL SERVICE — *Social Welfare Directories and How to Prepare Them*, National Council of Social Service, London, 1966.

NORTHCOTT, C. H. — *Personnel Management: Principles and Practice*, Pitman, London, 1960.

NUFFIELD PROVINCIAL HOSPITALS TRUST	*Waiting in Out-Patient Departments,* Oxford University Press, 1965.
PALMER, C.	*Student Guidance,* Longmans, London, 1965.
PERRY, P. J. C.	*Report Writing,* British Association for Commercial and Industrial Education, London, 1961.
PETERSON, A. D. C.	'Towards a University of the Post', *New Scientist,* 1964, no. 421, pp. 714–715.
PRE-RETIREMENT ASSOCIATION	*Pre-Retirement Advisory Courses,* National Council of Social Service, London, 1964.
RODGER, A.	*The Seven Point Plan,* Paper No. 1, National Institute of Industrial Psychology, London, 1951.
RODGERS, B. N. and DIXON, J.	*Portrait of Social Work,* Oxford University Press, 1960.
ROFF, H. E. and WATSON, T. E.	*Job Analysis,* Institute of Personnel Management, London, 1961.
ROWE, Kay H.	'An Appraisal of Appraisals', *J. Management Studies,* 1964, vol. 1, no. 1.
SAMUELS, A.	*Law for Social Workers,* Butterworth, London, 1963.
SIDNEY, E. and BROWN, M.	*Skills of Interviewing,* Tavistock, London, 1961.
SMITH, R. G. and WESTON, R. J.	*Studies in Morale,* U.S.A.F. Human Resources Research Centre, 1951.
TAYLOR, Nancy	*Selecting and Training the Training Officer,* Institute of Personnel Management, London, 1966.
TIMMS, N.	*Social Casework,* Routledge, London, 1964.
VARAH, Chad	*The Samaritans,* Constable, London, 1965.
VERNON, P. E.	*Personality Assessment,* Methuen, London, 1964.
WALKER, N.	*Morale in the Civil Service: a Study of the Desk Worker,* Edinburgh University Press, 1961.

WALLIS, J.   *Counselling and Social Welfare*, Rout-
                              ledge, London, 1960.
WALLIS, J.   *Someone to Turn To*, Routledge,
                              London, 1961.
WELFORD, A. T. (ed.)   *Society: Problems and Methods of
                              Study*, Routledge, London, 1962.
WHITELEY, C. H. and   *The Permissive Morality*, Methuen,
  Winifred, M.   London, 1964.
WILSON, A. T. M.   'Some Contrasting Socio-technical
                              Production Systems', *The Manager*,
                              December 1955.
WOOTTON, Barbara   *Social Science and Social Pathology*,
                              Allen & Unwin, London, 1959.
YOUNGHUSBAND, Eileen C.   *Report of the Working Party on Social
  (Chairman)   Workers in the Local Authority Health
                              and Welfare Services*, H.M.S.O., Lon-
                              don, 1959.

Index